The Story Of Youth

The Works of Lothrop Stoddard

Volume Two

Revisions and Additions Copyright © 2025 by Liberty Bell Publications LLC

ISBN: 978-1-59364-035-4 Softcover

ISBN: 978-1-59364-037-8 Hardcover

All Rights Reserved. No revised or added part of this book may be reproduced in any manner without the express written consent of the publisher, except in the case of brief excerpts in critical reviews or articles. All inquiries should be addressed to:

Liberty Bell Publications
655 Sandifer Road
York, SC 29745
1-803-818-5407
dmartyo@protonmail.com

Liberty Bell Publications® is a registered trademark of Liberty Bell Publications LLC, a South Carolina Limited Liability Company.

Printed in the United States of America

Editors Note

    Liberty Bell Publications is proud to reprint this marvelous History book for the young, both male and female. It tells the stories of the Youth of the great civilizations and people during many ages and countries through the year 1928. It has been reproduced exactly as the original from scanned images of our copy of the book. The images have been cleaned up to remove flaws and the inadvertant spots and marks in the images. There will be some minor imperfections from flaws in the images which we could not correct.

    An index has been added for easier reference and to facilitate locating a variety of topics, people and locations and references cited.

Enjoy!

Liberty Bell Publications

THE STORY OF YOUTH

THE STORY OF YOUTH
By
Lothrop Stoddard
Illustrated by
William Siegel

COSMOPOLITAN BOOK CORPORATION
NEW YORK, MCMXXVIII

THE STORY OF YOUTH
Copyright, 1928, by,

Cosmopolitan Book Corporation
All rights reserved, including
that of translation into foreign
languages, including the Scandinavian.

Printed in the United States of America by
J. J. LITTLE AND IVES COMPANY, NEW YORK

To My Children

CONTENTS

I	Children of the Morning	1
II	Children of Old Greece	29
III	Children of Ancient Rome	56
IV	Children of the North	81
V	Children of the Conquerors	97
VI	Children of the Middle Ages	113
VII	Youth in the Elizabethan Age	164
VIII	Children of Cavaliers and Puritans	194
IX	Children of the Eighteenth Century	214
X	Children of Young America	255
XI	Children of the Dawn of Today	311

THE STORY OF YOUTH

Chapter I

CHILDREN OF THE MORNING

BABYLONIA

TWO or three score boys and girls sit on low stools in a big room. Each child holds a small tablet of damp clay in his left hand. The right hand grasps a pointed reed, with which the child dabs little wedge-shaped marks on the clay. The clay and the reed are their pencil and paper, and they are learning to write. We are in a Babylonian schoolroom, many thousands of years ago—perhaps before Abraham left this very region with his flocks and herds for distant Palestine. The newly risen sun of civilization is casting its first rays on the fertile lands of lower Mesopotamia, watered by the great rivers Tigris and Euphrates.

The children bend to their task. Now and then they will glance up at the "blackboard"—which is neither black nor a board, but a large clay tablet baked in the oven until it has become a hard brick. On that tablet the writing exercise has been traced in the same queer, wedge-shaped characters, done larger, so they can be easily read by the children. The exercise consists of wise maxims, such as: "He who would excel in the school of the scribes must rise like the dawn." We know this, because modern scientists, digging among the ruins of ancient Babylonian cities, have discovered some of those old, old "copy-books," which, being baked brick, have been preserved through the ages.

The brick tablet stands on a raised platform. And near it the schoolmaster sits in a comfortable wooden chair. He is a stout, thick-set man, with straight nose, wide nostrils, and square face, which, like his round head, is clean-shaven. Most of his pupils are of the same type, though some have hooked noses and look much like modern Arabs or Jews. The ancient Babylonians were a mixed stock, made up of a very old race, the Sumerians, mingled with Semitic blood which had come in from time to time.

The children's task is not easy, for Babylonian writing is very complicated. There are a great many of those wedge-shaped characters, which look much alike and thus have to be all learned by heart. Before the writing lesson began, the schoolmaster had read it aloud, made his pupils repeat it after him, and explained carefully the differences between the various signs.

These boys and girls try hard to do their best. Their parents have emphasized the importance of learning to read and write. The Babylonians set great store by education. Even the poorest among them respect learning. Among other evidence, our scientists have discovered a clay tablet on which the son of a humble peasant had written out a chapter from one of the Babylonian sacred books, baked it in the oven, and deposited it in the public library of the near-by town, "for the good of his soul."

These boys and girls also know that they will need education in their business when they are grown up. The Babylonians are great business people. They are keen traders, and every important transaction, from the sale of a piece of land to the purchase of any valuable article, must be recorded on a clay tablet and stamped with the seller's and buyer's personal seals. This applies to women as well as men. The Babylonian boy or girl who cannot read and write will not get far in the world.

Therefore, Babylonian children begin their school-days at the age of six, and are usually eager to learn. The school we are now visiting is for the younger boys and girls; it is what we should call a primary school. The room itself is done in light-colored plaster, laid over walls of sun-dried bricks, with a ceiling of palm-tree trunks chinked with clay. It is lighted by narrow openings high up near the ceiling, to ensure a good circulation of air. For the climate is hot, and the sun beats down fiercely outside. Flies swarm in through the open door, buzz around the children, and annoy the master by frequently lighting on his bald head.

After a while the master varies the session with a reading lesson. Babylonian "first readers" contained chiefly short stories, like the one recently dug up which tells about a certain orphan boy whom the king discovered by the wayside and adopted, presumably because of his bright appearance. The brick lesson-book states that the boy was rescued "from the mouth of dogs and ravens," and was then brought to a priest, "who branded the soles of his feet with his seal." After that decidedly painful episode, the boy was handed over to a nurse, the king promising to provide the boy's "bread, food, shirt, and other clothing for three years." Unfortunately, we know nothing more about the career of this promising youth, for at that point in the story, the brick is broken.

The noon hour arrives. Laughing and chattering, the boys and girls troop homeward, pausing to peer into the little boothlike shops where merchants and craftsmen ply their trades, or watching the busy street traffic—especially the heavily laden donkeys and the strings of dignified camels. The buildings are also a continual source of interest to children's eyes; for the stuccoed walls are decorated with bright-colored borders, the entrances have elaborately carved doorways, while the temple gates are guarded by stone lions or statues of winged, human-headed bulls. The temples themselves are sometimes several stories high, rising in successive terraces as though built of children's blocks, and each story is tinted a different hue. With their cornices of carved wood, ivory, and gold, those temples of Babylonia's many gods shine resplendent in the brilliant sunlight.

The homes to which the children scatter vary greatly in character. Some of them are exceedingly luxurious. The humbler homes are mere mud hovels with dome-shaped roofs. Here the hard-working mother gives her children a far-from-abundant meal, perhaps consisting only of goat's milk and flat cakes made of crushed grain, eaten sitting or squatting on the clay floor. However, the warm climate of Babylonia permits children to get along on a light diet and scanty clothing. That is lucky for poor children, who wear only a shirt or kilt, and always go barefoot.

The houses of the wealthy are marvels of luxury in that remote age, when nearly all the rest of the world is still plunged in savagery or barbarism. They are built of sun-dried bricks, because Babylonia has no other handy building material and no timber except palm-trees. Nevertheless, these dwellings are often large two-story mansions, containing many spacious rooms arranged about an inner court.

The walls are ornamented with colored glazed tiles, vermilion plaques, and frescoes of men and animals, while the floors are covered with rugs and carpets done in vivid shades. The rooms are well furnished with chairs, tables, footstools, and comfortable couch beds. We know so little about Babylonian cookery that we cannot tell exactly what the children ate for their noon meal. It must have been ample. If the weather was very hot, there were slaves with big fans to cool the air and keep the flies away from the dinner table.

In Babylonia, bright boys even of poor parents had a good chance of rising high in the world. In this oldest of civilizations boys seem to have had a freer range of choice in their future careers than was the case with other peoples down to modern times. There was no caste system in Babylonia, nor was there any law or custom compelling a son to follow his father's occupation. A talented, ambitious boy could therefore feel that he might be almost anything he chose. He might even become king, for Babylonian history shows more than one instance where a weak monarch was deposed by an able usurper of humble birth, who made himself king and was not ashamed to be known as a "son of nobody" —that being the exact term used in the Babylonian annals.

In Babylonia, success usually implied education. Even poor children learned to read and write, and girls as well as boys needed at least primary schooling for the every-day affairs of adult life. And with the wide-spread respect for learning, bright boys must have been eager to get not merely primary schooling but also what we should call "higher education."

All the recognized professions needed a careful educational training. If a boy wanted to become a lawyer, doctor, or priest, he had to attend a college devoted to one or another of those callings. Law was an elaborate study, while priests were supposed to be learned men, with knowledge of the stars and other "knowledge" about lucky or unlucky signs and omens, which the Babylonians thought most important.

Architecture and civil engineering were two more important professions. In a marshy land like Baby-

Ionia, all buildings of any size had to be carefully planned and constructed, while the country's flourishing agriculture depended on drainage canals and other engineering works of an elaborate character. Bankers and traders had usually received a good preliminary education, including the learning of several foreign languages. These were needed, because Babylonian commerce extended all the way from the Mediterranean to India.

There were certain purely learned professions, like that of librarian, which did not promise much money but which conferred honor and public respect. A king's son is known to have held the office of librarian, and to have been obviously proud of his profession.

The Babylonians were great letter-writers. Besides numberless formal documents, many private letters have been discovered, perfectly preserved because written on enduring brick. Some of these are even love-letters. And in nearly all cases the handwriting is good and the spelling correct. This indicates a high level of schooling in old Babylonia.

Much letter-writing means a good postal service. And there was, in fact, such a service, with regular couriers and post-offices throughout Babylonia and the lands under its control. It is somewhat hard to imagine mail-bags filled with bricks. However, the letter-tablets were usually thin, while the script was so compact that much could be said on a tablet of small size.

These curious letters were placed in "envelopes" consisting of an outer layer of unbaked clay stamped with the name and address of the person to whom it was being sent. The receiver just cracked the clay shell, and the letter, being of hard-burned brick, would appear intact!

In Babylonia the road to learning was paved with bricks, since books were of that material. These people loved books, and since their civilization lasted for thousands of years, the number of these queer volumes which could not be burned or easily broken must have become extraordinarily great Every town had its public library. And those libraries were often of notable size. In one provincial city of southern Babylonia a library was discovered containing some thirty-two thousand volumes, arranged just as they were kept five thousand years ago. If this was true of provincial libraries, the great libraries of Babylonia, the capital, at the height of its glory, must have been in proportion. In all probability, ancient Babylonia possessed more books than our own country did in the days of our great-grandfathers.

In libraries everything possible was done for the student's convenience. The books were arranged on shelves, so that a library must have looked much like a brick-yard. The title of each book was written on its base, so that students or library attendants could find it easily, after consulting the catalogue which gave its shelf location. These brick books were made as large as convenient handling permitted, yet they sometimes ran into many volumes. To save space they were written in such minute characters that modern investigators nearly strain their eyes out reading them. Near-sightedness must have been a common ailment among Babylonian students. We know that they tried to counteract this by using magnifying glasses. The Babylonian student with his big lens was probably as characteristic a sight in those old libraries as the bespectacled student is today.

It seems almost incredible that ages ago, in the very morning of history, we can discern a land covered with schools, colleges, and libraries filled with students of all ages, pursuing knowledge not merely for practical reasons but for pure love of learning. Yet such is literally the truth.

EGYPT

Probably no children of history have had a more joyous time of it than that group of boys and girls in ancient Egypt known as "children of the king's bringing-up." It was an established custom of the Pharaoh to invite great nobles to send their young children to court. These high-born boys and girls arrived as mere babies and remained in the royal palace until they were youths and maidens of marriageable age. Here they mingled familiarly with the Pharaoh's own children, and also with sons and daughters of foreign princes tributary to Egypt, whose offspring at the Pharaoh's court were polite hostages for continued loyalty.

The whole scheme was one of clever policy, designed to bind such children to the throne in after life by ties of gratitude and affection. For that reason, the children were given a wonderful time. In their earliest years they were kept in a nursery, managed by a large staff of trained nurses and attendants, and stocked with quantities of toys. As they grew older, the children were put in charge of tutors, called "father-nurses." These tutors were picked men of proved ability, who watched over their charges, supervised their sports and games, and taught them everything which then constituted a polite education.

When they returned to their parents, these lucky boys and girls were cultured men and women. And this court training was always gratefully remembered; for in the life-histories inscribed on tombs, we often read that such and such a person had been "a child of the king of his bringing-up."

These young people dwelt in an earthly paradise. The royal palace was a world apart—a fairy-land of luxurious comfort, elegance, and beauty, in which the children knew nothing of the cares and miseries of the every-day world beyond the high walls and strong gates which sheltered their abode. The palace was set amid charming gardens and spacious parks, cool with the shade of old trees and the glint of ponds dappled with lotus-blossoms.

And what sights those children saw! There were the royal officials and courtiers, in ceremonial robes and jewels. There were parades of the royal guard-regiments—mostly foreign mercenaries—in varied uniforms, marching with glittering standards to the music of pipes and drums, or careering in gaily painted chariots drawn by prancing war horses. There were processions of priests clad in starched linen garments and leopard-skin cloaks, bearing images of amazing gods with human bodies and heads of birds or beasts surmounted by globular golden crowns. There were glimpses of the Pharaoh himself, the divine ruler of Egypt, ablaze with gold and jewels, riding stiffly erect in his gorgeous chariot or seated impassive on his resplendent throne.

The ordinary children of the peasantry had to content themselves with humble sports, of which they have left us many relics.

Children of nearly all lands and ages have made mud-pies. But these modeled toys of many kinds from the rich, sticky mud of their native land, as they played beside the irrigation ditches or along the banks of the great river Nile. They made mud dolls, crocodiles, pigs, even tiny houses and boats. And they treasured these creations of theirs so lovingly that if they died their parents would lay the toys beside the mummy-cases in the tombs. In the Egyptian Room of any big museum may be seen some of these bizarre toys.

Such were the only playthings which children of the humbler classes ever knew; for the *fellaheen* of ancient Egypt were as poor as their successors are now, and lived in wretched mud huts just as the *fellaheen* do today. So the brown-skinned youngsters crawled and toddled about the huts, played with the family goat, and lived in their mud world. Their heads were shaven, save for a single lock of hair which the boys wore hanging down over one ear. Until they were five years old these children went naked, the little boys with linen cords tied about their waists, the little girls each wearing a papyrus charm round the neck. These were solely for religious purposes—to keep off the evil eye.

Children of well-to-do parents wore a shirt and had many playthings. Some of the old Egyptian toys that have come down to us would delight the hearts of children in any age. The girls had dolls of various kinds, some being of carved wood, with real hair and movable arms and legs. The boys had a great variety of toy animals. There were dogs and cats made of brilliantly colored pottery; monkeys and elephants of painted wood; wooden horses on wheels which could be pulled along by a string through their noses; lions and crocodiles which snapped; and a wonderful cat (now reposing in the British Museum) with inlaid crystal eyes and a movable jaw studded with metal teeth.

The Egyptians indeed loved and welcomed children. No matter how poor the family, the arrival of a baby was always celebrated with rejoicing. Besides the children's regular names, parents usually gave them pet names such as "Little Kitten," "Pretty Pussy," or, "We Have Wanted You."

As far as the family purse permitted, everything was done for the child's comfort and entertainment. In addition to toys, Egyptian children had numerous pets. Chief among these was the cat, which in parts of Egypt was worshiped as sacred. There were also tame birds, a species of small deer, and even beetles and grasshoppers, which were kept in tiny grass cages.

The nurseries of wealthy Egyptian homes were decorated in bright colors, with frescoes of cats driving geese, and fat hippos sitting on chairs around a table.

Egyptian children played many games. They had marbles, checkers, dice, and several varieties of ball. There were also sports such as running, wrestling, and sham battles, in which cavaliers rode at one another mounted on comrades' shoulders. Fathers often took their children on fishing trips and bird hunts. Besides the marshy delta country at the mouth of the Nile, ancient Egypt possessed many ponds and small lakes, which teemed with fish and wild-fowl. Penetrating the reedy recesses of these shallow lakes in light canoes, the hunters would get fine bags of ducks, geese, and other water-birds with their bows and arrows, with a sort of boomerang, and even by means of trained cats.

Egyptian children respected and loved their fathers, but they adored their mothers. This adoration was deserved, for the mother devoted herself

without stint to her sons and daughters. The poor peasant woman literally wore herself out in her children's service. *Fellah* mothers usually nursed their babies for three years, since children could not sooner digest the coarse sour bread that was the common people's staple food.

Even when engaged in heavy field-work, the peasant woman carried her child, lying on her neck and shoulders or strapped to her back. In most cases married and a mother before she was fifteen, the Egyptian woman of the peasant class faded early and was often a wrinkled grandmother by her early thirties. Upper-class women were not exposed to such hardships and had nurses to assist them; nevertheless, they, likewise, personally tended their children and watched over their upbringing most carefully.

This mother-love was repaid by the child's lasting devotion. Egyptians were proud to trace their ancestry through the maternal side, and their literature is full of precepts urging eternal honor and gratitude to one's mother. A certain wise man adjures his son in the following lines:

"It is God himself who gave thy mother to thee. From the beginning she has borne a heavy burden with thee, in which I have been unable to help her. When thou wast born, she made herself thy slave. During three years she nursed thee at the breast, and as thy size increased her heart never once allowed her to say, 'Why should I do this?' She went with thee to school, and whilst thou wert learning thy letters, she placed herself near to thy master, every day, with bread and beer from her house. And now that thou art grown up, and hast a wife and house in thy turn, remember always thy helpless infancy, and the care which thy mother lavished upon thee, so that she may never have occasion to reproach thee, nor to raise her hands to heaven against thee. For God would fulfil her curse."

In Babylonia a bright boy of poor parents had a good chance of rising high in the world. That was not true of Egypt. In the land of the Pharaohs, the lot of a poor man's son was a hard one. Occasionally a boy of humble birth would rise to wealth and honor, but this happened so rarely that he was merely the exception which proved the rule. As for his sister, she had no chance at all. The average Egyptian girl was given no education, was married at fourteen, and spent the rest of her life as a domestic drudge.

As soon as poor children could walk, their overburdened mother would set them various duties to lighten her labors. Peasant boys and girls were told to gather herbs, pick up sticks for fuel, drive the ducks and geese to feed, and take the cattle to pasture or to drink. Children of town workers were employed running errands or doing other minor tasks. These children were ill-fed on the heavy bread, eked out with onions, milk, and cheese. Meat was a luxury rarely tasted.

If a lower-class boy seemed bright and clever, his parents might send him to the village school. But he did not learn much there. The primary school was kept by some old fellow who himself knew little. The boys learned by heart passages from the sacred books, which the master read aloud and the boys repeated after him, shouting at the top of their lungs. The aim was primarily religious. The ancient Egyptians were very devout, and children were taught at home as well as at school to reverence their many gods and to perform many ceremonial rites needed to save their souls when they should die, be embalmed as mummies, and await the Judgment Day, when the god Osiris would weigh their deeds in a balance-scale and assign their rewards or punishments. Most Egyptians grew up so illiterate that they regarded reading and writing as magical accomplishments.

Even when the poor boy went to school, his "education" did not last more than two or three years. By the age of nine or ten he was apprenticed to his father's calling. And the chief work-producer was the stick. "Man has a back," says an Egyptian proverb, "and obeys only when it is beaten." Indeed, not only boys but grown men were beaten on the slightest provocation, the practice being looked upon as one of life's inevitable evils.

The poor boy thus had to resign himself to a hard existence of blows, low wages, and coarse food barely sufficient for himself and his future family. That every trade had its hardships is explained by an old Egyptian writer, who draws a melancholy picture of the trades to which boys were apprenticed at an early age.

"I have seen," he says, "the blacksmith at his work in the heat of his forge; he has the fingers of a crocodile, and is black as fish-spawn. The artizans of all kinds that handle the chisel, have they more rest than the peasant? Their fields are the wood they shape, their profession is the metal; even in the night they are called, and they work again after their labor of the day; even in the night their hut is lighted up, and they are awake. The stone-mason seeks his work in every kind of hard stone. When he has accomplished his orders and his hands are tired, does he rest? He must be in the work-yard at sunrise, even if his knees and spine break with his toil. The barber shaves even in the night; to be able to eat, to be able to lie down, he must go from district to district, searching for customers; he must overwork himself as well as his two hands to fill his belly: thus the honey is eaten only by those who make it. The dyer? His fingers stink with the odor of decayed fish, his two eyes ache with weariness, his hand never ceases renewing pieces of stuff, until he detests the sight. The shoemaker is very miserable; his health is like that of a dead fish, and he has nothing to eat but his leather."

However, the *fellah* of ancient Egypt was a docile, easy-going soul, content with little, and always ready to extract some fun out of his hard existence. He would laugh uproariously at the wrigglings of a comrade being beaten, he loved his mud hut of a home, and of an evening he would dance and sing over a jug of beer. Life was as the gods had willed it; he made the best of a bad business.

Children of rich parents also lived in a mud house; only it was a mansion instead of a hut. The mighty pyramids of ancient Egypt, the great temples were of stone, and the innumerable tombs laboriously cut in the solid rock. But those structures, fashioned for eternity, were designed for the gods and the dead. The living dwelt in houses made of sun-dried mud bricks, strengthened by the trunks of palm-trees.

This caused occasional domestic tragedies. Egypt is an almost rainless country. Water is "the gift of the Nile," whose flood alone keeps Egypt from being a lifeless desert. But once or twice in a century the heavens open, and it rains in torrents. Then those mud houses, great and small, would literally melt away, so that a populous city would in a few hours become mere heaps of black paste, with wooden beams projecting here and there from the mud.

The whole population then gets busy. In a few days the poor people have rebuilt their huts from the same mud, and within a few weeks the houses of the well-to-do have likewise risen from the ruins.

Except for such occasional visitations, ancient Egyptian houses were well suited to the hot, dry climate which prevailed. The thick mud walls kept them cool, the chambers were well ventilated, and the furnishings were comfortable—even luxurious. The floors were covered with rugs or reed mats. Low divans ran round the walls, while finely made chairs, stools, and tables stood about the rooms. Beds were provided with wooden pillows fitting under the neck. These kept the head cool.

Even upper-class children wore very little clothing. Boys wore a loin-cloth and a linen shirt reaching to the knees, girls a sleeveless linen slip, kept up by shoulder-bands and falling to the ankles. Sometimes these dresses were embroidered with blue or green thread. Both sexes wore sandals of palm-fiber or leather.

Boys of all classes wore the side-lock. This was cut off when the boy became a youth, and was piously preserved. One of the articles discovered in Pharaoh Tutankhamen's tomb was a beautifully finished box containing a plait of black hair inscribed: "The side-lock which his Majesty wore when he was a boy."

Youths and men kept their heads clean-shaven,

wearing wigs on state occasions or when exposed to the sun. Girls wore their hair in various ways at different times during Egypt's long history. At some epochs they let their hair grow in long braids; at other epochs they bobbed it at the neck; while at still others they kept it close-cropped beneath wigs.

The ancient Egyptians were a clean people. One of the first things taught children was cleanliness, which was enjoined as a religious duty. They bathed frequently in cold water, anointed themselves with oil, and kept their clothes carefully washed. These cleanly habits were made necessary by the hot climate and the dust-laden winds blowing in from the deserts.

The ancient Egyptians loved the good things of life, and got them whenever they had the price to pay for them. Rich families set a varied table. They ate beef, kid, wild game, and various kinds of fowl. Ducks and geese were fattened for market, and were much esteemed. Fish, on the other hand, was usually disdained by all except the poor. Children drank much goat's and cow's milk. Butter was not used in that hot climate, but plenty of cheese was eaten. There was a variety of vegetables, usually boiled; also many fruits, especially figs, dates, and grapes, which wealthy persons grew in their private gardens.

The Egyptians were ceremonially particular in their eating, and children in upper-class homes were carefully taught their table manners. The polite manipulation of food was quite an art, since forks were unknown and spoons did not come into common use until later times. Furthermore, the Egyptians would use only bronze knives, iron knives being considered an impiety to the god Set. Food was scooped up in the right hand and eaten therefrom. The fingers and mouth were then wiped on thin bread-cakes about the size of a small napkin. The dessert course consisted of cakes, made very rich with honey and fat, and sometimes sprinkled with aromatic seeds. After these sticky sweets, servants poured water over the hands.

As part of their social training, upper-class children were often allowed to be present at the formal dinner-parties which their parents gave. These parties were splendid affairs: ladies and gentlemen in robes of finest linen, decked with jewels and garlanded with wreaths of lotus-blossoms. Slaves renewed the flowers as they faded, and anointed the guests' wigs with perfumes poured from alabaster vases. At the banquet, professional entertainers enlivened the proceedings with music, dancing, and juggling acts with balls and knives. The only drawback from the children's point of view was that they were expected to be mere spectators, "seen but not heard," and forbidden to touch a morsel of the tempting dainties until the banquet was over.

Children of the king's bringing-up obtained an excellent education. This was one of the greatest of their bounties, for in Egypt there was no widespread schooling such as that of Babylonia. Court-trained girls were practically the only girls in Egypt who learned even how to read and write. And outside of those trained at court only a few boys like priests' sons received an education aiming at genuine learning and culture. Many Egyptian priests were deeply learned men; but they kept their wisdom jealously within their own ranks, since this was the chief source of the mystical authority which they wielded over the superstitious multitude.

Another thing which restricted education was the unwritten law that a son should follow his father's calling. Since Egyptian families were usually large, there were nearly always sons enough to fill all prospective vacancies in the higher and more desirable professions. Thus, even if a boy showed a strong bent for some calling other than his father's, his chances of success in it would be slim.

Under these circumstances it is not surprising that children even of well-to-do parents were given a rather mediocre education. Schools in towns and cities were, of course, much better than the village ones. They were known by the title of "The House of Books." Boys, beginning at the age of six or eight, found themselves under a strict master, whose motto was "A boy's ears are in his back," and who was firmly convinced that his pupils' wits were best sharpened by a liberal application of the palm-stick to their cringing shoulders.

The hardest task set Egyptian schoolboys was learning to write. The Egyptians did not have an alphabet with a limited series of letters; instead, they used a vast number of *root-ideas*, expressed by *hieroglyphs*—queer little pictures of gods, men, beasts, and other things. And to write thus, a boy would have to learn how to draw all those little pictures, memorize them, and know how to put them together in various ways to express particular meanings.

The average Egyptian schoolboy was required to learn only the principal hieroglyphs—and those mainly for religious reasons. Only boys destined for the priesthood had to become fluent in the sacred picture-script. However, ordinary schoolboys did have to learn another script, based upon the picture-writing, but simplified and condensed into a form of shorthand. This simplified script, called *hieratic,* was used for business documents and correspondence, the picture-writing being too slow and cumbersome for every-day purposes. Yet the hieratic script was complicated enough to need much study.

The usual writing material was papyrus-fiber—whence comes our word "paper." The papyrus was a plant which grew in shallow ponds and river-marshes, and which the Egyptians cultivated in regular crops, so as to have an adequate supply. The papyrus stems were beaten until they formed a fibrous mass, which was then pressed flat to make a smooth surface, and was finally cut into sheets of any desired size. The result was a tough, silky paper, which was written on with a reed pen dipped in black or colored ink. At first, boys were not allowed to use this rather expensive paper, but did their writing on whitewashed boards or limestone slabs, which could be cleaned of ink and thus used many times.

The schoolboy's writing exercises consisted of passages from the sacred books and sayings of wise men, such as: "Be not haughty because of thy knowledge; wisdom is harder to find than an emerald." The boy also wrote out many magical formulas, which were supposed to come in handy when aptly used. For instance, before fording a stream infested with crocodiles, the Egyptian was taught to pause and utter the following words: "Halt, crocodile, son of Set! Do not wave thy tail; do not move thy legs; do not open thy mouth; may the water become like a rampart of burning fire before thee! Halt, crocodile, son of Set!" If the magic phrase were correctly uttered, and no single word left out, the lurking crocodile would instantly lose his appetite, and a safe crossing was assured.

When a boy could read, write, and do a little simple figuring, his general education was over. This happened by the time he was ten or twelve years old. Most boys then followed their father's calling, whatever that might be. If the lad were a priest's son, he entered a temple school, where he would pass many years in learned studies. The only other career needing further schooling was that of a scribe. And a scribe's career was deemed so desirable and offered such unusual possibilities that it was the dream of most ambitious boys.

A scribe means literally "one who can write." That does not sound very impressive to us. But among an illiterate people, every such individual is held in some honor, and in ancient Egypt the scribes formed a professional class of genuine importance. Most scribes, to be sure, eked out a precarious livelihood as minor government clerks or as a sort of notary-public, drawing up documents, writing letters, and doing other clerical services for private individuals. However, a clever, capable scribe might attract the notice of his superiors, and from being a mere bookkeeper or tallyman he might ultimately rise to be governor of a province, rich and honored, though born of humble parents.

Egypt was a land of such restricted opportunities that the careers of these few "self-made men" cast a glamor of romance over the whole profession. "There is nothing like being a scribe," says an Egyptian proverb; "the scribe gets all there is upon earth." So boys rushed wholesale into this alluring profession, each hoping that he would be one of the lucky few who drew the big prizes.

Boys learned to be scribes partly by attending special schools and partly by apprenticing themselves to practicing scribes, whom they assisted in their professional duties. Little original thought was required. The apprentices needed chiefly to become fluent writers and to memorize the standard textbooks containing collections of sample documents of every kind. When a lad had memorized all the standard formulas, the master would give him detached phrases which he must join together in new formulas, so as to be ready for unexpected situations. This training, together with simple bookkeeping and arithmetic, qualified a boy to be a scribe. The master or the boy's parents would use their influence to get him a minor post—and there he usually stayed. Not a brilliant prospect; but, the Egyptians seldom displayed brilliancy or individual enterprise.

There was one other career which the government was very glad to see a boy take up. This was the career of a soldier. But few boys thought of soldiering—save with dislike and fear; for the ancient Egyptians, like their modern descendants, were a most unwarlike people. The Pharaohs forcibly conscripted their subjects, just as the khedives of modern Egypt did before the British occupation of Egypt half a century ago. A body of troops would tour the villages, seize well-grown lads, tie them with ropes, and drive them like cattle to the nearest garrison post, while their mothers and sisters wept, wailed, and mourned them as already dead. Naturally, these unwilling conscripts did not make good soldiers, so the Pharaohs hired foreign mercenaries, who formed the crack troops of the Egyptian army.

In early times the Egyptian nobility seem to have been of a fairly warlike disposition, and their sons furnished the officers for the Pharaoh's army. But as the centuries passed, even the young nobles appear to have lost their martial spirit. A story has come down to us about a lad of gentle birth who showed a taste for soldiering, but was promptly talked out of it by a family friend and persuaded to adopt the peaceful career of a scribe. The tale is so amusing and illustrates the Egyptian character so well that it is worth retelling.

Dazzled by the martial spectacle of troops assembling for a campaign in Syria, a certain boy of good family gets the war-fever—much to the annoyance of his family. He neglects his lessons, scribbles his writing exercises any old way, and when reprimanded by his father answers that he wishes he were an officer and did not have to bother his head with studies any more.

The father intends his son to be a learned scribe. But, being a politic man, he does not lose his temper. He tells his son to talk things over with a wise old gentleman for whom the lad has deep respect. "Ask him," says the father, "what he thinks of the fine profession you are so taken with. He is a good adviser, and you will do well to listen to him as though he were the god Thoth."

The lad seeks the old gentleman and tells him how his young heart has thrilled at the sight of the infantry regiments marching to the shrill music of the pipes and the deep roll of the drums. The old man smiles indulgently at the lad's enthusiasm, and replies: "Why, then, dost thou assert that an infantry officer is better off than a scribe? Come here, and I will tell thee the fate of an infantry officer, the extent of his sufferings. He is taken when still young, the lock still hanging over his ear, and is imprisoned in a barrack. He is beaten, and his stomach is covered with wounds; he is beaten, and his head is broken by a wound; he is laid down and beaten like a papyrus, and he is bruised all over with the stick.

"Come, now, whilst I tell you about his march into Syria, his journeys to distant lands. His rations and his water are upon his shoulder like the burden of an ass, and weigh upon his neck like that of an ass, until the joints of his spine are displaced. He drinks foul water—still perpetually mounting guard. When he reaches the enemy?—he is only a trembling bird. If he returns to Egypt?—he is no better than old, wormeaten wood. He is ill, and must lie down; he is carried home upon an ass, whilst robbers steal his clothes, and his servants run away. Therefore, O my child, change the opinion thou has formed upon the scribe and the infantry officer."

The lad is rather crestfallen, but he still has an argument in reserve. He remembers those gaily painted chariots, whirled along by spirited horses. Surely, says he, the charioteers cannot have so bad a time of it. But the old man shakes his head. "The chariot soldiers?" he sighs. "Now let me tell you the tiring duties of a charioteer. He hastens to choose his horses from his Majesty's breeding stud; when he has chosen two fine horses he rejoices loudly; he returns to his village and drives at a gallop; but he does not yet know the fate that awaits him. Having saluted his grandfather, he gallops away again. But he entangles himself in his reins and falls to the ground amongst the thorns; a scorpion stings his foot, and his heel is pierced by the bite. When his battered accouterments are examined his misery is at its height; he is stretched upon the ground and receives one hundred blows from a stick."

The lad's war-fever is by now quite dead. He gives up thoughts of soldiering, becomes a scribe, and by family influence doubtless gets a good job in the government civil service. Yet this pacifist spirit is ultimately fatal to his country. When powerful military empires arise in Asia, the unwarlike Egyptians cannot withstand their attacks. About 500 B. C. Egypt is conquered by the Persians, and the Egyptians have ever since bowed to a succession of foreign masters.

Chapter II

CHILDREN OF OLD GREECE

HELLENIC states tended to be of two kinds. There were some where most of the people dwelt in a walled city on or near the seashore, and who lived largely by trade and commerce. These city-dwellers had dealings with other peoples, knew about foreign lands, got a lot of new ideas, and were what we should call "up-to-date." The best example of this sort of city-state is Athens.

The other sort of Greek state is best represented by Sparta. In Sparta and the states like it, most of the people lived in villages or small towns. They were country-folk, and their state was usually away from the sea, in some valley among the mountains. These people led very simple lives. They were farmers, herdsmen, or warriors. They did not like strangers and did not welcome new ideas. They were "old-fashioned" in every way.

In ancient Athens during its great days, just after the Persian Wars, a slave comes out of a dwelling-house and hangs something on the knocker of the door. A new baby has arrived.

If it is a boy, he hangs an olive-wreath; if a girl, a knot of woolen thread. The olive-wreath would bring out all the neighbors, exclaiming: "A baby boy! How lucky!" The wisp of wool would rouse no enthusiasm, since girls are not so much wanted.

In any case, the new-born baby is bathed in warm water and olive-oil, and is then wrapped round and round in woolen bands, until only its face peeps out. It is then placed in a wicker cradle, shaped like a shoe, and hung by cords from the ceiling so that it can be easily swung to and fro.

This for an average Athenian baby. In Sparta the babies were treated differently. And at the time of which we write, it was quite the fashion in Athens to have Spartan nurses, who thought babies should be toughened from birth by having very little wrapped around them and by getting lots of fresh air. That was what happened to little Alcibiades and other great Athenians who had Spartan nurses.

Ten days after the birth of an average Athenian child all the relatives and family friends called to see the baby and hear it formally given its name. The guests brought gifts, and there was a big celebration. What the name should be was considered very important, and there was often a family row before parents could reach an agreement.

Until they were seven years old, Athenian boys and girls were brought up together, under the joint care of their mother and nurse. A little lamp always burned in the nursery at night, to keep off evil spirits which might enter in darkness. The Athenians, like most ancient Greeks, were very superstitious, and an important part of a nurse's duty was to hang various charms about the child's neck, to protect it against witches, hobgoblins, nymphs, and other supernatural beings who were forever on the lookout to do unguarded children some mischief or harm.

Greek children had toys much like ours. There were rattles, go-carts, and dolls with movable legs and arms, which could be dressed and undressed at pleasure. A modern child suddenly transported to an old Athenian nursery would find it practically the same as its own.

So Greek children crawled, and toddled, and played with their toys. Their parents were in no hurry to have them walk, to avoid all possibility of bow-legs. They were sung lullabys and nursery rhymes, and were early introduced to Æsop's Fables, which were considered the first step in every child's education. Children were also told simple tales about the gods and the Greek heroes, and were warned against the evil spirits which lay in wait for naughty boys and girls. Children were soundly spanked with the slipper on frequent occasions.

Athenian children did not see much of their fathers. Ancient Athens was half oriental in its domestic arrangements. The Athenian house had its special women's quarters, where the young children were kept. And to the women's quarters no men, except close relatives, were ever admitted. Only when there were no guests would the father eat with his wife and family. On such occasions the young children would be allowed to come to the dinner table for dessert, and when they were somewhat older they would sit primly under their parents' eyes while they were taught table manners.

Good manners in children were emphasized in Athenian families, and respect for elders was insisted upon. Children were told to stand in the presence of elders until given permission to sit; not to contradict their parents; and not to speak of their sire by such familiar nicknames as "Old Father Time."

However, Athenian children, though brought up strictly, were seldom abused or neglected. Indeed, throughout Greece, fathers were fond of their children and often played with them. Even so grim a warrior as the Spartan general Agesilaus is said to have spent hours in the nursery amusing his children and piping on a reed to please his boys. And it is related of another Greek general that an unexpected visitor caught him romping with his children on the floor. Somewhat shamefaced at having been discovered in so undignified a posture, the general made his visitor promise that he would not tell the story until he had children of his own!

Although Athenian children, when they went out of doors, were usually attended by a slave, there was one occasion when even small boys were escorted by their father. That was when they went to get their hair cut. The ancient Athenians were very particular about the care of the hair and hands, so barbers and barbershops played an important part in Athenian life. Gentlemen were accustomed to meet and chat there. Any man who had a barber come to his house was criticized by public opinion as a snob.

Demosthenes in one of his orations, condemns an opponent as "unsocial; he never visits any of the barbershops." And Aristophanes in one of his comedies has a line about "when the fathers tell the boys in the barbershops."

If Athenian boys were "real boys," they must have found those visits to the barbershops somewhat of an ordeal. For the Athenian barber not only cut your hair; he also manicured your nails and gave you a general dandying up. He would tuck a towel around you, click his scissors, trim your hair, and let you look at yourself in a polished bronze mirror while he gave you a careful manicure. Incidentally, we may remark that Athenian barbers, like modern barbers, were notoriously great talkers.

"How will you have your hair cut, sir?" a certain barber asked Archelaus the Macedonian:

"In silence!" Archelaus answered.

Those Athenian boys as they walked through the streets beside their fathers to the barbership must have looked like little men, for their clothes were small-sized copies of their parents'. This clothing was simple enough. Since Athens enjoyed a warm, dry climate, the Athenians usually wore only two garments—a sleeveless tunic or undershirt falling to a trifle above the knee, and an outer garment draped in graceful folds such as we see in old Greek statuary. In winter, these garments were of wool; in summer, of linen. City-dwellers ordinarily wore light sandals on their feet, but went about bareheaded. For rainy weather, there were long cape-like cloaks, leather shoes, and close-fitting felt caps. In the country, broad-brimmed hats and high boots were often worn.

Food, like clothing, was simple in character. Owing to the warm climate, the Athenian diet was moderate. Little meat was eaten, though there was plenty of sea-food, and the Athenians ate barley porridge, whole-wheat bread, ripe olives, goat's cheese, and fruits. Children usually drank goat's milk, though at a comparatively early age they were allowed a little well-watered wine. Modern beverages like tea, coffee, and cocoa were, of course, wholly unknown to the ancient world.

The half-Asiatic seclusion of women in ancient Athens applied to girls as well. Judged by modern standards, the lot of the female sex in old Athens was not an enviable one. In Athenian eyes, woman's place was most emphatically the home. Every Athenian house had its separate women's quarters, to which only the father and the closest male relatives were ever admitted. And women and girls never appeared in the rest of the house when male visitors were there.

Until the age of seven, Athenian girls had their brothers as playmates in the women's quarters. After that, their paths sharply diverged. The boys could go out to play and began going to school. For little girls, however, such things would have been most unbecoming. So they stayed in the women's quarters, playing with their dolls and their pet birds or tortoises.

The older the girls, the more strictly they were confined. They learned to spin, weave, and embroider; to do plain cooking and other domestic duties, so that they would know how to run a household and manage the slaves when they were grown up and had homes of their own. But they never had an "education" in our sense of the word. Many girls, even of good family, could not read a line of Homer or write their own names. Athenian men did not care to have their wives and daughters know much. Of course, there were exceptional women who were both wise and clever. But Xenophon undoubtedly voices Athenian public opinion when he wrote as his ideal of a girl's education: "To see as little as possible; to hear as little as possible; to ask as few questions as possible; and to have learned but one lesson—modesty."

So the Athenian girl grew up—a shy, secluded creature, rarely setting foot out of doors save on great occasions like public festivals and religious processions, when she appeared in public, walking demurely with half-covered face.

When she was fourteen, her parents bethought themselves of her marriage. She had no say in the matter. Marriage in ancient Athens was a family affair. The girl docilely accepted the man picked out for her who was apt to be considerably older than herself. This was thought wise, because, owing to the climate, and still more to a sedentary life, Athenian women soon faded and often lost their health at a comparatively early age. Almost all Athenian girls were married before they were eighteen. Closely veiled, the Athenian bride went from her parents' house to her new home, there to take up another phase of the same secluded existence she had always known.

Much more interesting was the life of the Athenian boy. At the age of seven he was taken from the care of nurse and mother, and was placed under the guidance of a personage known as the *paidagogos*. We cite that Greek term, because it means something quite different from our word "pedagogue." The *paidagogos* was neither a schoolmaster nor a private tutor. He was almost always an elderly slave of staid habits, whose duty was a general oversight of the boy placed in his charge.

The bearded *paidagogos*, wearing a special cloak and carrying a long stick, was one of the characteristic sights of Athens. He superintended his young master's manners at home, took him to and from school, and followed when the boy went out to play, to see that he did not stray too far from home or get into mischief.

When the *paidagogos* was up to his job, the institution seems to have worked well enough. But when, as often happened, he was a doddering old fellow, the boy got the upper hand and led the *paidagogos* a merry chase. A good example of this is the young Alcibiades, who bullied his poor *paida-*

gogos as he liked, and once broke the official stick over the old man's back.

Athenian boys played in the street in front of their homes, while the *paidadogoi* lounged in the background. The boys whipped tops, pitched round nuts as we do marbles, played games like blindman's-buff, and even threw dice in a primitive version of "shooting craps." Plutarch relates that one day young Alcibiades—that notorious "bad boy" of Athens—was playing dice in the street with a number of companions. Just as Alcibiades was about to "roll the bones," along came a loaded cart drawn by two horses. Alcibiades yelled to the driver to stop, but the man merely laughed at the boy and came on. Thereupon, Alcibiades threw himself face-down in the middle of the road, angrily daring the carter to run over him. The horrified carter reined up his horses just in time, while the still more horrified *paidagogos* rushed up to lift the young scapegrace out of the way! It was probably boys like Alcibiades that led Plato to make the general statement that the boy is "the most unmanageable of animals."

How were Plato's "unmanageable animals" to be transformed into worthy men? That was the problem which not only the Athenians but Greeks everywhere sought to solve by their system of education. And, during the best days of ancient Greece, the system worked remarkably well.

When we consider what wonderful things the Greek states did, and how deep a mark they have left on world-history, we can hardly realize how small they were in both area and population. Furthermore, the majority even of those small populations were slaves. The only people who really counted were the minority of free citizens. Athens was the only Greek state with more than 20,000 adult male citizens, while the number of adult male Spartans never exceeded 10,000.

These small states, ruled by still smaller minority groups, were jostled by jealous neighbors. Under these perilous circumstances, if a Greek state was to survive and prosper it must take care its sons grew up into strong, loyal, capable men. The root-idea of Greek education was, therefore, the development of citizens worthy of the state, who should carry on in the future the legacy of the past. Education was thus regarded as a training for right living even more than for correct thinking; and the educational system throughout ancient Greece aimed not so much at imparting knowledge as at producing healthy, law-abiding, patriotic citizens. Educational differences in the various states were merely differences in method; different ways of trying to bring about an end which all sought to attain. And in education, as in so many other fields, the Greeks were pioneers. No ancient people before them had ever thought out a genuine theory of education; while, in loftiness of aim, no people of later times has surpassed them.

In its scope, Greek education may seem to us oversimplified. There was no science, no study of foreign languages, practically no history or mathematics, and no preparation for the learned or technical professions.

Greek boys were educated in just three subjects: letters, music, and physical training. And, as already stated, the aim even in these few subjects was, not their technical mastery, but their effect upon individual character and citizenship. The ancient Greek wanted to be a well-balanced "gentleman amateur," and dreaded anything like "professionalism." It is said that Alexander the Great, who had a decided talent for music, once proudly showed off his skill in playing on the lyre before his father Philip of Macedon. When Alexander had finished, his father remarked: "My son, aren't you rather ashamed to play so well?"

This dread of professionalism comes out even more strongly in the field of physical training. We know what a great part athletes played in Greek life, culminating as they did in the famous "all-Greek" contests known as the Olympic Games. Yet, in the best days of Greece, desire to win was not allowed to obscure the thing really aimed at in physical training, which was—better men and better citizens.

At the period we are considering, professionalism was just beginning to creep into Athens. Leading Athenian writers, from Euripides to Plato, bitterly condemn professionalism in athletics, asserting that it was making Athenian youth coarse, brutal, fit for nothing else, and spoiled by the applause of the multitude.

Later, as Greece declined, not only athletics but all education became more and more "professionalized." The educational aim became, not so much the making of good citizens as the fitting of youths for various professional careers. In the end, lads of good family no longer competed in public athletic contests, which were monopolized by paid professionals, who often won big prize-money, made up from gate-receipts paid by the crowds which flocked to those popular spectacles.

The ancient Athenians set great store by education. When King Xerxes and his Persian hordes drove the whole Athenian population into temporary exile, one of the first matters attended to was the establishment of extemporized schools in the Athenian refugee-camps, so that the education of the rising generation might not be interrupted.

Although education was not compulsory by law, and although the parents had to bear the expense, even the poorest Athenians managed to give their boys what we would call primary schooling. Fortunately, this was inexpensive. Anybody who had complied with a few simple legal regulations could set up a school, and schoolmasters were numerous, though usually ill-paid. Athens was thus dotted with small schools, attended by the boys of the immediate neighborhoods. They were all day-schools, boarding-schools being unknown.

The school day began early. Sunrise saw the streets of Athens thronged with boys, all the way from seven to sixteen years old, attended by *paidagogoi*, on their way to school. The schoolrooms were extremely simple. The master sat on a raised chair. The boys stood before him as they recited, or sat on stools as they practiced writing exercises. Every schoolroom was equipped with a *white*-board, on which the master would write with dark-colored chalk, which could afterwards be erased by a sponge.

The little boys began by learning their A-B-C's. Then followed reading, some very rudimentary arithmetic, and writing exercises. At first the boys wrote on wax tablets with a sharp-pointed metal instrument called the stylus. These tablets were like our slates, since the wax could be smoothed over, and the tablets thus used many times. The Greeks had no true paper; instead, they used rolls made of papyrus-fiber, which was fairly expensive. So it was only when the boys could write well that they were allowed papyrus rolls, writing in ink with a reed pen.

As soon as boys learned to read, they were set to studying Homer (which was the Greek Bible), together with others of the Greek classics. Boys had to memorize many passages from these writings of an especially moral and patriotic nature.

Music, the second branch of Greek education, did not usually begin until a boy was twelve or thirteen. The Greeks thought music a vital part of a boy's training. The object was a moral one. Technical knowledge and skill were neither attempted nor desired. All that was expected was ability to intone the songs of the great Greek poets, to a simple accompaniment on the lyre. The moral effects of this musical recitation were supposed to be most important.

About noon, the boys went home for their midday meal. The afternoon was devoted to physical training. The importance of sound bodies, not only for good health but also for patriotic service, is evident. Athens was often at war, and every ablebodied citizen would probably be called on to fight by land or sea.

Physical training consisted in running, jumping, wrestling, and gymnastics. As boys grew older, this training was supplemented by other athletic exercises, such as throwing the disk and the spear. At Athens there seem to have been no sports like baseball, cricket, and football, involving team-play.

The athletic-fields and gymnasiums were located just outside the city walls. Today, Athens is surrounded by a bare and dusty plain. But in ancient days the city was set amid groves of trees and running streams. In those pleasant surroundings the Athenian boys passed their afternoons in vigorous exercise, under the eye of professional instructors.

At the age of sixteen, "schooldays" were over. Most boys were then apprenticed to the trade or calling in which they planned to earn their living. Only the sons of well-to-do or wealthy parents could afford what we would call "higher education." This was a two years' course in general culture, under dignified professors who charged high fees for their instruction. The youths learned rhetoric, elocution, and deportment, in order to be able to speak in public and take part worthily in the great civic processions and religious festivals. There were likewise courses in literature, art, music, and philosophy, and further athletic and gymnastic training.

From this two years' "college" course, the young

Athenian emerged a "well-turned-out man," who knew the best of what there then was to know, and who could bear himself correctly and gracefully on all occasions.

At the age of eighteen, all free-born Athenian youths began their military service. This corresponds with the system today prevailing in most nations of continental Europe. Except for physical defects, there were no exemptions in ancient Athens. The wealthiest and the poorest served in the ranks together.

Military training began with a solemn ceremony, when the whole annual "class" of recruits marched to the Temple of Athena on the Acropolis to take the soldier's oath of loyalty and obedience. The conscripts then underwent a combined military and naval training, spending part of their time in garrison duty on the frontier and part at the port of Piræus. Athens was even more of a naval than a military power, so citizens had to be ready for sea as well as land duty.

Those two years of military service were strenuous ones. Discipline was strict, while drill and training in the use of weapons was a complicated affair. The Greek "hoplites" were heavily armed soldiers and fought in regular formations, which had to be carefully learned. The slightest confusion in the ranks might crack the battle-line and involve a whole army in disaster.

When at the end of their two years' intensive training, the young troops, clad in full armor, marched proudly back to Athens, a body of well-trained soldiers, they were given a chance to show their mettle, for their service ended in a grand review and public parade. Thereafter, they were considered grown men, and were reckoned as full-fledged Athenian citizens.

In the rugged peninsula of Peloponnesus, many a league of hill and moor from Athens, lay a fertile valley nestling under a great snow-crested mountain-range. The mountains were "high Taygetus"; the fertile valley was "hollow Lacedæmon"; its winding river was the Eurotas; and that straggling, unwalled town was Sparta—the home of the sternest breed of warriors that the world has probably ever seen.

The contrast between Sparta and Athens is amazing; the two peoples seem poles asunder. Partly, no doubt, because the Spartans dwelt in a remote mountain valley, while the Athenians lived on the seaboard and in touch with the outer world. Yet there was also an undoubted difference in race. The Athenians of that period were a blend between the slender dark-haired race that first inhabited Greece and a tall fair-haired race which had conquered the country some centuries before.

The Spartans were later arrivals in Greece. They, like the former conquerors of Athens, were fair-haired northerners, but they seem to have been made of much sterner stuff. Instead of mixing with the original inhabitants, the Spartans held themselves strictly aloof. The dark folk were reduced to the most abject slavery. They were slaves, not of individuals, but of the Spartan state. Contemptuously termed "Helots," they cultivated the fertile land, but had to turn over most of what they raised to the

Spartan authorities, who divided it among the free citizens.

The Helots hated the Spartans as much as the Spartans despised them. And since the Helots greatly outnumbered their masters, there was danger that they would rebel. But the Spartans realized this danger, and in order to forestall it, they lived like a camp of warriors, ready day and night to fight. And in order to keep up this warlike spirit, they imposed upon themselves the strictest discipline that can possibly be imagined.

The Spartans were nothing less than a whole people perpetually under arms—an army that never disbanded. They lived by and for war. This little nation, which could not put 10,000 genuine Spartans in the field, was the terror of all Greece. For many generations they never lost a war, and they even humbled the Athenian power. Unlike most Greek towns, Sparta had no city wall. This was done deliberately. The Spartans thought that the protection of walls made men careless and cowardly. The best defense, said they, is not stones but men.

The Spartans, as we encounter them on the streets of their capital, are tall, lean folk, mostly with light hair and gray or blue eyes. Both men and women are clothed in woolen garments, somewhat like the Athenians', but of plainer cut and with no decoration. They speak seldom, and then in short, pithy sentences; though their words have a dry humor which shows they are keen and intelligent.

There is here no seclusion of the female sex. In Sparta, women and girls walk about freely, with uncovered faces. What a difference between them and their Athenian sisters! Here are no timid, self-conscious creatures. Spartan girls look much like English or American girls of the "athletic" type, with their fresh complexions, strong bodies, erect walk, and frank, fearless gaze. In the girls' athletic field and gymnasium they exercise as strenuously as their brothers. Indeed, they spend part of the afternoon watching the boys at their sports, applauding winners and chaffing losers—which keeps the boys on their mettle every moment. For Spartan girls are taught to spur the boys to utmost skill and bravery.

A Spartan dwelling is very different from an Athenian house. The rooms are large and airy, but there is no attempt at artistic decoration, and the furnishings are plain and simple in the extreme. No luxuries. If any were wanted, there would literally be no money to pay for them; because, in Sparta, the currency consists, not of gold and silver, but of iron ingots, and it would take a wagonload of Spartan "money" to buy anything costly.

In this Spartan house there are no separate women's quarters, as at Athens. The husband treats his wife as an equal. He talks over the most important matters with her, and values her opinion. He addresses her respectfully as "Mistress." And she certainly is mistress of the household. Domestic matters are her province, and if the husband should try to meddle, he would probably be told to mind his own business. But he probably has no wish to interfere in domestic details, because his wife is an excellent housekeeper. In fact, she and her daughters do most of the housework. The Spartans do not approve of domestic slaves. They say a lot of servants make women lazy and spoil children. So, save perhaps for a single Helot serving-wench in the kitchen, the wife and daughters attend to everything. Especially does the housewife take pride in caring for her babies herself. She will have no slave-nurses about, to pamper young children and put un-Spartan ideas into their minds.

This Spartan family seems much like a strait-laced British or American household. Yet there is one important difference. The man of the house never eats at home, while the boys above seven years old do not come home at all. They live elsewhere. The father eats with fourteen other men at a military mess. The fifteen messmates club together to provide the meals, each man contributing his share; the provisions are kept in a common store and served out in fixed rations.

Their food is of the plainest sort. The staple dish is the famous Spartan "black broth"—a kind of stew, made of meat and barley-meal. It is nourishing, but not tasty. Finicky epicures of the more luxurious Greek cities shudder when they even think of it. Over in Asia Minor, a certain king, always on the lookout for new dishes, heard of this black broth and hunted up a Spartan cook to make some for him. One taste was enough. Pushing away his plate, the king sent for the cook and asked him how in heaven's name his countrymen could relish that stuff all their lives.

"Humph!" grunted the Spartan, with the dry

wit characteristic of his race, "to enjoy that dish, you ought to have had a lot of hard exercise, topped off by a plunge into the cold waves of our river Eurotas."

A noted Greek epicure, also curious to try anything new in the food line, swallowed a mouthful of black broth, and then exclaimed: "Now I know why the Spartans do not fear death!"

Besides their black broth, the messmates eat goat's cheese and fruit, washed down by moderate draughts of well-watered wine. The only table luxury they get is when one of their number goes hunting and brings back some game. The men hunt often in the surrounding mountains.

So we find that a typical Spartan boy—Lysander, we will call him—is born to no bed of roses. His first bath is not one of oil and water, but of water and wine—the idea being that weakly infants cannot stand the shock and may as well quit life at once.

When he is a few days old, little Lysander is brought before what may be called a drumhead court martial. He is inspected by a committee of experienced old men, who look him over to see that he has no serious physical defects. Luckily for Lysander, he is a fine, healthy baby; otherwise, he would have been taken to the mountains of Taygetus, and there left to perish. The Spartans will not have their breed weakened by the sickly or deformed.

Having been given a clean bill of health, Lysander is left to his mother's care. She is a devoted mother, but most emphatically not an indulgent one. To wrap a baby up in swaddling clothes may suit those effeminate Athenians; her son is going to get plenty of fresh air. So Lysander is dressed in a woolen shirt and is laid on a blanket, free to kick his tiny legs and thus give his muscles full play.

Save at nursing time, the baby is left to himself. If he cries, he just cries, till he gets over it. Also, no light burns in the nursery at night. He must not be afraid of the dark; and his mother does not bother her head about evil spirits. For this same reason, as he gets a trifle older he is not scared by tales of witches and hobgoblins. Such superstitions are probably good for slavish Helots; a Spartan boy should not know the meaning of fear.

Lysander's military training begins even in the nursery. His mother sings him war-songs for lullabies and tells him stories of brave Spartans and their great deeds. As soon as he can play, his toys are tiny soldiers.

By the age of seven, it is high time Lysander, an unusually sturdy little chap, began the serious business of life. Therefore he leaves home and mother, and is enrolled in a boy-troop with perhaps a dozen other boys about his own age. This in many ways resembles a troop of modern boy scouts. The chief difference is that the Spartan troop lives together all the time. The troop is headed by a young man in his early twenties, whom we may call the scoutmaster. He is their constant guide and companion. He watches over his boys carefully, disciplines them strictly, organizes their sports and games, and keeps them generally keen and fit.

During these years, Lysander is certainly toughened in good shape. He sleeps on a bed of straw or river-rushes, mixed in winter with thistledown. He is allowed no blanket, even on the coldest nights. His only clothes are a woolen shirt and a rough woolen cloak. He dives into the Eurotas when it is skimmed with ice, and wrestles naked in the snow.

Although most of his time is taken up with physical training, Lysander gets a certain amount of what we should call "education." He learns to read and write tolerably well, and he is carefully trained in "music," as understood by the Greeks—that is to say, intoning patriotic songs and poems to the accompaniment of the lyre. As for "higher education" such as we found at Athens, it does not exist at Sparta. To read, write, and sing is enough "learning" for a gentleman-warrior of the Spartan breed.

Lysander almost never goes home and rarely sees his mother. But he does see a good deal of his father. Beneath a stern exterior, that father loves his boy and does his best to make a man of him. Certainly, Lysander's father would scorn to entrust his son to some old slave of a *paidagogos*, as they do at Athens. The scout-master is of course a young Spartan of the best type.

Almost every day Lysander's father fetches the boy to his military mess. There Lysander sits on a stool beside his father, who gives him bits of food from his own plate and bids Lysander observe his elders and listen to their conversation. The mess talk is mostly about war, hunting, and kindred topics. Other fathers have brought their sons, for the Spartans rightly consider this an important part of a boy's education—the more valuable because it is wholly unconscious and unforced.

When Lysander is twelve, he and his troop-mates join a larger company of older boys, up to the age of eighteen. This company, living, studying, and training together, curiously resembles an English "public school." There is even a sort of "fag" system. Every "senior" youth has a "junior" boy as his fag. The fag does various personal services for his senior, and looks to him for advice and protection against bullying by other older boys; the senior is held responsible for his fag's good conduct. This system seems to work well in Sparta. Close and affectionate relations between seniors and juniors are encouraged by the school authorities, and these boyhood friendships often endure through life.

After their twelfth year the Spartan boy's training becomes harsher than ever. They now discard their woolen shirts, retaining only their rough cloaks. Physical exercise of various kinds is redoubled. One of the most strenuous sports is the sham-battle, fought between various teams. The battle-ground is a small island formed by a dammed-up stream. The island is connected with the mainland by two bridges, on opposite sides. The teams of lads, stripped naked, gather on the landward ends of the bridges. At a given signal, they charge across, meeting on the island itself. In the fight which follows, practically anything goes. Pummeling, kicking, scratching, biting; the battle continues until one team or the other has been pitched, splashing, into the water, and the victors triumphantly hold the conquered island. The banks of the stream are crowded with spectators, spurring the combatants to the utmost and scornfully condemning the

THE STORY OF YOUTH 53

slightest sign of weakness or shirking. Those sham-battles and other sports are led by captains, chosen from among their number by the boys themselves. And ambition to become a captain is yet another spur to the boys' best efforts.

Probably the hardest privation Lysander is called upon to bear is short rations. The school messes, modeled on those of the grown men, are even more meager in character. The food served is just sufficient to maintain health; it is never enough really to satisfy a growing boy's appetite.

Like the rest of the Spartan training system, these short rations have a purpose. Their object is to sharpen the boys' wits and develop qualities like craft and resourcefulness. So the hungry Lysander and his comrades are shown a way to satisfy their gnawing appetites; they are bidden to steal their extra food!

At early dawn and after nightfall, Spartan boys go slinking about dwelling-houses, butchers' shops, poultry yards, orchards, and vegetable gardens, intent on stealing food. If they succeed, they eat their fill in their messes, praised by their instructors and envied by less fortunate companions. If they are caught in the act, they are flogged and deprived of one of their regular meals, for having thieved so ill.

One of the most noteworthy features of the Spartan state was its legal prolongation of "boyhood" and "youth." Lysander was considered a mere "boy" until he was eighteen. Schooldays were then over. But during the next two years, he occupies a special legal status termed "approaching youth."

During this two-year period, Lysander undergoes a phase of military training peculiar to Sparta. He becomes a secret agent of the military police-bureau charged with keeping the Helot population in due subjection. Over the territory held by Sparta, Lysander travels, familiarizing himself with the country and obeying the commands of his superiors. The craft and keenness gained in his food raids here stand him in good stead. For his job is to spy upon the Helots, to discover any who may show dangerous, seditious tendencies. When he observes such a man among the Helots, he reports the circumstances to the police authorities, and he is probably ordered to waylay the fellow and kill him on the spot.

After two years of this strange life Lysander returns to Sparta, bronzed, travel-hardened, and experienced. Yet even now he is not considered a grown man; he is only a "youth." And this "youthful" period is to last ten years!

All that time he is a soldier in active service. Lysander is drilled and maneuvered until he has learned to perfection the minutest detail of the art of war and instinctively knows just what to do on all occasions.

No wonder that the Spartan heavy infantry was the terror of Greece; and that Leonidas and his immortal three hundred hoplites composedly combed their long fair hair and calmly completed their elaborate battle toilet in face of Xerxes' astonished Persian host, before the supreme death-grapple at Thermopylæ!

From a boresome barrack existence of endless drill and iron discipline, actual warfare came as a joyous sort of vacation. For, once on campaign, the Spartan soldier had a relatively easy time of it. Drill was moderate, rations were abundant, and officers permitted many unusual liberties. As Plutarch well says, "the Spartans were the only people in the world to whom war gave repose."

And Plutarch goes on to paint a striking picture of a Spartan army going into battle. "When," he writes, "their army was drawn up in battle array, and the enemy near, the general sacrificed a goat, commanded the soldiers to set garlands on their heads, and the pipers to play the tune of the hymn to Castor, and himself began the pæan of advance. It was at once a magnificent and a terrible sight to see them march on, to the tune of their flutes, without any disorder in their ranks, any discomposure in their minds, or change in their countenances; calmly and cheerfully moving with the music to the deadly fight."

So the long years of his militant youth pass, until at length Lysander reaches his thirtieth birthday. Then, at last, he is declared a "man," and is admitted to full Spartan citizenship. He can attend the public assembly, hold office, join a man's mess, have a house of his own, marry, and raise a family.

Those thirty long years have set their mark indelibly upon Lysander. He is hard, grim, dour; a harsh unsympathetic person if you will—but a man.

Chapter III

CHILDREN OF ANCIENT ROME

THE first streak of dawn, and Caius rose from his couch-bed, donned his toga, and hurried to the atrium. Caius was a Roman boy who lived in the early days, when Rome was yet a small city of hard-fighting, plain-living folk with whom early rising was a virtue. So when Caius entered the atrium, he found most of the family up and dressed before him.

The atrium was a spacious oblong chamber. It was the living-room—the center of family life. The old walls and pillars were black with smoke from the hearth-fire, which finally found its way out through a hole in the roof. In former days even the cooking had been done there, though now there was a kitchen in the back of the house. Caius listened eagerly to the sound of servants bustling about in the kitchen, preparing breakfast, for he was a healthy boy and decidedly hungry.

Before breakfast, however, there were certain ceremonies to be gone through. First, the paterfamilias or "house-father" had to be duly saluted. The paterfamilias was the oldest man of the family, and a very important personage. In this case he was Caius' grandfather—a dignified old senator who sat gravely in a round-backed chair awaiting the family salutations. Caius' stalwart father greeted the old man as respectfully as the youngest member of the household, for all were alike subject to the paterfamilias' authority. And the household was large, since it consisted of the senator's two grown sons, their wives, and numerous children. Little Caius and his sister Caia approached the old man when their turn came and wished him the prescribed "Good Morning." The senator then rose, went to the altar, and offered prayers to the family gods, Caius acting that day as altar-boy.

Thereupon, breakfast was served. It was a substantial meal. There were wheaten porridge, fruit, ripe olives, cheese, and great round loaves of whole-wheat bread just out of the brick oven, where they had been slowly baking overnight. This bread was coarse and crisp enough to exercise the jaws and keep the teeth white. With it the children drank cups of warm, fresh goat's milk.

Breakfast over, the children of the household were inspected by their mothers to see that their purple-edged togas were neat and clean before they set out for school.

Though the sun has not yet risen, the streets of Rome are thronged with boys and girls between the ages of seven and twelve, trudging schoolward.

They do not display must eagerness or enthusiasm. They know what awaits them! The stern discipline of Rome is nowhere shown better than in the schoolroom.

The master sits in a raised chair, scanning every move of the pupils, who sit on wooden benches beneath him. A ferrule, a birch rod, or a cat-o'-nine-tails hangs conveniently beside his desk, and is in almost constant use. The slightest fault brings a whack in its train. And boys and girls are thrashed with complete impartiality. For, unlike Athens, old Rome believed in coeducation; as in modern America, Roman boys and girls sat side by side in the primary schools.

If a whack with the ferrule be the penalty for minor errors, we can imagine the thrashings administered when a pupil really shirks his tasks; or when, as sometimes happens, boys try to get out of their lessons by putting oil in their eyes, or feign sickness by chewing cummin seeds which cause them to grow startlingly pale!

This severity of the schoolmaster lasts until the days of the empire. Centuries after Caius' day, a Roman poet of somewhat convivial habits curses his luck because he has chosen lodgings near a school. For, when he has attended a gay party the previous evening and wants to sleep late next morning, he is rudely awakened at sunrise by the sound of blows and the dismal howls of boys.

The poet Horace had such vivid recollections of his schooldays with a master of this type that he wrote a poem about them, giving Orbilius, the teacher, the dubious nickname of *plagosus*—which means "the giver of stripes and welts."

In early Rome schooling was little more than what we would call "primary education." As in Greece, the Roman child traced its letters with a stylus on waxed tablets. During the early republic, Rome had as yet produced no worth-while literature. Reading was taught chiefly so that the child might be able to read the laws of the land. These laws were committed to memory, the pupils reciting them in a singsong drone.

Arithmetic was a study of real importance. The Roman system of numerals, in which values are expressed by different combinations of letters of the alphabet, was a decidedly clumsy method. Little Caius, to get his sums straight, used an abacus, or counting-machine, besides a queer method of reckoning on his fingers. And the master kept him at it till he could "figure" well—as a practical, business-like Roman should.

School let out at noon, and the children trooped homeward in time for dinner, then served at midday. After dinner, the younger children romped about the spacious atrium, teased their pet dogs, and played with their toys.

Yet there were limits to the fun Caius and his playmates were permitted. Whenever they got too boisterous, the old grandfather or some other grown-up member of the household would be apt to raise a reproving finger and point solemnly to the ancestral masks ranged along the atrium wall.

Those wax masks represented many generations

of departed ancestors, and their glass eyes were forever gazing severely down upon the doings which went on in the atrium below. Perpetual guardians of the household, they symbolized the strict family discipline which prevailed in early Rome. The old Romans, like the New England Puritans, took life "hard." So their children were taught from earliest years to cultivate a grave and serious demeanor.

Though Caius' boyhood was somewhat lacking in gaiety, it was far from dull. The life of an old Roman household was full of interesting doings, especially the religious ceremonies. Boys and girls assisted their elders at the daily sacrifices to the family gods, took part in wedding and funeral processions, and especially enjoyed the complicated rites which occurred when a new member of the family arrived. In Caius' home, when his aunt had borne a son, the household all assembled in the atrium, everyone, even the slaves, and awaited the appearance of the new-born boy. The nurse presented the baby to the paterfamilias for his inspection, and when the senator had bowed approval, she laid the infant at its father's feet.

That was a tense moment, for the old Roman law permitted a father to refuse to recognize a new-born child as his, in which case it would be taken from the house and left in some public place, where anyone might appropriate it. But this seldom happened, for children were much wanted in early Rome; so Caius saw his uncle raise the baby proudly in his arms, thereby formally acknowledging the child as his and pledging himself to rear and cherish it, as a Roman parent should.

To the old Romans, this meant, among other things, that the new arrival must get started right with the supernatural powers. So the first weeks of the baby's life were filled with complicated religious rites, in which Caius was actor as well as spectator. Many minor gods and goddesses, especially concerned with children, had to be propitiated. There was one goddess whose sole function was to watch over the ceremonial lifting of the infant in its father's arms. Another goddess guarded its cradle; while still another graced the celebration when the baby was given its name. A god made its bones grow straight and strong, and a second god saw to it that the child's mind was alertly receptive to parental instruction.

In addition to those special deities of childhood, there were the family gods to be considered. These were the kindly Lares and Penates. Their little shrines, set in the walls of the atrium, were always decked with garlands and votive offerings. When a baby arrived, the Lares and Penates were showered with extra gifts and especially besought to look after the newcomer. Caius was very careful to offer cakes and to pour libations of wine in just the right manner.

Finally, there were the ancestors. The Romans believed that the spirits of the dead hovered about their former abode, and the glass eyes of their waxen masks watched every action of the household. Therefore, the ancestors' favor and protection too were needed for the new-born baby.

The climax of these religious ceremonies was the presentation of the *bulla* and the *crepundia* to the new member of the family. The *bulla* was a circular medallion of gold or gilded bronze, containing a sacred charm against sickness or misfortune. Once hung about a baby's neck, it was never taken off until a boy reached man's estate or until a girl was married.

The *crepundia* were a collection of little trinkets, presented by relatives and even by the household slaves. Their function was to ward off witches, goblins, and the evil eye. The Roman playwright Plautus describes in one of his comedies a typical set of *crepundia:* a tiny gold sword with the name of the father; a gold ax with the name of the mother; a silver sickle; two clasped hands; and a miniature pig. These trinkets were treasured throughout childhood, and their formal relinquishment on coming of age signified the entry into adult life through a "putting away of childish things."

Never did Caius forget the day when his cousin Festus came home. Festus was sixteen and had been serving as a military cadet under his father, an officer in the Roman army campaigning against the Greek cities in southern Italy. Caius' father was likewise an army officer, and for more than three months the fighting-men of the family had been in the field. Caius had listened feverishly to the war talk of his elders and had devoured every scrap of rumor bandied about the streets as he went to and from school. But no certain tidings had come for some time.

Then, at last, about sundown of that memorable day, Caius started up from a game of marbles as he

heard the porter's glad cry, and ran to greet Festus just as the stalwart lad strode through the street door into the atrium, in his gleaming bronze helmet, clashing armor, and with big oblong shield.

"Victory!" Festus shouted, as the household swarmed about him. "That stubborn Greek city is taken! The army returns, and there will surely be a Triumph!"

A few days later the Triumph was celebrated. So excited was Caius that on his way to the Capitol with his family, he got lost in the crowd, was roughly jostled by the milling plebeian mob, and was cuffed by a guard when he darted out into the thoroughfare cleared for the triumphal procession.

Despairing of making his way through the crowd, Caius caught sight of some boys perched upon the top of a wall. A moment later he had scrambled up beside them, and with dangling legs contentedly looked about him. As far as he could see, every house was decked with bunting and garlanded with flowers, while the windows and even the roofs were thronged with men and women in their best togas, newly whitened for the occasion.

Suddenly, far away, a deep roar of cheering burst forth, as the procession entered the city gate leading from the Campus Martius, the great exercise and drill ground outside the walls of Rome. Nearer and nearer came the cheers: *"Io triumphe! Hail to the Victors!"* And presently, down the long street, the head of the procession came in sight: first the magistrates and the senate, walking with dignity; then a blaring corps of trumpeters, proclaiming the spoils of the campaign. Caius gazed at the booty of a rich Greek city—silks, tapestries, bronze and marble statues, coffers of gold, and much more besides. After this walked a hecatomb of milk-white oxen with gilded horns—victims destined for the sacrifice before the temple of Capitoline Jove.

THE STORY OF YOUTH 65

Then, amid a frantic burst of cheering, passed the victorious general, clad in robes of purple and gold, crowned with laurel, and standing stiffly erect in a magnificent chariot drawn by four spirited horses. Last came the legions, the invincible infantry of Rome. Endlessly, they tramped by, in serried masses, a blaze of helmets and glittering spear-points, making the street tremble at the crash of their hob-nailed tread. Caius watched the standards rising and falling to the rhythmical swing of the march, and he longed for the day to come when he would be a soldier too.

Caius' father, back from the wars, became his boy's constant companion. The old Romans believed in family training, and devoted much time to their children's up-bringing. When the father held a morning reception to clients in his atrium, Caius stood by his side. When he sought the Forum, the son also listened to the orators and gained a firsthand knowledge of politics. So far did the Romans carry this practical training that in the earliest days of the republic, sons of senators were actually present at meetings of that body, until boyish lips told tales of secret sessions and so ended the practice. To teach them good manners, Caius and his sister Caia were present at most social occasions. Even at formal dinners, they and their young cousins often sat at table or helped with the service. This did not mean late hours, since the principal meal in early Rome was at noon.

Caius' father saw to his son's physical development. Was it not a Roman who uttered the famous phrase: *"Mens sana in corpore sano,* A sound mind in a sound body"? But the Roman father had a strictly practical object in view. There was none of the Greek cult of grace and physical beauty and virtually none of the Greek love of sport. Caius never saw a gymnasium, and never heard of organized athletics. Nevertheless, he got plenty of vigorous exercise. Often, his father would take him to the Campus Martius, the broad stretch of level land by the river Tiber. On sunny afternoons, the field was thronged with men and boys, out for a swim in the river or engaged in impromptu sports such as running, wrestling, jumping, or throwing the javelin. These matches did not culminate in public exhibitions like the Greek Olympic Games; the Campus Martius was primarily not an athletic-field, but a drill-ground for the legions. A true Roman boy always remembered that he was a future soldier of the republic, and that his training aimed at hardiness and vigor of frame. The athletic sporting spirit was not in him.

Caius now saw little of his sister Caia. Caia was closely under her mother's wing; for, as Roman fathers trained their sons, so Roman matrons trained their daughters. There was much for a Roman girl to learn, and none too much time in which to learn it. Girls were then married at fourteen or fifteen, and a Roman matron would have felt disgraced if a son-in-law should complain that a daughter of hers had proved an incompetent helpmeet.

The Roman maiden was therefore expected to understand every branch of domestic science, so that she would know how to manage a large household. And in addition to her general responsibilities, she must personally perform certain domestic duties, particularly the care of children and the making of the family wardrobe. To spin, weave, and sew the garments worn by all members of her immediate family was for a Roman matron a point of honor. It was the recognized test of good housewifery, and the tradition persisted for centuries. The Emperor Augustus prided himself on wearing only garments made by his wife and daughters; and the same was true of other "good" emperors who, in Rome's degenerate days, sought to revive old-fashioned virtues by their personal example. Caia had little time for dolls or childish games, but spent most of her time in the kitchen or at the loom "minding her wool," as the saying went in those days.

Another notable event in Caius' boyhood was his cousin Festus "donning the white toga." A few months after his return occurred his formal coming-of-age; for on his seventeenth birthday, the Roman youth was declared a man and a citizen, with impressive ceremonies. First Festus' father removed the *bulla,* the sacred talisman which had hung about the lad's neck since infancy, and consecrated it to the Lares in the presence of the assembled family. After prayer and sacrifice, Festus laid aside his boyish toga, edged with purple, and was solemnly invested with the *toga virilis,* the plain white robe of Roman manhood and citizenship. Thereupon the household went in procession to the Forum, where Festus was formally presented to the people as a new citizen of Rome. His name was then inscribed on the voting-list, a sacrifice was offered at the public altar, and the great day closed with a feast attended by family and friends.

The sun was rising when Marcus yawned, stretched himself, and gazed in lazy contentment about his room. It was a comfortable chamber, handsomely furnished in the Greek style, with oriental rugs on the floor and costly Babylonian hangings at the doorway. Marcus was a Roman boy, but over four centuries had passed since Caius' day, and this was the mansion of a moderately wealthy gentleman during the reign of the Emperor Titus.

Times had changed in those four hundred years. No getting up at the crack of dawn for the son of a wealthy Roman of the empire. And no hustling to the atrium for family prayers. Marcus would breakfast in his own chamber. A suave Greek slave appeared in the doorway with a silver tray. This he set down on a low table by the bedside.

It was a breakfast much like ours, and not at all like the morning meal of old Roman times. Instead of hot porridge and coarse home made bread flavored with garlic or goat's cheese, there was fruit, rolls crisp from the bakery, and eggs daintily prepared. Instead of coffee, Marcus drank well-watered wine.

As Marcus finished his breakfast, a second Greek slave appeared. He was a valet, and had come to assist his young master in getting dressed. Clothing was about the only thing that had not changed much since early Roman times. Marcus donned a purple-edged boy's toga similar to that Caius had worn.

Dressed for the morning, Marcus pushed aside the hangings of the doorway. His room was on the second story and overlooked a patio-like court, around which were grouped the other sleeping-chambers of the family. The court was floored in mosaic, with a central water-basin of white marble. In the basin floated a miniature galley—a toy of Marcus'. The patio was his favorite playground. It was unroofed, surrounded by a marble colonnade, and adorned with statuary and potted plants. In summer an awning excluded the glare. A Negro slave-boy was now busy with this awning, grinning good-naturedly as he caught sight of his young master.

Descending to the court, Marcus walked to the front part of the dwelling and entered the atrium—no longer the family living-room, but a formal reception hall. Here he saluted his father, who sat in state, holding the customary morning reception to a crowd of clients and acquaintances. This atrium was walled with colored marbles, lined with statues, and roofed with an elaborately carved and gilded ceiling.

It was time for Marcus to start for school. Though partly educated at home by a Greek tutor, he attended a fashionable day school in the neighborhood for boys of his own age and rank, though many wealthy boys were at that period wholly educated at home by private instructors.

By the porter's lodge at the street door, Marcus found waiting the slave who conducted him to and from school. That conductor, with his beard, cloak, and long staff was an exact copy of one of those old *paidagogoi* of Greek boys in the great days of Athens.

The whole system of Roman education under the empire was closely modeled on that of Athens. Roman children now learned Greek with their A-B-C's from Greek teachers, and studied the Greek classics as their principal textbooks. Marcus chatted in Greek with his *paidagogos* as they walked along, as fluently as he talked his Latin mothertongue.

A great admirer of Hellas and its culture, like most Roman gentlemen of his day, Marcus' father, Lollius, was daily expecting the arrival of an Athenian friend, who was bringing with him his son Charicles, a boy about Marcus' own age. When Marcus had been at Athens with his father the year before, the two boys had become friends. Now Marcus would show him the sights of Rome. Charicles was due to arrive at just the right moment, for the Emperor Titus was about to inaugurate the Colosseum (the huge amphitheater which had been so long a-building) by a series of games and gladiatorial shows, which would be the most splendid in living memory.

Like all Roman boys of his day, Marcus was crazy about horse-races and gladiators. He knew the names and records of famous jockeys and fighters in the arena as well as English boys of today know about celebrated cricketers or American boys follow the heroes of the diamond. Lessons that day were a farce, for the boys could think of nothing except the approaching games. But Marcus and his comrades got off with mild penalties. The head master, a wily Greek freedman, knew how to temper justice with mercy when dealing with sons of wealthy parents, who did not like to have them too severely punished, and he declared a holiday during the festive period.

When Marcus reached home, the porter informed him that Nikias of Athens and his son had just arrived. Marcus ran in search of Charicles and the two boys were soon chattering together, both talking excitedly at the same time. Marcus proudly showed Charicles his treasures—the galley in the patio pool, the bronze figures of animals, the toy chariots with real wheels, the little ivory statuettes of gladiators, and more besides. He told about the approaching games, which he asserted would be absolutely the most wonderful that the world had ever seen.

A slave now announced luncheon, for the Romans had by now abandoned the old-fashioned custom of having their dinner at midday. The luncheon was, like breakfast, a remarkably "modern" meal, consisting chiefly of cold meats, vegetables, and a salad.

Afterward, the hosts, father and son, took their guests on a sightseeing tour. When they emerged from the street door, they found awaiting them Lollius' two best litters with their bearers. These litters were comfortable conveyances, with soft mattresses wide enough for two persons to recline side by side, and with curtains which could be closed or pushed back, as desired. One set of bearers (four in number) were Cappadocian slaves; the other set were Negroes. Both sets were well-matched, and Lollius was as proud of them as a man today might be of fine spans of horses. Lollius bowed his friend Nikias into the first litter, the two boys scrambled into the second, and the bearers started off, preceded by a pompous servitor, who waved a staff and proclaimed his master's rank and dignity, to clear the way through crowded streets.

Rome was then the Mistress of the World, and her streets were thronged with traffic of every kind. The main thoroughfares were filled with fashionable ladies and gentlemen, reclining in litters borne by slaves, or riding in chariots drawn by horses. Mingled with the Roman citizens in their white togas was a cosmopolitan multitude of strangers and slaves from every corner of the known world. Greeks, Gauls, Syrians, Egyptians, Jews, Spaniards, North Africans, and Negroes, jostled one another on the Roman streets, their national costumes emphasizing their foreign origins. Now and then the boys would toss copper coins to the ragged street-urchins running alongside the litter begging for alms.

Sightseeing in Imperial Rome was a hot, dusty business, so the trip ended at the pillared portico of a public bath. The friends disrobed in a large, airy dressing-room. Clad in sheets, they went through the warm and the hot rooms, much as in a modern Turkish bath. After a good sweat, the boys lay down on stone slabs and were massaged by a bath attendant, who scraped their bodies with a wooden instrument called a strigil. Finally, they entered a swimming-pool dotted with bathers. Emerging from the pool, the boys were given a rub-down so vigorous that their bodies were rosy and tingling as they returned home.

THE STORY OF YOUTH 73

Dinner, served about sundown, was a quiet family affair. Yet it consisted of several courses, and so restful were the couches on which the boys reclined while eating that, long before the meal was over, they were drowsy, and Lollius smilingly bade slaves take them off to bed, while he and Nikias tarried in the lamplit dining-room, talking of Athens over their wine.

The next day the festal period was to begin with a series of chariot-races, to be run, not at the Colosseum, but in the Circus Maximus—the great Roman race-course. In this way, the Emperor Titus planned to rouse public enthusiasm and to whet his people's appetite for the gladiatorial games and spectacles which were to inaugurate the opening of the Colosseum itself.

Chariot-racing was conducted by four corporations, known by their colors as the Blues, Greens, Whites, and Reds. Every Roman, young or old, was a champion of one or another of those colors. Marcus was an ardent "rooter" for the Blues, rather priding himself on differing from his father, who was a "Green."

The Circus Maximus next day, seating over 100,000 spectators, was jammed with a multitude, rising tier on tier to the topmost seats surmounted by a marble colonnade. The circus was an immense oblong, like a Greek stadium, rounded at one end and square at the other—where were the gateways from the horse-stables. Down the middle of the enclosed space ran a long stone barrier, called the spina, adorned with shrines, obelisks, and other decorations. The chariots started from the entrance gates, rounded the farther end of the spina, and came back along the home stretch on the other side; seven laps made a race. Four-horse chariots (*quadrigæ*) were ordinarily used.

Marcus and Charicles had seats directly opposite the imperial box. They would have a good sight of the Emperor Titus when he appeared. And behind the far side of the circus rose the Palatine Hill, crowned by the magnificent Palace of the Cæsars. Even as they watched, the imperial box filled with courtiers, and presently, at sight of a commanding figure, the whole vast audience rose to its feet, cheering wildly for Titus, the Divine Emperor of Rome.

Cæsar's coming gave the signal for the races. From the entrance gates appeared columns of chariots, each drawn by four horses, matched in teams of white, black, roan, dapple-gray, and other shades. The charioteers, braced erect as they held in their teams with taut reins, wore the colors of their respective companies. Four abreast and over a hundred strong, the chariots paced slowly round the stadium in stately procession. Then all save the four which were to enter the first race disappeared. The contestants lined up; a trumpet sounded; the umpire dropped a white flag; and they were off!

Down the long straightaway they sped, reined in sharply at the curve, rounded the farther end of the spina, and came tearing down the other side. Marcus cheered wildly for the Blue team, which was in the lead, but at the fifth lap, Lollius touched his excited son on the shoulder, smiling ironically, for the Green charioteer had forged into the lead, kept it and won the race. At the next race, Marcus had his revenge, for the Blue charioteer won by a neck from the Green team. The third race was marred by one of those tragedies which often happened in the circus. As three chariots started to round the spina at the same time, the innermost team was pressed against the wall. Crash went a wheel, and chariot and horses piled into a tangled heap, from which the limp form of a Red charioteer was taken by attendants a few moments later. Thus, all that day, the chariots raced: by fours; by eights; finally, a dozen at a time. A frenzied, harassing day it was; yet Marcus went home well content, for the Blues had won the most races, and Charicles had become a rooter for the Blues.

Next morning the two boys were awakened early by a penetrating murmur which filled the air—a deep hum like a vast swarm of bees. The great day had come! The new Colosseum was to be formally opened to the public, and all Rome was swarming like a hive. Although Lollius had ordered the litters early, to avoid the crush of the last-moment crowds, they had difficulty in making their way through the turbulent throngs, pressing in from all directions on the center of attraction.

At last the Colosseum loomed before them—a huge bulk of stone, ornamented by arcades and numberless statues. The bronze gateways were held by prætorian guards in crested helmets and shining armor, to keep gangs of rowdies from stealing in. At Lollius' approach, however, the centurion in charge of that gate saluted, the ticket-taker bowed respectfully, and an usher promptly showed our party to their seats.

The great circle of the amphitheater was already well filled, to the topmost seats under the colonnade. Sailors were stretching an immense blue awning to shield the spectators from the sun. This awning was spangled with gold stars to represent the sky, while in the center had been woven the figure of a gigantic eagle—the symbolic bird of Rome. As the awning swayed in the breeze, the eagle appeared to flap its wings and gaze fiercely down at the sanded arena, which was soon to drink such torrents of blood.

The Greek boy was not so keen for the sights of the arena as he had been about the chariot races. Like most Greeks, he had an instinctive dislike of the bloodshed and brutality of gladiatorial shows. Marcus, on the other hand, being a true Roman, was quite callous to such things. He had already seen many gladiators fight in the arena, and saw only the pomp and thrill of the spectacle. So he chaffed Charicles good-naturedly and told him he would soon get over his qualms—just as a Spanish boy of today might reassure an American or British friend who was about to witness a bull-fight for the first time.

The crowd had begun to grow impatient when a flourish of brazen trumpets announced the coming of the emperor. As Titus appeared in the imperial box, escorted by lictors and followed by a train of courtiers, the vast multitude shouted, again and again, *"Ave, Cæsar! Salve, Imperator!"* The Roman people were in the best of humors; they had a great day before them!

When the cheering had at length died down,

Titus raised his hand for the games to begin. To another flourish of brazen trumpets, the show was on. It began with an act by two clowns, wearing grotesque masks. One clown was short and fat; the other, lean and prodigiously tall. The mob in the upper galleries roared with laughter at their antics.

Then followed a series of "short turns" by acrobats, jugglers, and bareback riders, animal-trainers with trick-dogs, dancing bears, and snarling panthers which sprang through hoops: much like the acts of a modern circus. The crowd began to grow impatient again. They were getting thirsty for a taste of blood! The master of ceremonies sensed the popular mood. The trained animals disappeared. A deep silence fell. The real business of the day was about to begin!

A third flourish of trumpets, and into the amphitheater strode a column of stalwart men: the gladiators. The procession circled the arena and paused before the imperial box. The famous cry rang out: "Hail, Cæsar! We who are about to die salute thee!"

The long column, over a thousand strong, filed back to the main gateway into the arena and momentarily vanished. Then, the first batch of contestants reappeared—twenty-five pairs of gladiators, armed respectively as "Thracians" and "Samnites." The Thracians were lightly armed with small round shields and wicked-looking crooked swords. The Samnites wore elaborate plumed helmets, and carried short, straight swords and oblong shields. The contestants were planted in pairs all over the arena, and a circle was traced in the sand, within which each pair must fight and die.

A moment later, they were at it. The vast crowd howled, and cheered, and made bets as the fighting went fiercely forward. When a gladiator fell, if merely wounded, his victor placed a foot on his neck, while the prostrate man raised his hand for mercy. The spectators decided his fate. Thumbs up and waving arms spelled life; thumbs down meant death. Chance popular likes and dislikes played a great role. Marcus preferred Samnites; so he always raised his arm for them, and invariably gave a wounded Thracian "thumb down."

After the survivors had departed and slaves with baskets of sand had effaced the pools of blood, the next act took place. Two famous gladiators fought a duel, mounted on war-horses. Spurring their steeds, they charged one another like whirlwinds, displaying marvelous skill as they caught sword-cuts on their shields. After a few moments, a chance stroke killed the horse of one of the gladiators, who was thrown heavily on the sand. This was so obviously not his fault that the crowd unanimously held "thumbs up," and the dazed man was led off, to fight another day.

The noon hour had come, and an intermission was declared for lunch. Up and down the aisles of the Colosseum went hundreds of venders, selling light refreshments and cold drinks. Marcus' party was served a good luncheon, brought from home and now produced by a slave.

The afternoon show opened with some sensational wild-animal acts. Such rare creatures as giraffes and ostriches had been brought at great expense from the almost unknown depths of Africa, and made a hit with the crowd. A troop of archers staged a mock hunt, chasing the terrified animals across the expanse of sand, and shooting them down with arrows.

Next came a duel between two gigantic bull elephants—one from Asia, the other from Africa. Of different species, the monsters instinctively hated one another at first sight, and charged together like thunderbolts. Twining their trunks like monster serpents, they slashed with their long tusks, which had been tipped with steel for more deadly effect. Soon the African elephant, somewhat the more powerful of the two, fatally gored his opponent, and the Asiatic giant fell dying on the sands. The attendants had a tough job getting the huge carcass out of the arena.

Thereafter followed a long series of gladiatorial shows—heavy-armed *secutors* against agile *retiarii* equipped with tridents, who strove to enmesh their ponderous opponents by a cast of their whirling nets; *dimachæri* brandishing curved sabers in either hand, against *murmillos* encased in dolphin-shaped helmets and thrusting with long bronze blades; Gauls, Britons, Germans, and Numidians, armed and matched in various ways.

Poor Charicles grew white at the unaccustomed sight of blood, while his father Nikias, though politely refraining from turning away his head, frequently closed his eyes. But Marcus watched the bouts with unflagging enthusiasm, and Lollius was quite unmoved, until at last be became slightly bored. Observing that his Greek guests did not relish the spectacle, he decided to leave before the end, to avoid the departing crowds. So they sought their waiting litters, refreshed themselves at an almost deserted public bath, and went home to dinner. The great day was over.

Chapter IV

CHILDREN OF THE NORTH

A NEW-BORN baby boy lies on a wolf-skin spread upon a hard-stamped dirt floor. The women have just laid him there, in the warmth of the glowing log fire, to be inspected by his father, whose heavy footfall has been heard outside. The father enters, followed by two companions bearing the hindquarters and antlers of a stag—the trophies of a successful hunt.

The father strides over to the wolfskin and looks down at the baby. He is a huge man, with long blond hair and a great tawny beard. He is dressed in a bearskin; his legs are wrapped in woolen bands, and his feet are encased in stout leather shoes. He leans upon his spear and gazes steadily at the baby with fierce blue eyes set in a ruddy face, weather-beaten by wind and cold.

No one speaks; neither the women beyond the fire, nor the men by the door. In the silence, you can hear a cow lowing and pigs grunting in the nearby stable, while a distant wolf's howl echoes through the forest.

Then the father takes his spear and thrusts the

butt-end toward the child. As the wooden shaft touches it, the tiny hands clutch at the weapon. "Ha!" exclaim the onlookers in satisfied tones. As for the father, his blue eyes gleam and his stern features relax in a grim smile. "Good!" says he, "The bairn will be a man of his hands!" He stoops and lifts the baby in his strong arms, girt with bronze or golden bands. As he rises, an old woman approaches carrying an earthenware crock. The father dips a finger into the jug and smears the baby's lips with honey.

The old woman now takes the baby and ducks it into a bucket of cold water. The infant yells lustily, but seems none the worse for its chilly bath. Again the father smiles: "Good! He will be a true man." After this, the baby is wrapped in woolen swaddling-clothes and laid in a rude cradle near the fire. He has passed his first tests, and is now a recognized member of his family and tribe in good and regular standing.

That is a typical scene in Old Germany and Scandinavia—the home of those tall blond peoples who poured forth from their northlands in a series of conquering waves during many centuries. The first of these waves overran the decrepit Roman Empire. Another wave of Anglo-Saxons from north Germany transformed Romanized Britain into "Engle-Land." Then, when those Germanic peoples had settled down in their new homes, a final wave of Scandinavians, the vikings, burst upon them, and the process of conquest and settlement was resumed. That long turbulent period, lasting roughly from 400 to 1000 A. D., is known as the Dark Ages.

The little German or Scandinavian in his original northland home was a sturdy child. He was also a decided blond. The old Nordics set great store by their racial type. The gods and heroes whom the children learn to reverence from their earliest years are of fair complexion. Odin, the "All-Father," has long fair hair; Thor the Thunderer, he of the mighty hammer, has a great red beard; Balder the Beautiful is described in the sagas, or heroic poems, as "so fair to look upon that light streams from him, and the whitest of all flowers is likened to his eyelashes."

An ancient saga tells us that the boy of good family should have "yellow hair, his cheeks rosy, his blue eyes as keen as a young serpent's." Dark hair and swarthy skin are signs of low birth. When a certain Norse noblewoman bears twins of brunette appearance, the husband flies into a rage, calls them "hell-skins," swears that some wicked elf or troll must have played him a trick, and refuses to recognize the babies as his own.

The old Nordics were a warrior-race, and from boyhood, children were trained and toughened to become strong, fearless men and women. The very names given them by their parents echo the clash of arms. Boys were called by such warlike names as *Gerhard*, "The Spear-Bold"; girls received equally martial names like *Brünhild*, "She Who Fights in Armor," and *Gertrude*, "The Spear-Strong," after the Valkyries, Odin's divine war-maidens, who hover over the battle-field to "choose the slain" and bear dead heroes away to the delights of Valhalla. A boy's first solid food was given him by his father on the tip of a sword or spear, to signify that he was to win his way in the world by force of arms and end his life in battle as a brave man should.

Children led an open-air life. The primitive Nordics hated crowding and abhorred the very thought of towns. The Old Germans despised the Romans for living cooped up in cities, which, they declared, "rob even wild beasts of their courage." When the Anglo-Saxons conquered Britain they sacked many fine cities and then left them desolate, building their wooden houses at a distance, refusing to use even the stones and bricks of the Roman ruins.

Nordic child-life was strikingly like that of American pioneer children. The home was a farmstead, the wooden dwelling-house standing with its rude barns and sheds in a forest clearing, isolated or within hailing distance of other farms. Houses of chiefs were relatively large and solidly built, with stag's horns over the painted doorways. The houses of simple freemen were often lightly built of wattle, chinked with clay and half sunk into the earth for warmth in winter. Such were always the abodes of bondmen—usually captives taken in war.

Home-furnishings of all classes were simple in the extreme. At mealtimes, the family sat on benches about a table made from rough-hewn logs, ate with fingers and knives from earthenware, and drank from cow's horns. However, they slept on comfortable beds and pillows stuffed with goose-feathers. Children wore linen shirts reaching to the knee. Only out-of-doors in winter-time did they put on woolen clothing and furs.

Food was usually plentiful. These men were great meat-eaters. Besides wild game of all sorts, the favorite meats were pork and horse-flesh, the latter being considered a sacred food especially good for warriors. Beef was rarely eaten, but milk, cheese, and butter were mainstays of the family larder, as were oatmeal porridge and barley bread. The common vegetables were beets and turnips. The great delicacy was honey, used for sweetening as we do sugar, and also as the basis for a fermented drink called mead. A thin beer was also brewed. Children were allowed mead and beer in moderation.

Children of all classes played together on a footing of perfect equality. The boys of chieftain and bondman were playmates, and Tacitus, the Roman writer, expresses his surprise at seeing German children of nobles and serfs, equally dirty and ill-clad, running about the farmsteads or tending the cattle. However, it was the honest dirt of the country "barefoot boy," for the Old Germans believed in bathing, and at stated intervals the whole family would be scrubbed up in a hot bath akin to the famous "Saturday night bath" of our immediate forefathers.

From their earliest years boys were brought up to be fighting-men, and girls to become the mates and mothers of warriors. The German women would bring their babies and young children near a battlefield, so that the youngsters might get used to the sights and sounds of fighting. When, as often happened, a Teutonic tribe migrated in search of a new home, the women and children would be packed into great covered wagons, drawn by oxen. If the scouts reported an enemy, the wagons would approach close to the prospective battlefield and would then be drawn up in a hollow square. The women and children would keep up a wild chant, to hearten the war-

riors and remind them of the penalty of defeat. For in that case the women and half-grown children would furiously defend their wagon-fortress, killing themselves and the babies at the last to escape the intolerable disgrace of capture and slavery. It all sounds like the "covered wagons" of American pioneers or South African Boer *laagers*, besieged by

Indians or Zulus. Under similar conditions, the customs of our primitive Nordic ancestors reappear, practically unchanged.

Roman writers, from Cæsar down, comment on the early age at which German children were taught the use of arms. Some German tribes seem to have had wooden rocking-horses on which small boys could practice riding exercises before they were big enough to sit a horse, while Seneca speaks of "tender children brandishing the spear."

Fathers often took small boys on hunts against dangerous beasts like the wolf and the wild boar. In Scandinavia, boys would sometimes refuse to play with a newcomer in the neighborhood, until the strange boy had proved that he had killed at least one wild animal on a hunt. Also, there were the blood-feuds which frequently broke out between families, and which were waged with a fury surpassing even the feuds of Scottish borderers or Kentucky mountaineers. One of the Norse sagas tells of a boy only nine years old who could boast that he had killed three men in a feud, while the Norse hero, Olaf Tryggvason, at the same age took up a feud and successfully avenged his foster-father.

Of A-B-C's and books, the primitive Nordic child knew nothing. The Scandinavians did develop a sort of writing called *runes*, but those mystic characters were employed chiefly for magical purposes like engraving charms on amulets or swords. The absence of books was made up for by an extensive literature handed down by word of mouth. Boys and girls had to learn by heart many long epic poems about the gods and heroes, mighty deeds, and even the rules of conduct for every-day life. This literature was being constantly added to, because these people were fond of composing poetry and would often make up odes, composed and chanted according to certain established rules.

Most of this oral education was imparted to the young in the wintertime. In Northern Europe the winter days are very short, while in Scandinavia winter is practically one long night. So the Old Germans and Norsemen would sit or lie for hours about the glowing fire, while outside the storm-winds howled and the snow drifted high. The girls would learn to spin and weave wool or flax, dyeing and embroidering those fabrics whose artistic beauty the Romans recognized and prized. The boys would help the father mend or fashion arms and hunting-gear, after the farm chores were done and the cattle had been fed and bedded down.

Often the father or mother would tell some old folk-tale or chant a heroic saga, the children listening intently and reciting snatches in turn. Thereafter there would probably be a silence, as the whole family fell into revery, pondering what they had heard as they gazed into the flames and the shimmering caverns amid the burning logs. This fireside education would sink deep into young hearts—to be later translated into deeds.

This education laid stress on certain high qualities: courage, honor, loyalty, duty, and contempt for death. Those were the virtues continually instilled into the child in such tales from the Norse sagas as that of Ragnar Lodbrok:

The famous viking, Ragnar Lodbrok, having "fed the ravens" (slaughtered his enemies) in many lands and countless battles, is at last captured by foreign foes, horribly tortured, and finally thrown into a pit of venomous serpents. Despite his sufferings, the hero never once loses his iron nerve, but spends his time extemporizing a death-song so skilfully composed that it becomes a literary classic. This epic poem recites his great deeds, heaps scorn upon his foes, and ends with a defiant laugh.

While the boys were musing upon this splendid example, their sisters would hear a story like the tale from a Norse saga concerning a young wife whose husband quarreled with her family and slew all except one of her brothers. The wife is thus faced with two apparently conflicting loyalties—to husband and to kin. She is true to both duties by first aiding her brother to triumph over her husband; then, when her husband lies wounded in his burning house, she calmly enters the flaming hall, to die at his side, as a Norse wife should.

Again the children thrill to fireside tales like that of Siegfried's hunting in the "Niebelungenlied." The blasts of the hero's horn ring loud and clear through the forest; the baying of his hunting dogs is heard from afar. Siegfried is everywhere, laughing and joking, until at length in sheer sport he catches a huge bear alive and binds it to his saddlebow. Returned to camp, he lets it loose in a Homeric jest. The bear dashes through the camp-kitchen, upsets the food among the ashes, and scares the cooks half out of their wits. Then, as the bear makes tracks for the forest, Siegfried pursues, still laughing, kills the beast, and brings it back to the camp-fire for a fresh meal.

Honey was so important an item in their diet that our primitive forefathers early learned to keep bees. Nevertheless, wild honey was always a grateful addition to the domestic supply. To discover its whereabouts, a boy armed with a small pot containing honey would go to a forest glade or meadow frequented by bees. A bee would soon light upon the pot, drink its fill, and fly away. The boy would note the direction of its flight, which would always be in a "bee-line,"—straight, toward the hive. He would also note the time which elapsed between the bee's departure and its inevitable return with other bees.

The hunter would then walk a short distance in the direction indicated, and repeat the process as the bees went back and forth, checking up constantly on direction and distance. When the hive was located in some hollow trunk or limb, upon that tree the boy would put his mark. It was then *his* tree; and no one, not even the owner of the land, could touch either honey or tree until the discoverer had removed the treasure—which he was supposed to do within a reasonable time.

In New England today, bee-hunters track their quarry by just the same methods, and their rights of discovery are protected by definite legal clauses on the statute-books of the New England States. I myself have seen a Yankee woodsman track wild bees in the New England "North Country"; and when I recall that tall, silent man and his two tow-headed boys, I realize how a change of clothing would have fitted the trio perfectly into a German forest thousands of years ago.

Toughened and trained since boyhood, the Nordic boy grew into a bold and hardy youth. Hunting and farmstead duties were supplemented by instruction in the use of arms. The Old Germans and Scandinavians had regular military exercises, of which the most picturesque was an elaborate war-drill, similar to the Pyrrhic Dance of the ancient Greeks, who were their distant kinsmen. In full battle-array, with sword, spear, ox-horned helmet, and great wooden shield, the young warriors would leap, charge, form the "shield-wall," and go through all their maneuvers, to the sound of martial music furnished by drums and the grunting notes of huge "ludr-horns."

These sham battles would be watched by an admiring audience, especially by the young maidens, toward whom the youths were taught to adopt an attitude of respect verging on reverence. The Nordic woman was believed to possess certain mystic powers, and chosen maidens became priestesses and oracles who were deeply venerated. The wife and mother had many hard duties, but she claimed and obtained universal respect.

Before he could be reckoned a man and a full-fledged member of his tribe, the Nordic lad usually served an apprenticeship in actual warfare. Lads while still very young often performed brave deeds in battle, and until they had thus proved their mettle they could expect scant regard from the fair sex. A Norse saga relates how an earl's daughter is

seated at table beside one a trifle younger than herself. Angered at having been assigned a dinner partner who seems a mere boy, the young maiden remarks scornfully: "Thou hast never given a warm meal to the wolf [slain men in battle]."

But the boy answers proudly: "Aye, but I have walked with bloody brand and whistling spear, with the wound-bird [the raven] following me!" Such were the credentials useful among young people in good Norse society.

When the Nordic youth had proved himself to the satisfaction of his elders, he was admitted to full manhood citizenship by a custom termed "the gift of arms." This was a formal ceremony conducted before the popular assembly of the freemen of the tribe. It was as much binding upon the son of a chief or noble as upon the son of a simple freeman.

A story is told about the youth of Alboin, the King of the Lombards and founder of their realm in Northern Italy shortly after the fall of the Roman Empire. Alboin, while yet a lad, had challenged the son of the king of a rival tribe to single combat, and had come off victorious. The Lombard warriors thereupon clamored that the youthful hero be admitted by his father to the royal table. But the king, controlling his fatherly pride, shook his head. "No," said he, "you know our custom that a king's son may not sit at meat beside his father till he has received a gift of arms from some other king."

Among the Scandinavian Nordics at the height of their power and glory—the Viking Age—the warlike spirit was just as strong as among the Old German tribes. But there was a higher culture and a far wider outlook on the world. The vikings were fierce men of war, but they were relatively civilized.

A typical "sea-king" is Hrolf (Rollo). He was

the leader of that host of Northmen who overran and settled the region of northern France which was thenceforth called "Normandy," and which produced the extraordinary line of dukes, one of whom, William, was to conquer Anglo-Saxon England at the battle of Hastings.

Hrolf came rightly by his warlike genius, for his father Jarl Rognvald was also a noted viking leader. Hrolf grew up in a great rambling wooden mansion, whose lofty hall was decorated in somber magnificence with booty won by the sword in distant lands overseas. The walls, smoke-grimed from the roaring hearth-fires, were hung with rich silks and tapestries. The dining-tables were laden with gold and silver plate and were lighted by tall candlesticks crusted with gold and jewels. All this and much more had been looted from towns and monasteries all the way from Ireland to Italy—wherever the restless Norsemen followed the "path of the sea-birds" over the foam-crested waves.

Almost every year during his childhood, as soon as the furious winter storms abated, Hrolf's father would launch his black long-ships with their gilded dragon-prows and fare forth on the "viking-path" to harry England, Ireland, France, or Odin alone knew where. Impatiently dreaming of the day when he, too, would go "viking faring," little Hrolf spent the months which followed fitting himself to be a sea-king. He learned to wield the sword with either hand, throw two spears at once, draw the bow, and mend his armor at the smoking forge. There was athletic training also: running, jumping, swimming, wrestling, and riding bareback—though in later years Hrolf grew so huge in stature that no horse could carry him, whence his nickname, the "Ganger," because he had to "gang" afoot. Finally there were the varied arts of seamanship, from steering a longship to the ticklish feat of leaping lightly along a bank of laboring oars.

With this practical training went a learning of many polite accomplishments; for the sea-kings were fine gentlemen, in their way. They could compose poetry, sing, play upon the harp, and were skilled at games like chess. They were also fastidiously neat and clean; their long fair hair was kept carefully combed; and great attention was paid to the details of their rich clothing, adorned as it was with a profusion of enameled brooches, jeweled swordbelts, and massive arm-bands of gold.

In late autumn, the long-ships would return heavy-laden with spoil, and grizzled Jarl Rognvald would smile proudly in his tawny beard as he observed how straight and tall his son had grown. There would be great feasts in the hall, with visiting jarls from neighboring fjords. Huge joints of swine's flesh and sacred horse-meat would disappear between strong jaws, washed down by endless horns of mead, and foaming beer, and even sparkling wine plundered from the southlands. Bards would sing lays of mighty deeds, amid roaring choruses, tumultuous clamor, and occasional brawls which might end in sudden death. And young Hrolf, watching it all, and listening intently to the songs and tales, would clutch his dagger-hilt till his knuckles grew white and his gray eyes blazed, yearning to do his part in that fierce viking world.

At last a spring came when the tall stripling went forth like a sea-eagle from its nest. The black long-ships slid down the rollers into the blue water; the burnished shields along the bulwarks glittered above the banks of oars, which churned the waters into white foam; the gilded, grinning dragon-prows pointed seaward; the gaily striped sails swelled to the breeze; and Hrolf and his comrades, aboard ships bearing heart-stirring names such as Deer of the Surf, Gull of the Fjord, and Raven of the Storm-Wind, took the viking-path.

And as Hrolf the Ganger, so went countless other bold lads, generation after generation, upon their half-piratical, half-mystical quest. No Norse lad of mettle failed to make at least one viking-voyage. It was part of his education, needed to stamp him a true man in the eyes of his fellows.

Some returned home, rich and honored; others settled abroad and founded colonies; still others met death in battle or in the sea-depths. But whatever their fate, their stern spirit never failed them. Those fierce sea-rovers so harried Europe that throughout Christendom priests and monks chanted a special litany: *From the fury of the Northmen, deliver us, O Lord!*

The vikings even scoured the distant Mediterranean, fought turbaned Saracens, and plundered the galleys of the Greek emperor almost beneath the walls of Constantinople, which the Norse called *Mikklegard*. A few youthful vikings, perhaps the most venturesome of all, turned their backs on the known world, and sailed north and west to Iceland, Greenland, and that mysterious region of the uttermost west, with its "singing-beaches" and sunny clime, which Lief the Lucky named *Vinland the Good*.

Chapter V

CHILDREN OF THE CONQUERORS

THE fierce Germanic warriors who overran the Roman Empire presently came to appreciate the civilization they had conquered. They accepted Christianity, and the church taught their children the learning that had survived the wreck of the ancient world. Manners and customs became less rude, and a new civilization began to evolve.

But the process had many set-backs. Fresh invasions of Northmen upset everything, and the process had to be repeated. So it went for some six centuries, until this confused "Dark" period brightens into the clearer light of the "Middle Ages."

Our Anglo-Saxon forefathers were among the first to settle down in the new ways. When they landed in Britain from their piratical long-ships, the Anglo-Saxons were wild warriors, intent on plunder and destruction. Yet less than three centuries later we find them practicing the arts of peace and producing learned scholars.

A clear picture of Anglo-Saxon child-life at that time is furnished by the boyhood of a famous monk known as the Venerable Bede. A hundred years before Charlemagne undertook to tame his rough Franks across the Channel, Bede (then not in the least "venerable," but a little towheaded boy) was learning his lessons in the school attached to a monastery in northern England, on the coast of the North Sea.

In one of the learned works which were to make him famous, Bede himself gives us a modest sketch of his early life. "I was born," he writes, "in the territory of the said monastery [Jarrow], and at the age of seven I was, by the care of my relatives, given to the Reverend Abbot Benedict, to be educated. From that time I have spent the whole of my life within that monastery, devoting all my pains to the study of the scriptures; and amid the observance of monastic discipline, and the daily charge of singing in the church, it has ever been my delight to learn or teach or write."

Bede was born as early as the year 673 A. D., and his long life of placid study was untroubled by any intrusion from the rough outer world. But the instability of the age is shown by the fact that a whole century after Bede's death, the monastery of Jarrow was sacked by the Northmen, who turned northern England into a Norse colony, so that for at least a generation the children grew up in the wild old ancestral life, knowing nothing of books, and worshiping Odin and Thor.

Bede's school at Jarrow was not an exceptional institution. Every monastery and abbey-church had its school for boys, while nunneries conducted girls' schools. An early decree of the church in England commands that "bishops, abbots, and abbesses do by all means take care that their households do incessantly apply their minds to reading. . . . Therefore let the boys be confined and trained up in schools, to the law of sacred knowledge."

Education in Anglo-Saxon England was far from being universal. Most children never saw the inside of a schoolroom, but learned merely a few prayers and religious formulas from the parish priest, which, as they were in Latin, they understood only in a general sense. Usually, only children living near a monastery went to school. Boys of good family, however, were often sent from a distance to a monastic boarding-school.

Such boys probably envied the day-pupils from the neighborhood, who lived at home, for boarding-school discipline was strict. The little fellows wore rough woolen robes and ate their meals in silence at long refectory tables, while a monk read edifying passages from some great leather-bound tome, its pages of crackling parchment scrawled with "black-letter" writing in a crabbed monkish hand. Discipline probably had to be strict, for Saxon boys seem to have been an unruly lot, preferring the rough, hearty life of "the world" to dull studies in the alien Latin tongue. Only gentle, studious souls like Bede came to love the monastic life, and made it their own.

It was to render education more practical and less repellant that Bede and other learned teachers added to the old Roman schoolbooks some new ones written by themselves. These new schoolbooks, designed for Anglo-Saxon pupils, were a genuine blessing to many generations of children. They are often written in the form of dialogues—a series of questions and answers between pupil and teacher. There are also learned riddles, and mathematical problems, of which a typical instance is: "A swallow invited a snail to dinner: he lived just one league from the spot, and the snail traveled at the rate of an inch a day. How long would it be before he dined?"

Some of those old schoolbooks give an excellent picture of child-life in that period. In a dialogue composed by Brother Aelfric, a teaching-monk of Winchester, the scene opens with a group of boys from every walk of life, gathered together for schooling. They are represented as so eager to learn that one boy states he would prefer flogging to continued ignorance. After this decidedly unnatural sentiment, however, the dialogue gives more trustworthy testimony about conditions of the time; for the master proceeds to ask each boy questions concerning his daily life, and receives most varied answers.

The shepherd-boy relates how he watches his flocks, accompanied by his dog to guard against wolves, and describes how he makes cheese from ewes' milk. The herdsman's son is frightened by cattle-thieves raiding from their haunts in the deep forest. The farmer's boy tells about getting up before dawn to do the chores and yoke the oxen to the plow. Sons of huntsmen and fowlers say they sometimes swap game and trade dogs. A fisher-boy names the kinds of fish he catches in the river to sell to townsfolk; but when asked if he does not want to go to sea and catch a whale, he answers emphatically: "I do *not!* Whaling is too risky a business for me." Then there are sons of salt-makers, cobblers, blacksmiths, and tailors, whose replies show Anglo-Saxon craftsmen as handy fellows; while a merchant's son reveals the fact that even thus early, England had foreign trade and imported the luxuries of the age.

Aelfric's dialogue likewise tells us the diet of young children: a little seven-year-old says he isn't allowed meat, but eats eggs, fish, cheese, butter, cabbages, and beans; his usual drink is water, but he likes ale when he can get it.

What Anglo-Saxon children learned in school was merely a foreshadowing of the educational system elaborated in later medieval times. Aside from the "Three R's," children were taught "grammar" and "rhetoric" in the old Roman sense of those terms, together with sacred music, some church history, and a weird kind of geography and astronomy, in which the stars spun about a square world, flat as a pancake and with sharp corners.

School reading and writing methods were primitive. Books (all hand-written upon parchment) were so rare and costly that children could seldom even handle them. Therefore the master would ordinarily write words and sentences on a blackboard, the children first reciting them aloud, and later, when they could write, tracing them on wax tablets in the Roman fashion.

Young children are natural conservatives, and the Christianized Saxon nursery was filled with mementoes of the heathen past. Many of the rhymes and tales told children by Saxon mothers and nurses are of great antiquity. Some have survived to our own day. The lullaby beginning "Bye, baby bunting, father's gone a-hunting," probably goes back to the forests of Germany, while Old King Cole has been identified with a very ancient British chieftain.

At bedtime came a curious blend of Christian and heathen rites. The little Anglo-Saxons would dutifully say their "Our Father" and "Hail Mary," but before dropping off to sleep they would peek from their cribs to see if the fairy-wife were washing her elf-baby in the basin of water which the nurse had carefully left, with a clean towel, beside the fire. Unless this were done, who could tell what pranks the "Little People" might play on sleeping children before morning?

Of course, Anglo-Saxon children had the simple toys such as rattles and dolls that are common to most peoples. They also had a variety of games, including checkers, chess, and a sport played with long wooden bats and wooden balls. As the Anglo-Saxons were fond of hunting, youngsters of good family had their hawks and hounds and horses at an early age.

Boys wore tunics and went bare-legged in summer; in cold weather they put on a short cape, breeches, or leg-bands, stout shoes, and a peaked cap of leather or velvet, sometimes trimmed with fur. Their fair hair was trimmed in a sort of Dutch-cut. Girls wore long petticoats, and the costume of upper-class girls included long sleeves, a train, and little flat caps. Their flaxen locks either hung in two long braids or was combed down over the shoulders.

Even in early childhood, Saxon boys were toughened and taught the use of weapons. The warlike traditions of Old Germany were still fresh, and fathers fostered the qualities of strength and courage in their sons. One of the first tests of a small boy's mettle was to put him on a sloping roof. If he hung on, without crying, he was hailed as a "stout herce"—a brave boy.

The most famous of all Anglo-Saxon boys was Alfred, later surnamed "the Great." This noted hero and savior of Saxon England from the Northmen was born in the year 848 at the royal "burgh" of Wantage, in southern England—he being the fourth son of Ethelwolf, over-king of the Saxon peoples. The infant was given the good old Saxon name of Aelf-rede, which means "Elf's Wisdom."

The "burgh" of Wantage was a rambling structure girt by a palisade and surrounded by a village of wooden houses, built in a style similar to Norse farmsteads today. We can imagine how the newborn baby was carried by its royal father into the great smoke-grimed hall, crowded with strapping freemen and bluff, fair-haired country gentlemen in blue cloaks, who raised their muscular, gold-braceleted arms in loyal salute.

Alfred was born to stormy times. He spent his first years following his father from one royal manor-house to another as the king sought to repel Norse raiders. Perhaps Alfred's earliest recollection was that of his father returning in triumph at the head of his troops after a victory over the Northmen. This visit gave pious King Ethelwolf a breathing-space which he employed in a pilgrimage to Rome. And with him went little Alfred, then five or six years old. The journey across France and Italy must have quickened and broadened a young mind, which already had shown unusual promise. Constant travel did not leave time for schooling; it is said that Alfred could not read till he was twelve. However, he had the desire to learn; and a pretty (though somewhat doubtful) story is told about his mother promising him a book illuminated with colored pictures as soon as he could read it.

About that time his father died, and Alfred came

under the charge of an elder brother who presently became king. This brother was a pious, studious young man, more fitted to be a monk than a king in that rough age. However, he saw to it that Alfred got the best possible education. A learned monk was assigned the boy as tutor, and Alfred showed scholarly zeal. By his mid-teens he was collecting and editing old Saxon tales and epic poems, and had translated the Psalms of David. Perhaps it was during this period that he invented a rude horn lantern to shield his flickering candle-flame from the drafts in his bed-chamber, so that he might pursue his studies at night.

Yet Alfred was no bookish recluse, for he also showed such strength and skill in athletics, hunting, and the practice of arms that he became the hope of his countrymen. At eighteen he was declared heir-apparent to the throne, and began his life-long struggle against the invading Northmen. About this time he was married, and a picture of his wedding-feast is typical of the banquets of that period.

The great hall is a scene of rude comfort and hearty jollification, such as the Saxon dearly loves. The walls are hung with hides and bearskins, a large woolen tapestry being draped along the upper end of the hall behind the royal board. The hall is filled with noisy feasters, sitting on benches at long trestle-tables bearing massive dishes heaped with stews, fish, bread, and fruits. No forks or spoons: the diners eat with their sheath-knives, hacking off chunks from the various roasts that servants bear about the hall. Those roasts of pork, beef, mutton, and wild game are impaled on giant skewers and come sizzling hot from the kitchen fires.

The banquet lasts for many hours. Most of the revelers drink ale and mead from polished silver-mounted cows' horns. Only the royal party at the high table quaff wine from goblets of silver and gold. Harpers recite old lays and improvise new ones in honor of the bridal pair. As barrel after barrel of ale is emptied, the torch-lit scene grows wilder and more barbaric. Brawls break out, but there is no bloodshed: before the banquet all guests except the chief nobles were told to leave their weapons outside. Perhaps the king has laid his naked sword in front of him upon the board, as a hint to hot-heads not to go too far. A few blows and buffets do not count, and in no way mar the joyous harmony of the occasion.

Charlemagne, the great Frankish monarch, was born about a century before English Alfred. Although his father and grandfather had so extended the Frankish realm that it had become a powerful kingdom, including western Germany and most of France, young Charles grew up amid barbaric surroundings, and was almost as devoid of formal education as his heathen ancestors. The little that we know about his boyhood shows us a sturdy youngster learning the use of arms, hunting, and taking part in a campaign with his royal father when yet in his early teens. Shortly afterwards he was sent by his father to govern a province, thus serving an apprenticeship in government as well as in war.

Charlemagne had a deep respect for learning,

and as soon as he could, he seized every spare moment for study. In the winter seasons, between campaigns, this big, hearty man with the great blond beard would puzzle over tomes in Latin and Greek, and make pathetic but vain attempts to write. As the years passed, Charlemagne became really learned for his times. He loved the society of scholars, summoning wise men from distant lands, creating a palace-school in which his children were well educated, and making it the model for a system of schools which he fostered throughout his empire. Before his death, he had the satisfaction of seeing the children at least of the upper classes growing up far better educated than their fathers had been.

Charlemagne was at the height of his power when a strange procession wound its glittering way southward through France. There were proud Frankish nobles in armor astride massive chargers, fair ladies, grave priests and monks, and long columns of sturdy spearsmen. The central figure of all this brave array was a three-year-old boy, in gorgeous miniature robes, wearing a tiny crown of gold. It was Charlemagne's son, Lewis, en route for his "kingdom" of Aquitaine. Such was the majestic send-off which the father gave the son who was destined to succeed him as ruler of the empire carved out by his sword.

The little "under-king" of Aquitaine certainly lacked no advantage in his up-bringing. Where his father Charles had grown up rough and illiterate, Lewis was reared and educated with every care that an all-powerful parent could bestow. His very place of residence made this the more certain; for Aquitaine was a region in southern France, where the imprint of Roman civilization remained far stronger than in the Germanized north. So Lewis grew into a cultured lad, learned and accomplished vastly beyond most young nobles of his times.

But Charlemagne had planned *too* well. In those Dark Ages, there was danger in too much book-learning and polite culture for any boy who planned to live his life in the world. Lewis' training was well suited to the cloister; it ill became a future king. In his own superb self-confidence, Charlemagne never seems to have suspected that his talented son was more a scholar than a soldier, more priest than prince. For Lewis was so intelligenet and so dutiful that as long as his father stood behind him to give orders, he did well enough. But when great Charles was dead, the imperial crown proved too heavy for Lewis' mild brow. Did not his subjects dub him Lewis the Pious? A dubious compliment, that, in those days!

So, little by little, the ill-compacted empire of Charlemagne got out of hand. At length, Lewis' own sons (who seem to have had more of their grandfather's tough fiber in them) rebelled against their parent, deposed him, quarreled among themselves, and split the empire to fragments. The light of learning and culture which Charlemagne had fostered proved a false dawn. His school system went to pieces with everything else, and children grew up ignorant and unlettered once more. And upon distracted Western Europe fell—the fury of the Northmen!

A hawk-nosed, hard-faced man stands before a crowd of equally hard-faced barons. Beside him is a sturdy seven-year-old boy. The man suddenly raises the child in his arms, exclaiming: "I do not propose to leave you masterless. Here is my son. He is little, but he will grow, and by God's grace he will one day be able to rule you. Therefore, I command you, by the loyalty you owe me, to swear true faith and allegiance to him as your feudal lord!"

It is Duke Robert who speaks—the heavy-handed ruler of Normandy, whom men whisperingly call Robert the Devil. Stricken with remorse for dark deeds accounted crimes even in those wild days, he has suddenly resolved to purge his soul of sin by pilgrimage to the Holy Land. And the little boy is William, destined to become the conqueror of Saxon England.

The masterful pair are the descendants of Hrolf the Ganger. And those turbulent barons are likewise descended from the viking host which Hrolf led to the conquest and settlement of the French province to which they gave the name of "Northman's Land" or Normandy.

Hrolf (his name altered to "Rollo") has been dead a hundred years, and the transplanted Northmen, become Normans, are outwardly much changed. They now dwell in stone castles, go clean-shaven, cultivate the social graces, and are as zealous Christians as their forebears were champions of Odin and Thor.

Yet their Christianity is of an ultra-militant brand, for the Normans have by no means lost the old Norse fire. They send forth swarms of young adventurers, often mere lads in their teens, who range far and wide. It is the old "viking-faring" under a new guise. And at home, Norman turbulence is restrained only by iron-handed dukes—as boy William is to discover as soon as his father, Robert the Devil, gone on his pious pilgrimage, dies in a foreign land.

Little William has already shown the warlike stuff that is in him. At the age of five he delighted his father by his passion for toy soldiers, and when Robert leaves home, William has begun to enjoy reading Cæsar's campaigns.

Little William leads a life of hairbreadth escapes. The turbulent barons rise in revolt. His guardians hurry him from castle to castle, to shield him from his enemies. Once, assassins creep into the chamber where William and his tutor lie sleeping. In the darkness, they pick the wrong bed; so dawn finds the tutor knifed to death, but the boy awakes unharmed.

William never forgets his terrible childhood. In after life he remarks to a friend: "Often, my guardians, fearing for my safety, would rouse me in the dead of night, and to save me from the wretches who sought my blood, I would be hidden in a peasant's hut." William finally finds refuge in a remote castle, where he spends several years. And all that time he fits himself to be a ruler, as his ancestor, Hrolf the Ganger, did many generations before. An old chronicler remarks of boy William: "Within his childish breast waxed all the vigor of a man."

Presently he comes forth from his retreat; a tall youth, hard as nails and full of fight. His subjects note his spirit, rally round him, and follow his standard gladly. Before he is twenty, he has crushed the rebel barons in a great battle, and is master of Normandy. In his late thirties, he conquers England and becomes one of the most powerful monarchs of the age.

The Conqueror had three boys, and they proved a great trial to their father, who grew stout and short-breathed with advancing years. Robert, the eldest son, was a daredevil, who bullied his younger brothers and delighted in fighting all the other boys in the royal castle. William, the second son, was nicknamed "Redhead," and had a surly, quarrelsome disposition. Henry, the youngest, was likewise strong and active; but, perhaps because of being much picked on by his elder brothers, he developed a shrewd cunning by which he always got the best of them in the long run.

Unlike Robert and Redhead, Henry was a good scholar, and despised his brothers for their brawling ways. Once when the father was excusing some wild prank of Robert's which had just been reported to him, on the ground that such high spirits betokened a two-fisted ruler, little Henry looked up from a book he was reading and remarked acidly: "That may be so, father; yet, to my mind, a know-nothing king is but a crowned ass."

That the Conqueror's household was a lively one is shown by the following story:

Angered by Robert's bullying airs, Redhead and Henry thought they would take him down a peg.

So as Robert was passing beneath a window, dressed in his best clothes and vastly proud of the new sword which he had just been allowed to wear, the two youngsters poured a bucket of dirty water over him. Raging with fury, Robert drew his blade, raced upstairs, and would very likely have killed his brothers, if the Conqueror had not burst into the room, puffing from the sudden sprint and roaring how the devil the young brats dared kick up such a row while he was trying to get a wink of sleep!

The brothers kept up their quarrels when they were grown men. And, as usual, Henry won out. For Redhead was mysteriously murdered, Robert died in a dungeon, and Henry at last gathered in the whole family heritage. So matters went in that rough "Dark Age."

Chapter VI

CHILDREN OF THE MIDDLE AGES

HE five hundred years from the close of the Dark Ages to the early part of the sixteenth century witness the rise and flowering of medieval civilization. It was a real civilization, though very different from ours. And there is the steady evolution toward a more complex, colorful existence.

One of the outstanding features of medieval life is the growing insistence upon good manners—especially table manners. During the Dark Ages, people had been gross feeders, "gobble and gulp" being almost everywhere the rule. Probably the best-mannered persons of that age were the heathen Norse sea-kings.

The whole household ate together. A baronial

hall might be crowded with scores on scores of diners, seated at various trestle-tables according to their rank. So the baron's children, seated at the high-table, would have very bad examples before their eyes as they watched what went on below.

They at first had only knives to aid those natural implements, the fingers. Spoons were for a long time uncommon, while forks were a great rarity until the close of the Middle Ages. A medieval chronicler relates as extraordinary the fact that a certain duke of Brittany used a silver fork with which to "pick up soppys."

Soups were drunk from earthenware bowls, while stews were dipped up with chunks of bread. Meats and vegetables were at first eaten from wooden "trenchers"—flat slabs of wood—and schoolboys became expert in building bread-dams around the edges of their trenchers to keep in the gravy. When platters were used, only one was ordinarily laid for every two persons, who ate off the same plate and drank from the same cup—made, not of china or glass, but of wood, horn, or metal. Napkins were unknown, thin slices of bread serving the purpose.

Under these conditions, dainty feeding was somewhat of an accomplishment. In the Canterbury Tales Chaucer describes the table manners of the sprightly prioress—evidently an uncommonly polite young lady, since he carefully notes how,

> "At meté wel y-taught was she with-alle,
> She leet no morsel from hir lippés falle
> Ne wette hir fingrés in hir saucé deep.
> Wel koude she carie a morsel and wel kepe
> That no dropé ne fille upon hir breste;

THE STORY OF YOUTH 115

> In curteisie was set ful muchel hir leste.
> Hir over-lippé wypèd she so clene,
> That in hir coppe ther was no ferthing sene
> Of grecé, whan she dronken hadde hir draughte."

One habit which was hard to break was the time-honored custom of throwing bones and scraps upon the floor, which was not carpeted but strewn with rushes, occasionally renewed. These bones and scraps would be promptly devoured by numerous dogs and cats, which acted as useful scavengers. Their growls, snarls, and fights were undoubtedly a source of amusement to their youthful masters and mistresses.

Children cherished these pets, and in earlier times had been wont to feed and fondle them at pleasure. How hard it was for young folks to give up the practice is seen by the old books and manuals of etiquette, all of which inveigh against such unseemly and uncleanly manners. Curiously enough, the cat is more condemned than the dog. One medieval writer terms the cat a "most onclenely beste." Another writer, apparently prejudiced by nocturnal serenades upon castle walls, says of the "wralling catte": "Her eyes glisten above measure, especially when a man cometh to see them on a suddain, and in the night they can hardly be endured for their flaming aspect." Moreover, the cat has "a peculiar direful voice." Or, as another foe of the feline tribe puts it: "He maketh a rueful noyse and ghastful when one proffereth to fight with another."

Small books or manuals of etiquette, written primarily for children and often rhymed, are surprisingly numerous throughout Europe, especially during the later Middle Age. One of the earliest is an Italian manual that consists of fifty rhymed "Courtesies." Some run as follows:

"Do not fill your mouth too full; the glutton who fills his mouth will not be able to reply when spoken to."

"Do not dirty the cup in drinking," and "wipe it before passing it on."

Those taking soup are admonished not to "swallow their spoons," nor to "eat noisily" at any time.

"If you should sneeze or cough, cover your mouth; and, above all, turn away from the table."

"Do not mix together on your plate all sorts of viands, meat and eggs; if any one should dine with me, and thus fish up his victuals, I should not like it."

"Do not wipe your fingers on the table-cloth. . . . Let the hands be clean, and above all, do not scratch your head at table."

Finally, as we might expect: "Do not, while eating, fondle dogs, cats, or other pets; it is not right to touch animals with hands which touch the food."

A German manual of etiquette is of wider scope, dealing with all aspects of child-life, including religious piety. Children are given careful directions on how to carry the head; not to wink, blink, or roll the eyes; and not to make unseemly grimaces. Sneezing in company is to be avoided if possible; yet, "if it may not be, to stop it were to prefer manners to health." Blushing and gaping are likewise considered bad form. In company, a child must not wriggle his shoulders, pick his ears, or scratch his head; neither should he speak till spoken to. Due reverence in church is emphasized, and the sign of the cross should be made on going to sleep and on awakening. Politeness is due other children as well as elders, for when sleeping with a brother a boy should keep still and not start trouble by pulling off the bedclothes.

Turning now to England, we find a whole series of manuals bearing such titles as "The Babees' Boke," "The Lytyl Boke," and "The Boke of Curtasye." In these medieval "juveniles," the child reader is urged not to lap up his soup, dip his meat in the salt-cellar, nor put his knife in his mouth. Also, politeness forbids a boy to fling himself upon the cheese or cast bones upon the floor. If these directions are observed, people will afterwards remark: "A gentylman was heere."

Perhaps the most amusing of these quaint volumes is a rhymed manual conducting a boy throughout the day, from the time he rises at "syxe of the clocke" until he retires for the night. On getting up in the morning, the youngster is told:

> "Make cleane your shoes, and combe your head,
> And your cloathes button or lace;
> And see at no tyme you forget
> To wash your hands and face."

There are many directions for general deportment. Among them, the boy is told not to "claw your head or back, a fleigh as thaughe ye sought"; and when spoken to by a grown person, not to "lumpischli caste thine head a-down, but with a sad cheer look him in the face."

The chief emphasis, however, is laid on table manners, as is evident from the following passage:

> "Burnish no bones with your teeth,
> For that is unseemly;
> Rend not thy meate asunder,
> For that swarves from curtasye.
> Dip not thy meate in the Saltseller,
> But take it with thy knife.
> And sup not lowde of thy Pottage,
> No tyme in all thy lyfe.
> Defyle not thy lips with eating much,
> As a Pigge eating draffe;
> Eate softly and drinke mannerlye,
> Take heed you do not quaffe.
> Scratche not thy head with thy fyngers
> When thou art at thy meate;
> Nor spytte you over the table boorde;
> See thou dost not this forget.
> Pick not thy teeth with thy knyfe
> Nor with thy fingers ende,
> But take a stick, or some cleane thing,
> Then doe you not offende."

During the early Middle Ages, the homes of the lowest rural classes, such as serfs and "cottars," bound to the soil like slaves, were miserable hovels of clay-daubed wattle, with dirt floors and thatched roofs. They were practically identical with the humbler dwellings of prehistoric times. Here babies rolled in the mud, children played with the pigs, and only the very hardiest survived.

Free peasants lived in better-built cottages, while yeoman farmers often possessed comfortable houses sturdily built of timber, brick, or stone, with slate roofs tight to the weather. Town houses of artizans were at first one-story dwellings of similar type, though later they were often several stories high and housed a number of families. The homes of prosperous townsfolk became large, well-appointed mansions in later medieval times.

Gentlefolk lived in "manor-houses," the lord of the manor being supported by the rents and services of the tenants and serfs on his estate. The manor-house might be anything from a rambling wooden structure of the old Teutonic or Anglo-Saxon type to a stone mansion almost as fine as a small castle. As time passed the manor-house became designed less for defense and more for residential comfort, until in the later Middle Ages houses of country gentlemen were much like European country residences—of today—minus certain very modern improvements.

Child-life in the early medieval castle was not, from our viewpoint, a joyous one; for those strongholds, built for defense against ever-threatening foes, were grim piles of masonry, surrounded by moats and almost without windows, which must have been abodes of gloom, damp, and chill.

The castle in time underwent the same development as the manor-house, evolving from defense toward domestic comfort, though of course on a magnified scale, until the later medieval castles became splendid and relatively luxurious abodes.

The most significant change was the development of private living-quarters for the master and his family. At first, the great hall was the center of all domestic life. There the master's children ate, played, and fought with the children of retainers and servants, and with the numerous dogs and cats of the household. Their sole privacy would be dark little sleeping chambers, while the other castle children would bed with the common herd promiscuously upon the hall floor, cleared of its trestle tables and turned into a dormitory as soon as supper had been cleared away.

The master's children probably did not particularly relish their night-time privacy, because their chambers could not have been cheerful compared to the hall, where fires always burned. Yet those same fires had their disadvantages. In early times when there were no chimneys, everybody must have been plagued by smoke, while a universal coating of soot added to the general dirt and gloom.

When chimneys had abated the smoke nuisance, it paid to brighten up the hall and master's quarters with tapestries and with paint and gilding on the woodwork and walls. Also, crusaders brought back a taste for oriental rugs and silken hangings. Another great domestic boon was window-glass, which permitted more light without sacrificing heat. Soon the master's family had a private living-room, known as the "solar," from its sunny windows; and later on came sleeping chambers, gaily decorated and furnished with huge canopied beds. By this time the master's young children had a jolly nursery, where they played and ate most of their meals. The great hall had ceased to be the center of domestic life, and was ultimatly used only for ceremonial occasions. In other words, castle life had been transformed, and was taking on a distinctly "modern" tone.

Medieval children were seldom spoiled by their

parents. Nurses, however, appear to have been kindly souls, since complaints were often made that royal or noble children had been overindulged by the worthy women in whose charge they had been placed. That the children themselves appreciated this treatment is shown by instances where such children, when grown up, made generous provision for their nurses. King Henry V of England settled a handsome annuity upon his Welsh nurse as soon as he ascended the throne.

Old records give us some interesting sidelights on royal nurseries. We know quite a bit about the children of Edward I, including several of their toys —a miniature crossbow, a little cart, and the model of a plow. The cart must have been roughly treated, for it soon needed mending, together with a mug, which had to be repaired and regilded.

Castle children probably had many homemade toys, fashioned by the good-natured carpenter, harness-maker, blacksmith, and other artizans always on the premises in those days when towns were far away and every great household had to be practically sufficient unto itself. For more elaborate toys, children eagerly awaited the fairs that were held periodically in every locality.

Medieval fairs were great events. Everything conceivable was sold at them by traveling merchants, and there were always booths full of sweets and toys. Dolls and gilt "gingerbread husbands" for the little girls; drums, pop-guns, hobby-horses, and kites for little boys; and peppermint drops for both sexes, are among the delightful articles which we know were then sold.

Another event was the bath. The Middle Ages was not a period when cleanliness was considered next to godliness. Indeed, many churchmen looked askance at the practice, and held total abstinence from bathing a pious mortification of the flesh. For this and other reasons, people were probably less cleanly than they had been in heathen times. A certain English abbot thus lays down the rule for his monastic household:

"A bath should by no means be refused to a body when compelled thereto by the needs of ill health. Let it be taken without grumbling when ordered by a physician; so that, even though a brother be unwilling, that which ought to be done for health may be done at the order of him who is set over you. Should he wish for one, however, when not advantageous, his desire is not to be gratified."

And, of course, in this connection, it is well-known that the bath given a youth about to receive knighthood was considered a solemn (possibly a unique!) event.

The children of Edward I were given baths about four times a year—notably on Easter, Whitsun, and Christmas eves. In many noble households baths were even less frequent, while in humble homes they were usually quite unknown. Voltaire had much justification for his celebrated jibe at the Middle Ages as "A Thousand Years without a Bath!"

Since lack of baths was only one aspect of the filthy, unsanitary conditions which then prevailed, there was an enormous death-rate among children of even the highest social grades. The waste of child-life was terrible, and medieval "medical science" was so grotesque that doctors probably killed as many patients as they cured.

Of Edward I's children, we find no less than seven dying at an early age. Here is the course of medical treatment given one of the ailing youngsters, Prince Henry: First, a "bathe medicinable," containing, besides water, a gallon of wine and diverse strange herbs. Next, a learned doctor dosed little Henry with "Triasandal," "Letwar," "Diaboriginal," and other weird concoctions. After such formidable, and probably nauseating, medicines, it is not strange that his stomach refused to be tempted by larks, partridges, pears, and other dainties proffered to stimulate his appetite. Medical science having failed, and the little prince being seriously ill, the saints were now called upon. Tall wax candles were burned before the most celebrated shrines in England; but the saints availed as little as the doctors, and the boy soon passed away.

Probably one cause of illness among upper-class children was the rich, heavy food with which they were often indulged as soon as they were old enough to eat with their parents. The art of cookery became very elaborate in medieval times. Old cookbooks startle us with their strange recipes. The mighty roasts of the Dark Ages, borne about on giant skewers, went out of fashion. Their place was taken by "mortrews"—amazing combinations of meat and fish, boiled, cut in small pieces, brayed in a mortar (whence their name). When reduced to a pulpy mass they were further blended with egg-yolks, highly spiced, sweetened with honey, colored with saffron, decorated with nuts and chopped-up hard-boiled eggs, and eaten with sharp sauces.

The variety of meats and fish was very great, including about "every comestible animal," as a contemporary put it. And there were many kinds of sweets, including rich cakes and cookies, tarts, buns, pancakes, and fritters. The sweetening basis, as in former times, was usually honey, though sugar was introduced into western Europe by the crusaders and was ceasing to be a luxury for the very rich by the close of the medieval period.

One writer of the time (possibly a sufferer from dyspepsia) utters the protest: "What an Hodgpotch do men that have Abilities make in their Stomachs, which must wonderfully oppress and distract Nature." He enumerates a long list of varied foods and seasonings, and continues: "Jumble them together into one Mass, and what eye would not loath, what Stomach not abhor, such a Gallemaufrey? Yet this is done every Day, and counted Gallent Entertainment."

Children of lesser station were not exposed to such temptations. Middle-class children seem to have had abundant but healthful fare. Poor children, however, suffered the opposite extreme by not getting enough to eat or by having a monotonous, ill-balanced diet. In his celebrated lament, Piers Plowman states that he and his family have only cheeses, oaten cakes, beans and bran, onions, parsley, and "many cabbages," upon which last item, we infer, his household relied to tide them over their hard times. Piers tells us that other poor families lived on vegetables cooked without meat, a coarse sort of bread, and nothing but water to drink; while from other sources it appears that many poor households subsisted chiefly on bacon and beans, or even on bread and herrings.

In no way is the growing luxury and love of display of medieval times better shown than by the way people dressed. And children dressed almost exactly like their parents; distinctive garments for children were then unknown.

Rich children (especially girls) probably enjoyed the costly materials and gay colors of their clothing, but many of the extreme styles must have been most uncomfortable, especially at playtimes. Boys were as badly off as girls; for if girls wore long gowns with trains, and towering head-dresses shaped like crescent moons or foolscaps draped with veils, boys were sometimes decked out in flowing sleeves, skintight hose, and shoes with pointed toes so prodigiously long that they had to be fastened to the knees with little gold or silver chains.

Of course, every-day folk did not dress in such exaggerated fashions. Still, toward the close of the Middle Ages, increased prosperity enabled middle-class and even lower-class persons to ape their "betters." From that period dates a complaint of a courtly writer that it is no longer possible to know lords from other men by their "array," because "knaves copy the guise of lords." So we presume that children of nearly all classes must have been made stuffy and uncomfortable—at least on "dress-up" occasions.

The relations of parents and children during the

Middle Ages appear far from ideal. Not only were children brought up very strictly; they were often treated with rank injustice and revolting cruelty. Such parental conduct seems to have been taken more or less as a matter of course; whereas, any notable degree of kindness and consideration for children was apt to be reproved as "fond cockering and apish indulgence"—to use the terms employed by one stern medieval writer.

"Spare the rod and spoil the child" was a maxim firmly believed in and universally applied. Even youthful kings were not exempt; for when a father's untimely death made a certain small boy "Henry VI" of England, his guardian, the Earl of Warwick, felt that this fact should not relieve the little king from the customary beatings. At the same time, the earl was somewhat apprehensive lest his ward should bear a grudge and take it out on him later on. Warwick, therefore, seeks to share the responsibility, and lays his problem before the royal council in the following language:

"That consideryng howe, blessed be God, the Kyng is grown in years, in stature of his persone, and also in conceyte and knowleche of his heigh and royale auctoritie and estate, the which naturally causen hym, and from day to day as he groweth shall causen hym more and more to grucche with chastysing and to lothe it"; therefore the earl, fearing lest the king bear malice, prays the council "trewely to assisten hym in the exercise of the charge and occupacyoun that he hath about the Kyng's persone; namely, in chastysing of hym for his defaults, and support the said Earle therein."

If this were the discipline deemed necessary for a prince whom we know to have been a rather mild-mannered boy, the treatment accorded ordinary youngsters can be imagined. A letter has come down to us from an English lady to a schoolmaster concerning her son, in which the lady urges the master to "belash" the boy well; while another lady drags her recalcitrant son to school on a dog-leash, after beating him with a dog-whip.

And such harsh punishments were not confined to young children. Well-grown lads and maidens got the same treatment. Agnes Paston, one of the principals in that celebrated collection of correspondence known as the Paston Letters, had a daughter in her late teens whom she resolved to marry off to a wealthy man of fifty. As he was also deformed, the girl refused to obey her mother's command; whereupon Agnes shut her up and beat her so severely that the unfortunate girl was seriously injured.

Parents likewise seem to have had scant notion of even-handed justice within the home, discriminating openly between children as these happened to win or lack their favor. A striking instance of this is the boyhood of Bertrand du Gueschlin, the famous French general. One of a large family, his homely features and odd disposition earned him the dislike of his parents, so that he early became the butt of the household, including the very servants. But little Bertrand showed the spirit which was to make him invincible in battle, and fiercely resented this treatment, no matter how severe his punishments. On one occasion, when only six years old, he rebelled against being debarred from the family board by jumping on the table and loudly demanding the same rights as his brothers and sisters. When his mother angrily threatened him with a beating, Bertrand promptly kicked over the table, laden with dishes and food!

Another proof that medieval parents felt little tenderness toward their children is the widespread practice of sending them away from home when they were only seven or eight years old. Upper-class children were placed at court or in noble households as pages, or as "bower-maidens" in attendance upon the Lady Chatelaine. Middle-class children were sent to boarding-schools and convents. Even lower-class children were often apprenticed to strangers at a tender age.

The Paston Letters give us a glimpse of medieval parental feeling (or rather, lack of it) where Margaret Paston reveals herself in a letter as thoroughly bored with her growing daughters and anxious to be rid of them at the earliest opportunity. "We be eyther of us werye of other," she candidly admits.

Thus reared, it is not strange that children seldom showed deep love and devotion for their parents. Outward deference was paid. But formal protestations ring hollow, when we know that bitter quarrels between parents and grown children often occurred (usually over money matters) in which parents were sometimes violently assaulted by their enraged offspring.

The custom of child-marriage is one of the amazing aspects of medieval life. It was due, not to any religious ideal as among some oriental peoples, but solely to the selfish greed of parents or guardians, seeking to profit themselves at the children's expense. For this reason, child-marriage was confined mainly to the upper classes; the poor, having little to bargain with, let their children grow to a reasonable age before seeking to make matches for them, and even gave lads and lassies some say in the matter.

But a baby born to broad acres and a rich inheritance was not so lucky. Even before it was born, the parents would probably be match-making; while the terms of marriage-contracts might be hotly debated over the infant's cradle. A great heiress like Jacqueline of Holland was a center of marital intrigues from the day of her birth. Little Jacqueline was almost engaged before she had cut her first tooth, and was formally betrothed when she was four years old!

Children were held capable of "consent" to a marriage ceremony when they were seven, though the marriage was voidable until girls reached the age of twelve, and boys the age of fourteen. Sometimes the "bride" or "groom" died very early in life, when there would ensue ridiculous yet pathetic spectacles like that of a certain English duchess, wife and widow at nine, romping in the garden blissfully unaware of her bereavement and climbing cherry trees in her widow's weeds.

Those boys who left home between the ages of seven and ten, to be reared at a king's court or in the almost equally imposing household of some great noble or churchman were nearly always of noble or gentle birth, though occasionally the son of some wealthy townsman would be admitted, if he were a boy of unusual promise whose father had gained the favor of the patron who graciously granted the privilege.

Such a boy was the English churchman, Thomas à Becket, who was placed by his father as page to an Anglo-Norman noble, and who acquired at that personage's castle the manners of a gentleman before he embraced the religious life. Indeed Thomas never forgot his courtly up-bringing; for, at the height of his power, he maintained a splendid household and welcomed many boys of good family, whom he reared and trained in polite accomplishments as well as in scholarly attainments. The households of courtly churchmen represented the best examples of "polite learning" which the Middle Ages could show.

Such clerical households were, however, rather exceptional. Most church dignitaries were too austere to attract any but boys predestined to a religious life.

The average boy of good family, therefore, went to court or castle and became a page. He found himself in the company of other boys, sent there by their parents with similar intent. And we should realize that even upper-class parents who genuinely loved their sons and might have wished to keep them at home were almost obliged to send them away, if the boys were to get the rearing necessary for success in later life. Left at home, in some country manor-house or remote feudal castle, the boys would have grown up without those polite accomplishments and ability to bear themselves worthily among their social peers which were indispensable for a youth who wanted to be a gallant knight and to make his way in the medieval world. So every court or great household was a sort of fashionable boarding-school, where boys were carefully trained. Furthermore, a clever, likable boy might win the special favor of his royal or noble patron, would make lasting friendships with fellow pages of influential families, or even with the royal children themselves; and these social connections would smooth his path in life.

Page-boys received some education in our sense of the word. Learned priests, attached to court or castle as tutors, would teach them to speak Latin, to read and write both Latin and their mother tongue, and to be punctual in their religious observances.

Yet "letters" played, after all, but a minor part in a page-boy's education, which was primarily directed toward making him "a very parfait gentil knight." And, to become a "parfait knight," a boy had to begin young. Chivalry was a fine art, needing not only physical strength but also great skill, attained only after long years of patient effort and constant practice.

So the little pages at once began their chivalric apprenticeship. Their teachers were numerous. First, there were "esquires"—youths who had once been pages themselves, but who, with ripening years, had become aspirants for the golden spurs of knighthood. Also, there were bluff men-at-arms, corresponding to a combination of modern drill-sergeants and professional athletic trainers. Lastly, there were knightly instructors, who, like present-day college coaches, directed and supervised the entire course of instruction.

In sunny castle-yards or in the armory on rainy days the page-boys learned sword and dagger-play with miniature blunted weapons, and the same boys took riding-lessons on the green meadows outside the castle walls. As soon as their little bodies became strong enough, they accustomed themselves to the wearing of armor and the nice management of lance and shield.

Thereupon, they were introduced to the exciting and strenuous exercise known as "tilting at the quintain." This was nothing less than a mock tournament. Regular "lists" were built, consisting of a smooth riding-course with a low wooden barrier down the middle. At one side of this barrier stood a dummy figure, usually that of a hated "Paynim Saracen." The dummy Saracen, fully armed with a shield on its left arm and a wooden saber or club in its right hand was hung on a pivot fixed to a pole in such a way that it turned very easily. The tilter charged down the lists on horseback, his lance couched, seeking to strike the Saracen in the face. If he did so, all went well. If, however, he missed his aim and struck any other part of the figure, the Saracen whirled round and gave the boy a whack.

Another sporting exercise was tilting at a ring. This required even greater accuracy of aim if the lance-tip were to bear off the coveted trophy. Combat afoot was mimicked by "Fighting at the Pell"—

an attack on a post shaped like a human body, which was hacked and stabbed with sword and dagger in approved fashion.

Besides these martial exercises, boyish muscles were developed by athletic sports of a more familiar kind. Pages learned to wrestle, run, jump, and swim. They also played various games of ball, a primitive form of tennis, and even a forerunner of golf, termed cambuc, in which a small ball was hit with a curved bat called a bandy.

On rainy days and in the evenings before bedtime, pages played many indoor games, usually in company with the little "bower-maidens."

Two quaint games very popular in the Middle Ages were hoodman blind and hot cockles. The first was a forerunner of blindman's buff. One of the players was blinded by a hood pulled down over his face, while the other players would try to hit him with their hoods without being caught by the blindman's clutching fingers. In hot cockles, one player knelt blindfolded, holding the hands behind his back. The other players would strike at the hands until the blindfolded "it" would guess the name of the striker, who thereupon became "it" in his turn. As might be expected from the spirit of the age, both games were apt to be played in strenuous fashion. The hoods were often knotted to give stinging slaps, while the striking hands of cockle-players tried to knock over the "it" with the force of the blow.

However, there were "parlor-games" of a milder sort. One curious pastime was ragman's roll. In this game a roll of parchment was used, on which various verses were written, describing the characters of the players, each verse having a string and seal attached. These seals hung down from the rolled-up parchment, and each player drew one of the seals and had to take on the grotesque or unflattering character portrayed in the particular verse.

Games of "forfeits" and questions-and-answers were also played, while there was much dancing, apparently similar to old-fashioned square-dances and Virginia reels. Some of these were danced out-of-doors, especially after picnics, which were frequent.

The daily life of a medieval page was certainly a full one. From the moment he jumped out of bed and slipped on his fine clothes embroidered with the household coat-of-arms in time for early mass, every minute not earmarked for lessons and physical training was at the service of his lord and lady, whenever they might have need of him.

The old books of etiquette give us minute details of the page's household training. When they came into their lord's presence, the boys were to salute the company and say, "God speed!" Their entrance into the lord's chamber must be done gravely, head erect, while the greeting should be uttered kneeling on one knee. Thereafter, they must pay attention when spoken to, not whisper, snicker, or swap stories among themselves, nor yet stand sulky, but "have ever a blythe visage and a spirit diligent."

Other rules for correct deportment are: "Answer shortly and to the point; stand until you are told to sit; bow to your lord when you answer him; give place to your betters, and turn your back on no man." When told to sit, the little page must do so at once; but if praised, he is to stand up and give thanks "with demeanor meek yet cheerful." When his lord and lady talk together, he is to keep discreetly in the background, but ever watchful, ready on the instant to hand an article required, hold a

taper, or do any other service. Moreover, he must be able to amuse his lord and lady by singing a ballad to the accompaniment of harp or lute, reading or reciting some romance or poem, or gracefully execute dance-steps in company with his fellows and the bower-maidens attached to his lady's service.

At meal-times the page's code of etiquette was nicely defined. Meals in a great medieval household were very ceremonious. When the lord, his family, and honored guests had taken their places at the high-table upon the dais, the hall rang with a blast of trumpets and the assembled pages filed gravely in, bearing basins, ewers, and towels with which the folk at the high-table washed and dried their hands. The page in attendance upon the lord next is instructed: "Put the salt on the right hand of your lord; on its left, a trencher or two. On their left, a knife, then white rolls, and beside, a spoon. At the other end set a salt and two trenchers; cut your loaves equal, take a towel 2 and ½ yards long by its ends, fold up a handful from each end, and in the middle of the folds lay eight loaves or buns, bottom to bottom; put a wrapper on the top, twist the ends of the towel together, smooth your wrapper, and open the end of it before your lord."

As the page thus served at table, the great hall buzzed with talk, an orchestra played in the gallery at the opposite end of the hall, and the court "fool" capered about making jests at everybody's expense.

These were the meal-time diversions in any noble household. At splendid banquets like those staged by the pleasure-loving Dukes of Burgundy, the tables were covered with black velvet embroidered in crimson and gold, were decorated with marvelous objects—windmills with whirling sails, churches with bells that rang, tigers that wagged their heads, and falcons that beat their wings, and a mammoth pie might suddenly open, disclosing, not four-and-twenty blackbirds, but a band of fiddlers and bagpipers, scraping and blowing with might and main.

The page would end the day's service by seeing that the lord's bedchamber was in order, his final duty being to "dryve out dogge and catte, or els geve hem a clout."

The usual age when the page-boy became an esquire was sixteen, though lads of exceptional promise sometimes won the promotion earlier. That the average esquire was a doughty youth is indicated by the exploits of such medieval lads as "Prince Hal" or "Madcap Harry." Long before he became King Henry V, young Madcap Harry was chasing rebels over the Welsh hills and leading his troops to victory on the bloody field of Shrewsbury. Of Edward III's martial sons, the eldest, the famous "Black Prince," at the age of sixteen brilliantly commanded a wing of the English army at the battle of Crècy, while another, the celebrated John of Gaunt, was only ten years old when he stood beside his father on the deck of the royal flagship as she went into action in the great sea-fight off Sluys, while the trumpeters played a gay dance tune.

In an esquire's training the use of arms, horsemanship, and every other branch of chivalry, was thoroughly mastered. The esquire attached himself to some knight, serving him faithfully in every way, from buckling on his armor to carving and cutting up his meat at table—and even combing his hair!

Following his knightly mentor like a shadow, the esquire's time would be mainly divided between the tilt-yard and the hunting-field. For medieval gentlemen loved hunting and hawking almost as much as they did jousting and fighting. The arts of falconry and the chase were as precise and elaborate as the art of chivalric warfare, and under ordinary circumstances, no esquire could hope to win knighthood until he was expert in both.

The spirit of the medieval huntsman is expressed by an old-time master of the hunt: "Now shall I prove how hunters live in this world more joyfully than any other men. For when the hunter riseth early in the morning, and he sees a sweet and fair morn, and clear weather and bright, and he heareth the song of the small fowls, the which sing so sweetly with great melody and full of love, each in his own language in the best wise that he may, after that he may learn of his own kind. And when the sun is arisen, he shall see fresh dew upon the small twigs and grasses, and the sun by his virtue shall make them shine. And that is great joy and liking to the hunter's heart."

Girls of noble birth sent by their parents to court or castle to be reared in attendance upon queens or chatelaines, as the page-boys served king or lord, were often called bower-maidens, because "bower" is the old word for a lady's private chamber, but at royal courts such girls were usually termed maids of honor.

Trained to become accomplished gentlewomen, they seem to have been somewhat better taught in polite letters than were their page-brothers; for medieval chroniclers speak of several noble ladies as patronesses of learning who were able to speak and read two or three foreign languages.

Upper-class girls were sometimes kept at home and there educated by private tutors. Others were sent away to nunneries for their education; but the number of noble convent-bred girls was never large. Convent education was more for daughters of gentlefolk or of wealthy town burgesses. In fact, with girls there was no such general rule as there was with boys.

Home-bred daughters of nobles were sometimes as well-lettered as their court-trained sisters, though probably less versed in the airs and graces of high society. All girls of good family were expected to spend much of their time embroidering or weaving tapestry, and they frequently did skilled work of great beauty.

In the hunting-field hawking and falconry were the ladies' specialties; though some young Dianas hunted the stag, and one old manuscript contains a picture of a lady thrusting her spear down a boar's throat.

At the beginning of the Middle Ages, education was almost entirely confined to the clergy and a few enlightened nobles, the rest of the population remaining ignorant and illiterate.

Before long, however, matters began to mend. Not only the lesser gentry and well-to-do townsfolk (whom we may collectively term the medieval middle classes) but also artizans and peasants wanted their children to get some education. Therefore, there was a steady development of educational institutions, all the way from primary schools to colleges and universities. Ambitious parents often make painful sacrifices for their children's schooling; fathers set aside legacies in their wills for their sons' education; and public-spirited citizens leave generous bequests for the assistance of poor scholars or for the salaries of schoolmasters who shall teach gratis those unable to pay tuition fees.

This educational development occurred mainly outside the cloister. Although monastic schools continued, they were intended chiefly for boys destined to become monks. The daily life and studies of such boys were practically the same as those we saw in the Anglo-Saxon monasteries many centuries before.

Convent schools for girls were somewhat more numerous, but their teaching methods failed to keep pace with the times. Girls seemed to have learned little there except needlework, singing, religious observances, and a rather mincing code of manners. They certainly did not get much Latin, because the nuns were often ignorant of it themselves. Furthermore, many churchmen looked askance at the presence of girls in convents who did not intend to take the veil. Such girls, with thoughts of a future "in the world," tended to disturb the strict discipline of nunneries which the church sought to maintain.

Although benevolent persons often left handsome endowments for the education of poor boys, they never made similar bequests for girls. Instead, they left girls marriage-portions.

Medieval ideas on the subject of female education are well expressed by a certain La Tour-Landry, considered a very wise man in his day and quite an authority on the matter. This knight says he desired his daughters to be able to read, and thought that "maydenes shulde be putte unto scole to lerne vertuous thinges of the Scripture, wherethorugh thei may the beter see and knowe thaire savement, and to duell and for to eschewe al that is evil in manere." But he evidently desires no further intellectual training for them.

Though medieval education emerged from the cloister, it remained chiefly in clerical hands. Most teachers were either priests or "clerks"—men who, though not admitted to the priesthood, wore the tonsure and had taken the minor vows. Some lay teachers there were, especially in primary schools; but the church looked on them with suspicion, and their number remained comparatively small throughout the Middle Ages.

Medieval primary schools were simple affairs, where young children were taught their A-B-C's. Reading was considered much more important than writing. Many persons grew up able to read both their mother tongue and Latin, yet compelled to "make their mark" because unable even to sign their names.

Primary schools were day-schools attended by both boys and girls of the neighborhood. Grammar schools, as those of secondary grade were called, were attended only by boys and were boarding-schools. Indeed, the scholars never went home on vacation, because long vacations did not exist. Holidays there were a-plenty. But holidays then meant literally holy-days, so scattered through the church calendar that the school term extended without a break through the entire year.

"Grammar" then meant the study of Latin; so a grammar school was one in which Latin was the principal subject taught. Grammar-schoolteachers used the same old textbooks which had come down from late Roman times, and medieval schoolboys learned their lessons by heart and scribbled on wax tablets just as Anglo-Saxon boys did in the days of the Venerable Bede.

The youngsters who attended these elementary and grammar schools seem to have been full of the "Old Adam"; and since masters believed in free use of birch and ferrule, medieval schools must have been lively places. Schoolteachers complain bitterly of the "necligent japing and disport" of their pupils. Schoolboys must have been pretty rough at times, for the authorities at the Winchester grammar school had to issue a special order forbidding ball-playing, stone-throwing, wrestling, and other horseplay in the school chapel, hall, and cloisters. Even more illuminating is a complaint lodged with the mayor of Exeter by the dean of the cathedral that ungodly youths, especially "in tyme of dyvyne service," played lawless games in the cloister, whereby the walls were "defowled" and the windows broken.

A medieval "bad boy" is described by the author of "The Babees' Boke." This gentleman certainly underwent a remarkable change of heart with advancing years, because he himself says that he was a very bad boy.

Frankly confessing his youthful misdeeds, he tells that he was "loth to ryse, lother to bed at eve"; that he went most reluctantly to school, "lyke a yonge colt without a bridle"; and that he "hadde a custom to come to scole late, nat for to lerne but for a countenance with my fellaws, reedy to jangle and to jape." Sometimes he played truant, spending his time in the following lawless manner:

> "Ran into gardyns, applys ther I stal,
> To gadre frutys sparyd hedge nor wal,
> To plukke grapys in othir mennys vynes
> Was moor reedy than for to say matynes.
> My lust was al to scorné folk and jape,
> To skoffe and mowé lyk a wantoun Ape."

The lashings and beatings given such boys seem cruelly severe. Furthermore, punishments were handed out so indiscriminately that the innocent must often have suffered with the guilty. The prioress of a certain nunnery, having been much annoyed by the depredations of mischievous boys in the convent grounds, issued a general order to all her tenants to give their children a sound beating every time similar acts occurred.

We can appreciate the avowal of one "sory ladde" that his schooling was "a strange werke," and that his first enthusiasm for learning had evaporated, because "the byrchyn twiggis ben so sharpe."

Another much-birched schoolboy rebelliously states:

> "I wold my Master were an hare,
> And alle his bookis howndis were,
> And I my self a joly hontere;
> To blowe my horn I wold not spare!
> For if he were dede I wold not care."

Most boys finished their education with grammar school. But those who wished to enter the learned professions went to a university—usually subdivided in several "colleges," as Oxford and Cambridge are today. The chief learned professions of the Middle Ages were: civil law, canon (church) law, theology, sacred music, and medicine. The general training was in all cases much the same. The cornerstone of the system was the so-called "Seven Arts," divided into the *Trivium* (grammar, logic, and rhetoric), and the *Quadrivium* (arithmetic geometry, music, and astronomy). To these should be added philosophy.

The medieval university course was for the most part a dreary grind which lasted an unconscionably long time. Seven years were usually devoted to the Seven Arts alone. The system proved more and more out of touch with reality, broke down of its own weight at the close of the Middle Ages, and has utterly passed away. Men thus trained were clever logicians and fluent debaters; but they were far fonder of hair-splitting subtleties and oratorical tricks than they were of true learning or constructive thinking.

Far more amusing than their studies is the daily life of those young fellows. They were of all social classes: wealthy youths, luxuriously housed, who squandered fat allowances and ran into debt; poor devils grinding away on a pittance barely enough to keep body and soul together.

There were no organized athletics or other rational recreations, and students usually gave vent to their high spirits in pranks or even brawls, often in much-frequented taverns.

University towns were continually disturbed by fights and "affrays." There were rows between different colleges; likewise, "town and gown" battles, which sometimes became serious riots in which youths of both sides were killed. The old records of Cambridge University contain many entries of fines paid by students who had "broken the peace" or committed other lawless acts.

At Oxford, in the middle of the fifteenth century, townsfolk dared not proceed against students for fear of being beaten up, and the lawlessness of Oxford students was brought to the attention of parliament in a petition stating that, "armed and arrayed in manner of war," riotous students had driven many men from their "lands and tenements," had threatened to beat and kill them, had hunted in game-preserves, and had threatened the gamekeepers in the same way. Yet nothing much seems to have been done about it.

About the workaday existence of poor boys, little need be said. Until toward the close of the Middle Ages most peasants were serfs, legally bound to the soil; so peasants' sons had to stick to the plow, because they could not leave their district save in exceptional circumstances. Sons of town artizans either followed their fathers' trades or were "bound out" as apprentices at an early age.

Yet poor boys had many sports, such as quoits, casting the stone, and a queer ancestor of modern football, sometimes played by hundreds of boys and young men on each side. This old-time football was an extremely rough sport, which the local authorities often prohibited for a season because of the fights and riots it occasioned.

The outstanding event in the life of a lower-class boy was probably fair-time. These fairs appealed to all classes and had attractions suited to the leanest purses. Along with the merchants went traveling showmen, who were forerunners of the modern circus. There were jugglers, acrobats, contortionists, and "freaks." There were also trained animals —dancing bears, trick dogs, and gibbering apes— whence the old-fashioned term jackanapes is derived. There were puppet-shows, of the Punch-and-Judy variety, where little wax figures were jerked about by the showman behind the scenes, while a boy stood in front pointing with a wand to each puppet as he told the tale.

The medieval church was an intimate part of child-life. "Mother Church" showed her tenderest side to her little ones, and did her best to win their love and devotion. In countless ways, children were made to feel themselves members of a great spiritual household. The church had its discipline, which could be strict and stern enough; yet it also had holidays, diversions, even games. The children's part in the many ceremonies of medieval Christendom explain amazing instances of youthful religious enthusiasm like the Children's Crusade and the career of Joan of Arc.

The most picturesque of these special childhood observances was the "episcopate" of the boy-bishop, which took place every year, early in the month of December. This was a very ancient custom, celebrated throughout Europe and persisting till the end of the Middle Ages. It was the high-light of a "children's season" which lasted from Saint Nicholas' Day (December 5th) to "Childermass," the Feast of the Holy Innocents.

For weeks before Saint Nicholas' Day, in every cathedral town, abbey, or church school, the boys were on their best behavior, since from among their number the boy-bishop would be selected. When some pious, intelligent lad had been chosen, he and his assistants were coached in their respective parts.

At last the great hour arrives. At vespers on Saint Nicholas' Eve, when the choir chants the words "He shall put down the mighty from their seats," bishop or abbot descends from his exalted place, which is immediately filled by a boy robed like a miniature bishop, with a miter of cloth-of-gold and a copper-gilt pastoral staff. For the next twenty-four hours, from vespers to vespers, children fill the offices and act the parts of the grown-ups, while grave ecclesiastics switch roles and solemnly hold candles or swing censers. On Saint Nicholas' Day itself, the boy-bishop appears in the pulpit, preaches the sermon, and blesses the congregation. The mass itself is celebrated by a priest, but in all other respects the ceremony is in child hands, and the usual processional order is completely reversed, the real bishop or abbot walking last and taking the lowest place. The child assistants of the boy-bishop are arrayed in copes and play the roles of the regular canons. After high mass, the boy-bishop rides on horseback through streets filled with joyous crowds, and as Saint Nicholas' Day draws to a close, his brief episcopate ends with a supper given him by the real bishop at the episcopal palace.

In the same month of December fell Christmastide, with its rites, some of Teutonic heathen origin, like the yule log and the Christmas tree. With the spring came the rogations processions, when the fields were blessed to insure a good harvest. After that came May-pole and its attendant games; next, midsummer night; while the autumn witnessed Halloween, and the Feast of Saints Clement and Katherine, when the apples were garnered. The children in this last-mentioned festival went about in procession, collecting apples and beer for the feast itself. At every farmstead or town burgher's house the children would stop and sing the following chorus:

> "Katherine and Clement be here, be here;
> Some of your apples and some of your beer;
> Some for Peter, and some for Paul,
> And some for Him Who made us all.
> Clement was a good man;
> For his sake give us some,
> Not of the worst, but some of the best;
> And God will send your soul to rest."

The year 1212 was "a time of signs and omens." Even the weather was unusual, for all over Europe the winter had been extraordinarily mild, while the spring marked the beginning of unprecedented heat and drought which was to last the entire summer season. And throughout Europe, people were in a highly excited state of mind. Some years previously, the "Paynim Saracens" had captured Jerusalem; and the Holy Sepulcher, which had been in Christian hands for a century after the mighty First Crusade, was again defiled by miscreant followers of the false prophet "Mahound." Ever since that disaster, the church had unceasingly thundered the call to

THE STORY OF YOUTH 149

a new crusade, and good Christians were stirred to the depths of their souls. The very air was charged with emotion.

Then, in the early spring of that year 1212, strange tidings bore a call addressed especially to the children. In France had arisen a wonder boy, a shepherd lad named Stephen, who had seen visions

and who even claimed to have been visited by Christ himself with a command to gather a mighty host of "innocents" to redeem His holy tomb. Within a few weeks the news had spread over Europe and produced startling results. In Germany, another boy prophet named Nicholas arose, with a similar tale, while everywhere boy preachers traversed the countrysides, proclaiming the Child Crusade. Before long, a host of children, forty thousand strong and including many girls as well as boys, had gathered about Nicholas at Cologne; while at Vendôme, in central France, a similar child host flocked to Stephen.

These crusading hosts were unarmed, for both Stephen and Nicholas asserted that victory would come through miraculous means. God was weary of the vain strivings of grown men, and so had commissioned innocent children to do His will. Taking as their text the passage of Scripture which reads, "Out of the mouths of babes and sucklings hast thou ordained strength, because of thine enemies, that thou mightest still the enemy and the avenger," the boy preachers asserted: "A new power enters on the scene—the white power of innocence! For the last time we have heard of defeat. Now shall children show mailed warriors and proud barons how invincible are youths when God leads them."

To reach the distant Holy Land would thus be easy, for the Mediterranean Sea would either dry up before them or divide like walls of glass, between which the child crusaders would march dry-shod to Palestine. And when they should thus miraculously appear from the waves, the Paynim Saracens would fall down converted, and all would worship together at the Holy Sepulcher. Such were the promises of Stephen and Nicholas to their youthful followers. And the child crusaders, carried away by a boundless faith, implicitly believed every word their leaders said.

This amazing religious enthusiasm among the

children was greeted by their elders with mingled feelings. Some men opposed it vigorously, declaring it to be a work of the Devil. Other men hailed it as rapturously as the children themselves. Churchmen were divided on the matter. The pope refused to commit himself, so clerical opinion was free to express itself either way. Generally speaking, bishops and parish priests seem to have looked askance at the strange business; whereas monks and abbots usually gave it their blessing, aided the child crusaders with food and money, and even joined the pious enterprise as guides and spiritual counselors.

Both crusading hosts were organized along similar lines. The rank and file were garbed like pilgrims in woolen robes, usually of gray, on which were sewn crosses of red cloth, which the little fellows (often only eight or ten years old) wore as proudly as a soldier does his regimental chevrons. Boys of noble birth, however, came attired as crusaders in white cloaks and riding ponies or even spirited horses. The German host was the more sober in appearance, perhaps because Nicholas seems to have kept to his role of shepherd prophet and avoided display. French Stephen, on the other hand, put on great airs, had himself hailed as "king," surrounded himself with a glittering boy body-guard, and lived in regal style.

Thus the child hosts gathered. Then followed the strangest and most tragic story of heroic but misguided youth in all history. The German children started first. It was in the merry month of May that Nicholas and his devoted "army" left the old city of Cologne and with banners flying and pilgrim staves uplifted in song, began their southward march up the valley of the Rhine. Day after day they tramped onward, gathering recruits as they passed through village and town, until they entered what is now Switzerland. In those days it was an inhospitable land, of rugged forest and untrodden snow-clad mountain-peaks, which the child host must cross before they could reach Italy and the Mediterranean Sea. Doggedly, the children struggled up over the tremendous barrier of the Alps; starving, freezing, and brutally harried by wild mountaineers. In that terrible crossing of the Alps, over one-half of the German host perished of cold and hunger. The ragged, starving remnants straggled across northern Italy until they reached the port of Genoa. This was the place where Nicholas had prophesied that the sea would dry up at their approach and make a miraculous roadway to Palestine. But the sea rolled and foamed as always, and no miracle was vouchsafed. Thereupon his deluded followers turned furiously upon Nicholas, who disappears from history, his end being unknown. In frantic despair, the wretched survivors of the German host scattered in all directions. Most of them perished miserably; relatively few ever returned home.

The story of the French child crusaders is much more eventful and picturesque, though in a way even more tragic in the end. About the time their German comrades were scaling the snowy ramparts of the Alps, "King" Stephen and his followers left Vendôme on their march across France, planning to reach the Mediterranean at the port of Marseilles.

They had a much easier route than the German children, since it lay through settled, friendly country, and there were no mountains to cross. Still, summer had now come, and the young marchers suffered cruelly from disease, and sometimes from thirst, large numbers dying on the road.

Nevertheless, Stephen's army must have been an imposing sight, a great child host of thirty thousand, inspired by a fanatic enthusiasm, making the very heavens ring with its songs and hymns. At its head rode King Stephen in a splendid conveyance, seated on rare oriental rugs bolstered with silken cushions, his royal head protected from the sun's rays by a canopy. He was a slim, dark-haired boy of fourteen, and he wore a shimmering robe of white silk embroidered with a big red cross; his black locks were bound with a band of gold for coronet; his dark eyes glowed from a pale, serious face. Thus he rode onward in his royal chariot, drawn by white horses and surrounded by a glittering body-guard of youths in armor, mounted on chargers.

What wonder that, as this gorgeous pageant came in sight, backed by the columns of the marching host, making the earth quiver beneath their tread and the air vibrate to swelling song or intoned chant, a prodigious impression should have been made upon a devout, simple-hearted people. Everywhere, they crowded to watch the crusaders pass. Peasants left their fields, and artizans their shops. In town and country alike, all business was suspended. Men cheered or stood with uncovered heads; women ran forth, snatching up little crusaders in their arms, covering their faces with kisses, feeding them bread and fruits, and giving them warm milk to drink from wooden bowls.

But all this was as nothing beside the excitement of the children along the route. Upon them, the passing of the crusading host wrought an emotional frenzy. From battlemented castles on the heights; from the winding streets of old towns; from the cottages and mud hovels of the countryside, children rushed in streams to join that devoted host—fated, alas, never to return. Appeals and commands of cooler-headed parents were usually quite in vain. Neither bolts nor bars could hold the frantic children. If shut up, they broke down doors or threw themselves from windows, yearning to take their places in those marching columns, whose crosses and banners, whose shouts, songs, and waving censers, seemed to the fascinated children the very summons of Heaven. If children were forcibly detained and so confined that escape was impossible, they wept and pined till they fell sick and sometimes died. Thus the young crusaders swept onward, gathering so many recruits that, despite heavy losses from death and desertion, its number probably kept up to its original strength of thirty thousand.

Incidents which have come down to us in the old chronicles reveal the pathetic ignorance as well as the boundless faith of the child crusaders. More than once, when the marching columns reached the summit of a hill and saw in the distance some large town or walled city, the little pilgrims would go wild with excitement, and, forgetting the sea they had to cross, would shout frantically: "Jerusalem! Jerusalem!" Only after long explanations could the deluded children be persuaded that they were still far from their goal. And when they actually came in sight of Marseilles, with the broad blue Mediterranean beyond, the weary marchers, unable to conceive the vastness of the sea, strained their eyes in hope of seeing the towers of the Holy City rising on the opposite shore. And all eagerly scanned the waters for the miraculous roadway through walls of glass formed by the dividing waves.

When the waves stubbornly refused to divide, a crisis arose, similar to that which had disrupted Nicholas' army at Genoa. King Stephen was reviled as a false prophet. Only his faithful body-guard saved him from being lynched. Thousands of disillusioned children streamed back over the roads they had just traversed, seeking their distant homes. It looked as if the whole strange business was over.

But at this crucial moment, help came from an unexpected quarter. Two wealthy merchants of Marseilles appeared before King Stephen and his counselors. These merchants stated that, profoundly moved by the faith of the child crusaders, they had resolved to offer Stephen the use of seven ships, in which, without price and solely for the love of God, they would transport the pilgrims to the Holy Land.

The news spread. Cheering and shouting, the children trooped to the waterfront. There lay the ships: big, clumsy hulks, with high bows and sterns built up like castles. Dubious craft they would have looked to modern eyes. To those children, they seemed magic barks, heaven-sent to bear them safe to Palestine. King Stephen was quite himself again. Haranguing his followers, he proclaimed that this was the fulfilment of his prophecy. Would not those ships divide the waves, so that they might pass the sea dry-shod?

This reasoning satisfied enough of Stephen's followers to jam the ships to their total capacity—five thousand souls. So that same day, before sunset, the seven craft, crowded with the stoutest-hearted of the child crusaders, sailed forth from the harbor of Marseilles, pennons flying in the afternoon breeze and trumpeters blowing fanfares of victory. From the rocky heights above the harbor mouth, crowds of citizens and ex-crusaders watched the little squadron sail onward until it vanished in the fading twilight—forever!

Yes, forever. For that gallant squadron was never seen again—at least by Christian eyes. Years passed, with no tidings of King Stephen and his crusaders, until grieving parents gave up hope and sadly set down the fate of their lost children as a mystery destined to remain unsolved.

Then, eighteen years later, there appeared an old, old man—with news! He was one of the monks who had sailed with Stephen as guides and counselors. But what a tale he told! That voyage, so blithely begun, had turned to swift disaster. On the third day out of Marseilles a storm had sunk two of the ships, and more than a thousand of the children were drowned. They were the lucky ones! For hardly had the skies cleared when sails appeared on the horizon and strange craft bore down upon the remaining five ships. Dark-browed Saracen pirates, brandishing curved scimitars, swarmed over the bulwarks, making the children prisoners—with no resistance offered by their "friends" the Marseilles sailors.

The awful truth came out: the "good" merchants were slave-dealers, who had deliberately sold these choice cargoes of picked Christian boys and girls to a fate worse than death—a lifetime of servitude among the hated Saracens!

The poor children were scattered all over the Moslem world, from Morocco to Bagdad. And there they lived and died. The aged monk chanced to be sent to Europe on a special mission by his Egyptian master. But not one of the child crusaders ever escaped. The tragedy was utter and complete.

According to the lowest estimates, at least sixty thousand families in France and Germany were saddened and bereaved, while nearly one hundred thousand children were sucked into the whirlpool of fanaticism, few of whom saw their homes again.

Six months from the moment the shepherd boy Stephen left his flock to preach his crusade, it was all over, and the wretched "king" and his despairing dupes were chained slaves. Within that brief span, the great throb of child-life rose, quivering—and passed into oblivion.

The same exalted spirit of youthful faith so characteristic of the Middle Ages came to a perfect flowering two centuries later.

Early in the fifteenth century, a little girl with dark hair and big blue eyes played about a thatched cottage in the village of Domremy, on the eastern border of France. Her name was Jeanne Darc, and her parents were well-to-do peasant folk.

Jeanne was born in evil times. France was overrun by the English invaders, and the air she breathed was filled with rumors of war. Night and day, a watchman in the church tower kept guard to warn the villagers of the approach of enemies. And when Jeanne was about twelve years old, a marauding band of Burgundians, allies of the English, swooped down on Domremy. Warned betimes, the villagers saved their lives by flight. But the village was sacked and burned, the peasants were reduced to poverty, and Jeanne suffered hardship and hunger for a season.

Brooding over the misfortunes of her own folk and her country, Jeanne became more and more serious and thoughtful. One day, while sitting under and apple-tree in the garden behind her cottage home, she felt herself bathed in a wondrous light. Dropping her needlework, she fell upon her knees and imagined she heard a heavenly voice bidding her be comforted. Overwhelmed with mingled emotions, Jeanne told no one of her strange experience, even when the vision came again. So, for a time, she led a dual life. Outwardly, she was a demure peasant maid, busy with her household tasks; inwardly, she felt herself the object of divine favor, and came gradually to believe herself called to some exalted mission.

Presently this mission was revealed to her. The Archangel Michael, leader of the hosts of heaven, came to her, clad in shining armor and panoplied in a blaze of glory. He announced to the trembling Jeanne that she was appointed by God to save France! Saint Michael visited her often, as she walked alone in the garden or among the woods and fields; and with him came Saints Margaret and Catherine, to comfort her and strengthen her faith. Jeanne lived in a world apart, accompanied by her "Voices," as she called her heavenly visitors. Still she concealed her inner life from her parents, knowing that her hard-headed peasant father and even her pious mother would deem her insane if she told them.

Her parents were already troubled about their daughter, for she had ceased to play with the other children and went about in a singular quietness— a far-away look in her eyes. Honest Jacques Darc feared she was going into a decline, and bought from a passing friar a holy charm, warranted to avert the "falling sickness." So matters went on for a long time.

Jeanne was now sixteen. Then, one day in the spring of 1428, Saint Michael informed her that the time for action had come. The state of France was desperate: its rightful ruler the dauphin barely maintaining himself south of the river Loire and debarred from reaching the city of Reims, where he should receive the crown before he could be termed king; Paris and all the northern provinces in the hands of the English and the Burgundians; and a powerful English army laying siege to Orléans, the bulwark of the French cause. If Orléans should fall, the English would sweep south of the Loire, and all would be over. Jeanne must begin her mission!

Acting always in accordance with her "Voices," Jeanne managed to leave home and, without her parents' knowledge, sought an interview with the Sire de Baudricourt, who held a neighboring fortress for the dauphin. When the slender peasant girl appeared before him and informed him that he was to send her to the dauphin's court, where she would lead the French army to relieve the siege of Orléans and open the road to Reims, the veteran warrior at first thought her mad. Jeanne calmly told him that he would believe later, and went home again.

But the story of Jeanne's interview with the dauphin's lieutenant and his curt rebuff got about. Domremy buzzed with gossip, and Jacques Darc felt himself made ridiculous. He threatened to lock his daughter up and tried to marry her off to a neighbor's son. Then the Burgundians descended upon Domremy once more, and the villagers had to flee, returning later to find their homes devastated. Yet Jeanne's Voices bade her to be of good cheer, and she seems never to have lost heart.

It was almost a year later that Jeanne again appeared before the Sire de Baudricourt, telling him that he must now send her to the dauphin, and adding the alarming tidings that the French army was even then being badly beaten. The officer was in a chastened mood. Since he last saw her, things had gone ill indeed for the French cause. Orléans could not hold out much longer. Further, Baudricourt had bethought him of an old prophecy that France, in its hour of direst peril, should be saved by a maid. This time, therefore, Baudricourt did not dismiss Jeanne with ironic laughter, but bade her stay until he had reflected upon her story.

A few days later came the news that the French army had indeed been beaten—a fact that Jeanne could not possibly have learned by any ordinary means. The Sire de Baudricourt was deeply impressed. Clearly, here was no ordinary peasant girl. Either she was bewitched, or she was the Maid! A priest sent to examine her, having vainly uttered the formula for casting out devils, declared her to be a singularly pious girl. Thereupon, Baudricourt acted quickly. A full report was sent to the dauphin, who ordered Jeanne sent to him.

Between that remote border stronghold and the dauphin's court stretched hundreds of miles of country, much of it in Burgundian hands, and all of it infested by robber bands which harried both sides. With an escort of one officer and six men-at-arms, Jeanne, disguised as a page in boy's clothing, set out on her perilous quest. For a peasant girl, barely seventeen years old, who had never sat a horse or handled a sword, that long ride across war-torn France seemed an almost impossible ordeal. Yet Jeanne stood the journey as well as the stoutest soldier of her escort; dangers and ambuscades were miraculously avoided; and she arrived safely at the dauphin's headquarters.

Yet her ordeal was by no means over. Charles, the dauphin, was a weak man, much swayed by his favorites. And several influential courtiers scoffed at Jeanne's mission, declaring her an impostor. So they induced Charles to play Jeanne a trick. When the girl entered the audience chamber, she found it crowded with courtiers, officials, and gay ladies, and she was told to kneel before the resplendent figure, in royal robes, who sat upon the throne. But Jeanne merely gazed at the throne with a puzzled air; then shook her head and looked searchingly about the chamber. A moment later, she knelt before a soberly clad young man concealed behind a knot of courtiers. The trick had failed. She had discovered the dauphin.

Marveling greatly, Charles nevertheless asked the girl for a second proof of her powers. Thereupon Jeanne whispered in his ear, word for word, a prayer that he had uttered that very morning— known to him alone. Amazed and awed, the impressionable Charles cried out that she was indeed the Maid, and promised her an army for the fulfilment of her divine mission. In a short time Jeanne set forth at the head of her troops to raise the siege of Orléans.

The French army marched as though to a crusade. The ancient prophecy that imperiled France should be saved by a maid was on every lip; and when the soldiers looked at Jeanne, riding upon a great black charger and clad in shining white armor, she seemed to them a glorious angel sent by Saint Michael himself. In such a mood of patriotic frenzy, the French army neared Orléans. The English lines were strong, and from their fortified camps the English soldiers cursed Jeanne; they called her a witch, told her to go back to her cows, and threatened to burn her if they made her a prisoner. But these insults merely infuriated her followers. Hurling themselves upon the English lines, the French carried all before them. The siege of Orléans was raised, and the English retreated. Following them up, the French defeated them in open battle, and sent the demoralized enemy flying northward. The spell of English invincibility was broken.

At the news of these astounding events, all loyal France went wild. The royal army marched, almost unopposed, to Reims; and there, in the old cathedral, Charles was crowned and anointed king—the Maid standing by his side. Within four months from the hour when she reached Charles' headquarters, everything which Jeanne foretold had come to pass.

And now, having accomplished all that her Voices had bidden her do, Jeanne felt her mission at an end. So, donning her peasant dress, she craved leave to go home to Domremy. But the king and his generals would not hear of it. Against her own judgment, the Maid was persuaded to continue her great work of driving the English invaders from the land.

Alas! The marvelous good fortune which had borne her onward now deserted her. The weak king, listening to envious favorites, withdrew his support from the heroic girl to whom he owed his throne. Surrounded by treacherous intriguers, Jeanne was presently defeated and captured by the Burgundians, who turned her over to the English, athirst for her blood. After two years of brutal ill usage, this saintly girl was burned alive in the market-place of the city of Rouen—only nineteen years old!

Chapter VII

YOUTH IN THE ELIZABETHAN AGE

F ever there was an "Age of Youth," it was the sixteenth century. The medieval pattern of life, which had been a-weaving for a thousand years until it was worn threadbare, was suddenly rent asunder; and a new life-pattern appeared.

Three new worlds simultaneously expand the narrowly medieval horizon. They are: the buried world of Greek and Roman culture, brought to light by the Renaissance; the unknown world of America discovered by Columbus; and the immeasurable outer world of the stars, brought by pioneer astronomers within human ken. Inspired by such momentous visions, men think new thoughts about everything—including their own children. So we are not surprised to find a new attitude toward childhood; while young people, in their turn, acquire a novel attitude toward life.

Now the best and fullest expression of this sixteenth-century spirit is found in England, especially during the reign of "Good Queen Bess." England was relatively free from the bloody religious turmoil which then afflicted continental Europe, and was entirely free from the curse of foreign invasion. Therefore, it is in England, safe behind her protecting "silver streak" of sea, that we may best note the child-life of the age.

Youth was freer and happier in Elizabethan times than it was in the seventeenth century, when Puritanism came to regard children as full of original sin, which must be chastised out of them by the most strenuous methods. The Elizabethan period is thus, for children, a joyous interlude between the old austerity of the Middle Ages and the austerity of Calvinism to come. The evolution of child-life in the sixteenth century is well illustrated by three examples: Sir Thomas More and his children, the boyhood of Sir Philip Sidney, and the boyhood of Lord Francis Bacon.

Sir Thomas More belonged in many ways to the medieval past. He was a grown man when the sixteenth century began. When he was a child, England was still in the Middle Ages, his boyhood being typical of that of boys who might have lived centuries before. He first attended a monastic school, was then placed by his father in the household of the Cardinal-Archbishop of Canterbury, and finally went to Oxford University, from which he was soon snatched back home by his pious, old-fashioned father, who feared that his son's love for the "New Learning" just coming into vogue might undermine the lad's orthodoxy.

The elder More need not have been alarmed; for despite a love of Greek and other aspects of Renaissance culture, young Thomas was then what he remained through life—a devout Catholic. Every day Thomas spent hours in religious exercises. He fasted, denied himself sleep in long vigils, wore a hair-shirt next his skin, and thought seriously of becoming a monk. He might have served as a pattern for youthful piety in the high noon of the Middle Ages.

Yet this austere youth in later life showed himself a fond parent, and his home breathes a lovingkindness practically unknown in medieval homes a century before. Although brought up to strict religious observances and an old-fashioned formality, Sir Thomas's children were obviously happy enough. We see an affectionate father stimulating the interest of his little daughters in their studies by showing them his collection of coins and curiosities, and rewarding their good conduct by taking a lively interest in their pets and games. Gentleman visitors are taken to see the rabbits and the monkey, while Sir Thomas proudly shows off his "Little Meg's" fluency in Latin. And when traveling, the father writes one of his daughters: "I have given you many kisses, but stripes hardly ever."

Sir Philip Sidney was born in 1554, only four years before Queen Elizabeth ascended the throne; so he grew up in the bracing atmosphere of the Elizabethan Age. His father was a man of wealth, intelligence, and liberal religious views, well representing the cultured, moderate Protestantism favored by the queen. Philip's boyhood was accordingly a singularly happy one. He was brought up in a beautiful old castle, "modernized" with all the comforts of the period. A quiet, dreamy boy, he early showed a marked taste for reading. In this he was encouraged by his father, who, delighted by his son's literary tastes, nicknamed Philip "The Light of the Family."

At the age of ten, Philip went to the grammar school at Shrewsbury. It was one of those "new model" schools then being established in accordance with the novel educational ideas—a very different place from the grammar schools of the Middle Ages. The teachers seem to have been capable men, and since Philip was a brilliant scholar, his schooldays were pleasant ones. Furthermore, since the school term now had vacation, and the school itself was not far from his home, Philip spent his holidays with parents who loved him devotedly.

This parental devotion is shown in their frequent letters written to him while he was away at school. One from his father begins with a serious exhortation to regular and attentive prayer, "thinking of Him to whom you pray, and of the matter for which you pray." He then reminds Philip of the noble blood which flows in his veins, telling the boy that only by a good life and upright conduct will he prove himself worthy of his heritage.

Then follows some common-sense advice, such as:

"Use exercise, but without peril to your joints and bones"; "drink wine but seldom, yet sometimes, lest, being unused, you should be quickly overcome when mixing with the world"; "be courteous of gesture and affable to all men, with diversity of reverence, according to the dignity of the person." Neatness of person and apparel is counseled, together with modesty of demeanor; for, says the father: "Rather be rebuked of light fellows for maiden shamefacedness than of your sad friends for pert boldness." And to this paternal letter is added a postscript from his mother, ending: "Farewell, my little Philip, and once again, the Lord bless you! Your loving mother, Mary Sidney."

Francis Bacon's boyhood was not so happy as that of Sir Philip Sidney. In most respects it should have been, for Francis's father, a high official, was a merry, easy-going man, who loved his son and did his best for him. The cloud over Francis's young life was his mother. This lady, though a woman of intellect and learning, was a religious fanatic, belonging to the extreme Calvinist wing. Narrowminded and self-righteous, she ruled her children with a crabbed vigor that increased with age. Since Francis was a delicate boy, he was educated at home, largely by his mother and developed into such a precocious little lad that when his father first took him to court, the boy's solemn demeanor caused jovial Queen Bess to dub him laughingly her "young Lord Keeper," in humorous allusion to the office held by his father, who was then Lord Keeper of the Great Seal. In Francis Bacon's maternal upbringing we glimpse a foreshadowing of that ultra-Puritanical sternness which was to prevail in so many households a generation or two later.

Leading educators of Elizabeth's reign, and enlightened men generally, uttered protests against the severity and brutal cruelty which still lingered as an evil legacy of medieval times. Loving parents and wise schoolmasters like those of Sir Philip Sidney's boyhood were not universal. Only too many parents and teachers kept up the customs of the "bad old times." A father could still legally flog a grown daughter, while boys and even well-grown lads were often mercilessly beaten at home and at school. Indeed, even in "advanced" households and "new model" schools, birch and ferrule were frequently used, though less vigorously wielded. The important thing to notice is that the best minds of the age protested against excessive harshness, and urged kindness and moral suasion as a sounder method than blows.

Two of the most outspoken protesters against traditional practices were Roger Ascham, one-time tutor to the queen, and Richard Mulcaster, head master of a famous boys' school. Ascham laments that school, which should be a stimulus and joy to the awakening child mind, is turned into a place of bondage and punishment—a veritable prison to the body, and a cramping strait-jacket to the mind. He denounces unsparingly the system of flogging, which dulled youthful wits by terror and brutality, so that boys often ran away despite the direst consequences.

According to Ascham, parents were sometimes

worse than masters, for he thus reports what Lady Jane Grey told him of her home upbringing. "One of the greatest benefits," says Lady Jane, "that ever God gave me is that he sent me so gentle a schoolmaster after such sharp and severe parents. For when I am in presence, either of father or mother, whether I speak, keep silence, sit, stand, or go, eat, drink, be merry or sad, be sewing, playing, dancing, or doing anything else, I must do it, as it were, in such weight, measure, and number, even so perfectly as God made the world, or else I am so sharply taunted, so cruelly threatened, yea, presently sometimes with pinches, nips, and bobs, and other ways which I will not name for the honour I bear them, so without measured misordered that I think myself in hell, till time come that I must go to Master Elmer, who teacheth me so gently, so pleasantly, with such fair allurements to learning, that I think all the time nothing, whiles I am with him."

This teacher of the new type is in sharp contrast with that terrible "flogging master" who drove even so doughty a boy as Peter Carew—afterwards destined to be a famous soldier—to run away from Exeter Grammar School, climb into a turret of the city wall, and threaten to hurl himself to earth if his master climbed after him. Peter's father, hearing of his son's predicament, had him seized, coupled to a hound, led home, and chained to a dog-kennel, where he was left, not until he repented, but until he managed to escape.

Another Elizabethan protest against cruel practices is a rhymed skit entitled: "A Pretie and Merie New Interlude called The Disobedient Child." In it, a rich father desires to put his son to school. The boy objects, asserting that the school in question is a prison, the master a brute, and that boys already there have told him:

> "Their tender bodies both night and day
> Are whipped and scourged, and beat like a stone
> That from top to toe the skin is away."

The father, who is evidently of the new type, condescends to argue the matter with his son, saying that the boys must exaggerate, since:

> "It is not to be judged that any Scholemayster
> Is of so great fiersenesse and crueltie,
> And of yonge Infantes so sore a tormentor
> That the breath should be about to leave the bodie."

But the boy answers by citing the case of a boy who was killed by the master's cruelty, being hung up by the heels and beaten, so that he "through manie stripes was dead and cold." The father thereupon gives in, and the boy does not go to the school. Of course, this is a satirical skit, obviously not dealing with actual events. But its whole spirit and purpose make it a valuable indication of the new temper of the time, which may be summed up in another phrase from Roger Ascham, that, because of much beating, "boys carry commonly from the school with them a hatred of their master and a continual contempt for learning."

The voluminous pages of Elizabethan literature contain many references to child-life. In one realistic little picture of an Elizabethan nursery, the mother enters in the morning and asks the nurse how baby has slept. The good woman replies that he was "somewhat wayward" in the night, and the mother suggests this may be due to an approaching tooth. Baby's "swaddling bands" are then undone, and nurse bathes him, while the mother gives advice, mingled with fond exclamations at her son's excellent appearance. Then baby is dressed in his "biggin" or little cap tied under the chin, and his undershirt. "Give him a coat of changeable taffeta and his satin sleeves," continues mother. "Now where is his bib? Where his little petticoat? Let him have his gathered apron with strings; you need not give him his coral with the small golden chain, for I believe it is better to let him sleep until afternoon. . . . God send thee good rest, my little Boykin."

Except for the taffeta and the satin sleeves, all this sounds quite up to date. Not so modern, however, were the queer rites celebrated after birth and the terrifying yarns that mothers and nurses poured into impressionable minds. Despite the spread of education, the masses remained very superstitious, and even the upper classes believed many things that to us seem incredibly foolish.

For at least a month after birth, baby had to be continually guarded against two dire perils: the danger of being stolen by fairies; and the danger of being "overlooked"—that is, bewitched by a glance of the evil eye. No baby was allowed within sight of an ugly old woman, lest she might prove a witch, while dark-browed strangers were equally suspect.

Fairies were an even more insidious peril. A hag

or an ill-favored stranger might be kept at a distance by due vigilance or proper "white magic." But who could keep away the fairies? They visited every nursery, invisibly rocked the cradle, and manifested their presence in other strange ways. True, few of the Little People were really bad or unduly mischievous; yet even good fairies might take an irresistible fancy to some especially pretty baby and steal it, leaving a "changeling" in the cradle. When-

ever a child did not live up to early expectations, but grew dull, ugly, or idiotic, the mother could comfort herself and salve her vanity by asserting that the baby must be a fairy changeling.

Enlightened men of Elizabethan times roundly condemn the old wives' tales told children, which implant superstitious fears and sometimes lead to lamentable consequences. One writer says that often "children are so afraid that they scarce dare go out of doors alone, lest they should meet with some evil thing." And he concludes: "It is not expedient so to terrify children. For sometimes through great fear they fall into dangerous diseases, and in the night cry out when they are fast asleep."

Another writer, toward the end of Elizabeth's reign, thus dilates upon the matter: "In our childhood our mother's maids have so terrified us with an ugly devil, having horns in his head, fire in his mouth, and a tail in his breech, eyes like a bason, fangs like a dog, and a voice roaring like a lion, whereby we start and are afraid when we hear one cry 'Boo!' And they have so fraid us with bullbeggars, spirits, witches, urchins, elves, hags, fairies, Kit-with-the-Can'stick, dwarfs, giants, imps, calcars, conjurers, Robin Goodfellow, the Sporn, the Mare, the Man-in-the-Oak, the Hell-wain, the Firedrake, the puckle Tom-thumb, Hobgoblin, Tom Tumbler, Boneless, and other such bugs [terrors], that we are afraid of our own shadows."

In the homes of Elizabethan children the tendency toward domestic comfort begun in the later Middle Ages goes on apace and spreads to all classes. Chimneys and window-glass banish soot and allow warm rooms relatively free from drafts. Furniture multiplies, so that even humble folk sit on chairs and sleep soft o'nights. One servant quit a place because his master will not provide him with a feather-bed.

A new and very modern type of home appears— what we would today term the "suburban villa." Multitudes of such comfortable cottage homes, with green lawns and pretty flower gardens, are built by well-to-do townsfolk, as the congested cities pull down their ancient walls and expand freely over the surrounding countryside, now that life has become relatively secure.

All this comfort appals some conservatives, who bewail its softening effects upon the rising generation and praise the salutary hardships of the "good old times." Says one of these moralists, writing toward the close of Elizabeth's reign: "When our houses were builded of willow, then we had oaken men; but now that our homes are come to be made of oak, our men are not only become willow, but many altogether of straw—which is a sore alteration. Now have we many chimnies, and yet our tenderlings complain of rheumes and catarrhs. . . . For as the smoke in those old days was supposed to be a sufficient hardening for the timber of the house, so it was reputed a far better medicine to keep the good man and his familie from the quack, wherewith very few were oft acquainted."

Here is a description of the beginning of a boy's day, as given by a writer of the time in a book called "The Frenche Scholemaister." The young son of a London merchant is roused by Margaret the maid, whose duty it is to see that the boy gets dressed, breakfasts, and starts off in time for school. Margaret warns him that it is past seven of the clock, and that he will get a taste of the switch if he does not hurry. The boy calls loudly for his doublet and hose, and is disgruntled when Margaret insists that he put on a clean shirt, warming it for a moment before the fire, as it is somewhat damp. After a wash and tooth-rub, superintended by the maid, the boy hurries downstairs, kneels for his father's blessing, gulps down his breakfast, and hastens off to school, "with his satchel and shining morning face." A second boy sketched by another Elizabethan writer is so loath to leave his snug four-poster that his tutor complains: "Guy is somewhat slow to rise in the morning, for one must call him three or four times before he come out of his bed." Whereat Guy's mother advises that "the best cure for the disease of sluggishness is to anoint the limbs with the juice of Birch, which is excellent for such a cure if you apply it but twice or thrice."

At the Elizabethan dinner table the contrast with the Middle Ages is startling. It is covered with a linen cloth, and before the end of Elizabeth's reign, up-to-date households use napkins and eat with table-knives, spoons, and even forks. The old individual sheath-knife, and the basin and towel for fingers which had served for forks, are no longer in good taste. And as another touch of refinement, the table-linen is usually perfumed.

This Elizabethan dinner table is also set with Venetian glassware, cut-glass from the Netherlands, even delicate porcelain—"China-ware," from the Far East. For the conservatism of the Middle Ages now gone, people are keen to adopt foreign novelties. One of the oddest Elizabethan fads is the craze for toothpicks. Often made of gold, with jeweled cases, toothpicks are ostentatiously carried by "smart" persons, and it is the height of good breeding to pick one's teeth frequently at table.

It is also a time of new foods and drinks, introduced from all parts of the world. Elizabethan sea-captains are told to "bring back with you the kernels and stones of fruits. Also seeds of strange herbs and flowers, for such seeds, coming from another part of the world, afar-off, will delight the fantasies of many." So fruits and vegetables from distant climes are acclimated to Elizabethan orchards and kitchen-gardens. Oranges become fashionable, sugar supplants honey as a sweetening-base, while from America comes the potato, "that sweete roote that far exceedeth our English parsnep."

Elizabethan cookery is more sensible than that of the Middle Ages. Young people are carefully taught the virtues of good taste and nice discrimination in food and drink, as in other matters.

One Elizabethan child describes her nursery meals: "Our breakfast is bread and butter and fruit. To dinner we have greens and porrige. If fish be reasonable in price, we have it fresh—if not, salt fish, but well soaked, and beans and pease. Some drink small beer and a few have wine well watered. After noone we have bread and raisons, almonds, apples, cherries. For supper, salad, with salt and oil and vinegar, boiled mutton with dry prunes, or roots and herbs. Or gallantine of minced meat—marvellous savoury! Sometimes we have roasted meat—and sometimes pancakes—and cheese and nuts. We have as much bread as we will, and other things sufficient for nourishment, but not for the over-filling of our bellies."

Table-talk has been enriched by new topics of conversation: tales from returned travelers on the Continent, or from "merchant-adventurers," who describe marvels of the Levant, the Spice-Islands of the Far East, the queer Muscovites of the frozen North, and (strangest of all) the "New World" of the Americas, with its fabled "El Dorado"—the Land of Gold. Smoking, introduced from America, was ceasing to be a mere sea-captain's whim, and showed signs of rivaling toothpicks as a fad of "smart" society. Boys curiously watch bronzed gentlemen from overseas lighting clay pipes, and perhaps steal a whiff or two when a good opportunity offers.

This period witnessed a series of fashions that for ugliness and discomfort are simply unbelievable. And Elizabethan boys and girls were cramped, stiffened, padded, and weighted down with absurd garments, as children never were before, nor since.

The prime object of Elizabethan fashions was apparently to disguise, distort, and disfigure as far as possible the human form. And these styles were not confined to smart society; every man or woman who could afford cheap imitations aped the craze, which, as one Elizabethan writer expresses it, infested the nation, "from courtiers to carters."

Among sartorial horrors was the ruff. That fashionable instrument of torture, worn around the neck, was a band of linen or other fabric, starched stiff as a board, and sometimes further strengthened by wires.

Sensible men poured forth scorn and ridicule upon both. Ruffs are denounced as work of Satan, and starch is termed "the Devil's liquor." Hats are described as "some, sharp on the crown, peaking up like a spear or shaft of a steeple, standing a quarter of a yard above the crown of their heads; others be flat and broad on the crown like the battlements of a house." The wearer of a three-ply ruff could hardly eat or drink; and we read of a French lady who was obliged to sup with a spoon two feet long!

Yet neither the scorn of critics nor the discomfort of wearers had any effect, and exaggerated ruffs continued to be the mode.

The entire apparel of both sexes was equally grotesque. Women pinched in their bodies with corsets to give themselves wasplike waists, and then suddenly expanded into enormous "farthingales"—a sort of hoopskirt, hung upon a framework of wire and whalebone which made the skirt jut out from the waist like a shelf and then fall rigidly to the feet. The farthingale made a lady look as if encased in a cloth-covered barrel, and so foreshortened the legs that she appeared deformed. Fashionable ladies, laments a critic, "seem not women of flesh and blood, but rather puppets or mawmuts, consisting of rags and clouts compacted together."

Apparently envious of the ladies' bulk, gentlemen began to distend themselves, from waist to knee, in similar proportions. The difference was that what women accomplished by wire and whalebone, men achieved by padding. Wool-wadding, horsehair, even bran, were used to enlarge one's breeches, and below the knee would be skin-tight hose, in which even a shapely pair of calves would appear pipe-stems compared to the "bombasted" breeches.

A story is told of one young gallant in whose enormous breeches "a small hole was torn by a nail of the chair whereon he sat, so that as he turned and bowed to pay his court to the ladies, the bran poured forth as from a mill that was grinding, without his perceiving of it, till half his cargo was unladen on the floor."

So angered were sensible men by this absurd fashion that Queen Elizabeth was persuaded to issue a proclamation forbidding the wearing of farthingale-breeches. But the edict was soon rendered of no effect by the acquittal of a culprit haled into court, whose trial and naive defense are perhaps the most ludicrous ever heard in a court of law. The incident is recorded:

"About the middle of the Queen's reign . . . so excessive were men herein that a law was made against them as did stuff their breeches to make them stand out; whereas when a certain prisoner was accused for wearing such breeches contrary to law, he began to excuse himself for the offense, and endeavored by little and little to discharge himself of that which he did wear within them; he drew out of his breeches a pair of sheets, two table-cloths, ten napkins, four shirts, a brush, a glass, a comb, and night-caps, with other things of use, saying: 'Your Lordships may understand that because I have no safer a storehouse, these breeches do serve me for a room to lay my goods in; and though it be a straight prison, yet it is a storehouse big enough for them, for I have many things more yet of value within them.' And so his discharge was accepted and well laughed at: and they commanded him that he should not alter the furniture of his storehouse, but that he should rid the hall of his stuff, and keep them as it pleased him."

The fact that children were dressed like grownups is typical of the Elizabethan attitude toward childhood. Parents then regarded them as "little men and women," and this parental attitude made the children old beyond their years. Shakespeare's witty, precocious boys and girls seem to us rather unnatural, but they are really true to the life of their time. Girls especially acquired a mature point of view, because they looked forward to marriage at an early age. While the child-marriages of the Middle Ages became rare in Elizabeth's reign, many girls were wives at fourteen, while marriage for girls at fifteen or sixteen was still more frequent. If a girl remained unmarried at twenty, she was considered a confirmed old maid.

In some ways the life of an upper-class girl remained much the same as it had been in the later Middle Ages. Besides domestic training, a girl of good family was taught a similar code of social graces; embroidery and fine needlework being an art which every young gentlewoman was supposed especially to cultivate. Girls were likewise expected to be thorough in their religious observances, though with the Reformation convent-training and the nun's ideal of the "religious life" naturally disappeared.

The new comfort was pronounced in a girl's bedroom. Girls now wore dainty "night-gear," and prinked before a dressing-table equipped with combs, brushes, pincushions, and a bewildering array of lotions and cosmetics; for Elizabethan ladies were careful of their skin, teeth, and hair, and were frankly strong on "make-up."

One result of the increase in primary schools which occurred after the Reformation was that most girls could now read and write. But there were no secondary schools for girls corresponding to the boys' grammar schools; so girls whose parents wished them to be well taught were usually educated at home. Such education was relatively inexpensive, because the great increase in educated persons had resulted in a large class of professional tutors, whose services middle-class families could afford.

During this period likewise appears the "governess"—a gentlewoman in straitened circumstances who teaches girls good manners and decorum and is often able to instruct them in Italian or French, the "polite languages" of the day. Indeed, the sixteenth century offers many examples of highly educated ladies such as Lady Jane Grey and the learned mother of Lord Bacon. Sir Thomas More's "Little Meg" grew up to be an accomplished classical scholar, while Queen Elizabeth prided herself on her Greek and Latin, to say nothing of her fluency in French, Spanish and Italian, and so set the pace for her court ladies and for the daughters of persons in good society.

Richard Mulcaster, the leading educational authority, says that girls should learn to read and write, sing and play, and recommends both the classics and modern languages. They should likewise be taught religion, and "civil and domestic duties." Girls may attend primary school at the same age as boys, though Mulcaster states that girls are "more forward and prattle sooner."

The degree of learning given a girl should accord with her social position. For upper-class girls, his educational ideal is as follows: "A young gentlewoman is thoroughly furnished which can read plainly and distinctly, write fair and swiftly, sing clear and sweetly, play well and finely, understand and speak the learned languages, and those tongues also which the time most embraceth, with some logical help to chop, and some rhetorick to brave."

Mulcaster is careful to add that the primary aim of a girl's training is "in respect of marriage," and he frankly states that the education of boys is a matter of more importance. Nevertheless, his ideas on feminine education are vastly more advanced than the views of even the most enlightened men at the close of the Middle Ages, less than a century before.

The Elizabethan Age ushers in a genuinely modern attitude toward education, alike in theory and practice. The invention of printing had amazingly multiplied books, while the Reformation broke the educational monopoly of the church and put teaching increasingly into laymen's hands. The whole outworn medieval educational system, from primary schools to universities, goes rapidly by the board, and a new system, more rational and more in touch with reality, begins to take its place.

The new spirit is nowhere more evident than in the attention paid by educational leaders like Ascham and Mulcaster to the hitherto neglected primary schools. Ascham states that the very best teachers are needed to start the child a-right. And Ascham, like other educators of his day, composed new textbooks for both primary and grammar schools, to supersede the old, dry-as-dust manuals, some of which had come down from late Roman times. Ascham urges teachers to make school pleasant as well as instructive, and to break the long hours by recess periods, during which the children should be encouraged to play games and be allowed to make as much noise as they like.

Furthermore, there emerges the idea of free, universal education—at least, for the primary grades. "Better unborn than untaught" was a maxim current at that time. And wealthy citizens did their best to supplement public agencies by endowing scholarships and founding new institutions. Harrow, Rugby, and other famous boys' schools date from Queen Elizabeth's reign.

College life changed far more than college studies during Elizabeth's reign. The students were much younger than they had been in medieval times. Fifteen was the ordinary age for Elizabethan freshmen. and bright boys of fourteen were often enrolled. Multitudes of youths sought admission, ranging from young nobles and scions of wealthy merchants to poor boys from country parsonages, and even "ragged weavers' and butchers' sons."

Lowering of age limits and overcrowding combined to make necessary a stricter college discipline. College lads were now forbidden to haunt taverns and were punished for many minor breaches of decorum. "Town and gown" rows still occurred, but they were no longer the wild and bloody riots of yore. The university authorities even tried to stem the tide of fashion. "Excessive ruffs" were denounced, together with "breeches of unseemly greatness." Here, however, college discipline failed. The tyranny of style is something which the strongest efforts cannot break.

The love of novelty and adventure characteristic of Elizabethan times led many youths to travel. Some serious-minded young men went for what we should call post-graduate work in German or Dutch universities. But most young Elizabethans went abroad for cultural polish and amusement. Indeed, a young gentleman's education was considered hardly complete until he had made a foreign tour. And his goal was usually Italy, especially Venice, which was then the pleasure-seeker's paradise.

He sometimes returned to England rather the worse for his Italian sojourn. One Elizabethan writer pithily remarks: "Our countrymen usually bring three things with them out of Italy—a naughty conscience, an empty purse, and a weak stomach." In one of his plays, Shakespeare satirizes the "Italianized" young Englishman by making a character say: "Farewell, Monsieur Traveller; look you lisp and wear strange suits, disable all the benefits of your own country, be out of love with your nativity and almost chide God for making you that countenance you are, or I will scarce think you have swam in a gondola."

However, the better type of young Elizabethan derived distinct benefit from foreign experiences. Of this, Sir Philip Sidney is a good example. Leaving Oxford at the age of seventeen, Sir Philip spent the next four years in travel and study abroad. He first went to Paris, where he lived at the English Embassy and spent some time in the cultured society of the French capital. He next went to Germany for study, stopped a short while at Vienna, and thence journeyed to Italy. Here, after some travel, he settled down in Venice, making the acquaintance of many eminent personages, though somewhat surprising his Venetian friends by his disinclination to the pleasures of gay society, so that they thought him rather too serious for a young fellow barely twenty years old. Sir Philip returned to England a model of social accomplishments and polite letters, and became the most popular young man of his day.

In a gay, pleasure-loving time like the Elizabethan Age, the number of youthful sports and games was legion. Most of the old favorites survived. Children still played hot cockles, lads "tilted at the ring," while youths and maidens hawked, and young bloods followed their sires in the hunting field.

The chief novelties in indoor games were backgammon and cards. Playing-cards were known by the close of the Middle Ages, but during Elizabeth's reign they became a "craze," and card-games innumerable were invented or were introduced from abroad. Billiards also were a rare novelty at the very close of the period.

There were hand-ball, tennis, "racquet"—a sort of ping-pong—"bandy-ball" or golf introduced from Scotland, "balloon-ball" played with a large inflated bladder, and old-fashioned football. That old type of football, which was popular in the Middle Ages, was as rough as ever. Played over a wide stretch of country, with a large number of players on each side, and with practically no restraining rules, it gave rise to so many accidents and brawls that attempts were made to abolish it. Oxford banned it absolutely, and none of the Elizabethan educators have a good word to say for it. Mulcaster, with his usual dispassionate spirit, believes that it would be conducive to health and strength if properly played, but adds that "as it is now commonly used, with bursting of shins and breaking of legs, it be neither civil nor worthy the name of any train to health." Another Elizabethan writer condemns it even more severely. "Doth not everyone lie in wait for his adversary?" asks this writer, "seeking to overthrow him and to pitch him on the nose, though it be upon hard stones, in ditch or dale, in valley or hill, or what place soever it be, he careth not, so he have him down." And he concludes by scoring football as "a bloody and murdering practice."

The rough temper of brisk lads in Elizabethan days is attested by another survival from medieval times. This was quarter-staff or cudgel-play. The object in this sport was to draw blood with a sharp rap on the head. Even young children had a decidedly painful sport called "Dun in the mire." Dun was a heavy log. Two boys would start to lug it away, and each would try to drop it on the other's toes—that being the object of the game.

In this Golden Age of "Merrie England," there was an extraordinary amount of music and song. As an authority describes it in the volume "Old English Popular Music": "During the reign of Elizabeth, music seems to have been in universal cultivation, as well as universal esteem. Not only was it a necessary qualification for ladies and gentlemen, but even the city of London advertised the musical abilities of boys educated in Bridewell and Christ's Hospital (foundling asylums), as a mode of recommending them as servants, apprentices, or husbandmen. . . . Tinkers sang catches; milkmaids sang ballads; carters whistled; each trade, and even the beggars, had their special songs; the bass-viol hung in the drawing-room for the amusement of waiting visitors; the lute, cittern, and virginals were the necessary furniture of the barber shop. They had music at dinner; music at supper; music at weddings; music at funerals; music at dawn; music at night. . . . He who felt not, in some degree, its soothing influence, was viewed as a morose, unsocial being."

"Gentle and simple" alike took every opportunity for singing, dancing, and celebrating. Many of the old church festivals survived the Reformation— shorn of some religious solemnity but not of the attendant merry-making. There was Yuletide, and the colored "Paschal Eggs" of Easter, and Maytime with its pole and morris-dances, and October's "cakes and ale." Medieval "mysteries" and morality-plays gave way to masques and "Interludes" of a secular character, and the children, instead of appearing as angels and "boy-bishops," now took part as fairies or little imps wearing comic heads.

There were the fairs still, and on gala evenings, children would be taken to see sights unknown in medieval times—fireworks, with banging powder-crackers, and sizzling "squibbs," and flaming "set-pieces."

Every-day life had its glamor, for the children of commoners as well as young aristocrats. Take Dick, the waterman's son, for example. In those days of unpaved streets and atrocious roads, the Thames was far and away the best avenue of London. The broad river teemed with traffic, and a waterman's son like Dick had before his eyes a constant pageant of which he never tired. Multitudes of light craft were constantly plying up and down stream; hundreds of rowboats ferried passengers from bank to bank; while now and then private barges of noblemen, with oarsmen in gay liveries, rowed swiftly along. The stately royal barge bearing the queen herself was a great sight, at which Dick always doffed his cap and set up a loud huzza.

Below London Bridge, with its arches crowned by ancient buildings, was yet another spectacle. For there lay a mass of shipping—a veritable forest of masts and sails. Dick loved to watch the ships, with their high, castlelike sterns, discharging cargoes brought from distant lands. He did not see as much of those ships and their bronzed crews as he would have liked, because his father usually ferried passengers above London Bridge, at one of the chief crossings of the Thames.

When the boat drew alongside the stairs of the landing-stage, Dick would jump nimbly ashore, help the ladies out of the boat, and assist waiting passengers for the next trip with such good will as earned him many a welcome coin.

The lads of the river-front were as much at home in the water as on land. Dick could swim like an otter and dive like a seal before he was ten. And as he grew older, he took part in the river-sports then so much in vogue. At Eastertide there were mock sea-fights, applauded by cheering crowds. Another favorite sport was water-quintain—an old game, handed down from the Middles Ages. A pole would be set up in the middle of the river, to which was fastened a shield. Then a lad, armed with a lance, and standing erect in the boat, would be rowed swiftly toward the target. If he struck the shield fair and shivered his lance without losing his footing, well and good. But a glancing blow would knock him overboard, and he would come up spluttering a moment later, to be hauled into a waiting boat with much chaffing from his friends.

Sometimes, during a hard winter, the river would be frozen over. Dick thought that great luck, for then there would be no work at all, and he could give his entire time to play. Sleds and skates were unknown. The riverside boys sledded on cakes of ice which slithered splendidly over the frozen surface, and skated on leg-bones of animals, bound to their shoes. By pushing themselves with iron-shod staves, boys equipped with such primitive skates could work up great speed; and in a rough game of ice-tilting, two lads, shod with bone-skates, and pushed by comrades, would tilt against one another, armed with lance and shield.

For another representative boy of the period, take Hal, the apprentice. One bright morning Hal might be seen being led through the streets of London by his father to the district known as Cheapside. He was on his way to be apprenticed to the goldsmith's trade.

In those days, masters of each craft plied their trade in a certain quarter of the town; so Cheapside was lined with goldsmiths' and jewelers' shops, old buildings with gables of weathered timber and whitewashed plaster. An ancient stone cross was in the middle of the way, and there was a bustle about the Mermaid Tavern—soon to be immortalized by Master Will Shakespeare and his cronies.

In one of the shops, Hal was presented to the master goldsmith. The trio walked to the town-hall, where the "indentures" or contract was signed by his elders and Hal was bound to serve the master faithfully for seven years, while he learned the goldsmith's craft. He was to be lodged and fed in his master's house. Thereafter, if he proved a competent workman, he would be admitted to membership in the goldsmiths' guild and might hope to become a master himself, with a shop and prentices of his own.

At first Hal was a bit homesick, but the goldsmith was a just master, and his wife was a kindly woman, who looked after Hal and the other two apprentices almost as though they were her own sons. Of course, the new apprentice had his troubles, got into mischief, and was birched by his master more than once.

The London apprentices of those days were an unruly lot. Each lad owned a stout cudgel, and apprentices from different crafts were always running foul of one another on the streets. A fight would start; the cry of "Clubs! Clubs!" would resound; prentice lads would pour from the shops armed with their cudgels; and a merry brawl would ensue, resulting in many bruises, and perhaps a broken head or two. Yet such mishaps were taken in good part. A fair fight left no bad blood.

The guilds had each their celebrations, when masters and apprentices would parade; and there were civic processions like the Lord Mayor's Show, when all the crafts would take part, dressed in their best, and walking proudly beneath their standards.

The greatest day in Hal's boyhood occurred in

the second year of his apprenticeship, when he watched Elizabeth's triumphal procession through London on the way to her coronation. Old records have left us an excellent description of what the boy saw.

First came a gorgeous group of royal heralds, proclaiming the new queen. Then came a glittering group of knights in armor. After them rode an even more resplendant group of lords and gentlemen; the sergeant-at-arms; the Lord Mayor of London with his scepter; and the Lord High Chamberlain with the royal sword. Then, the queen herself, in a magnificent litter borne by footmen in the royal livery and surrounded by the stalwart beefeaters— the Yeomen Extraordinary of the Guard, in the same uniforms which we see today.

After the queen rode more lords and high dignitaries of the realm, "in faire complete armour," mounted upon chargers trapped in cloth of gold— notable among them, the Lord Steward, "with a silver wand a yard long, commanding everybody." Next the Lords Spiritual—archbishops, bishops, canons, and prebends; and the Commons, in their parliament robes. Next, a full thousand men in armor, marching to the blare of trumpets and a thunderous roll of drums; ten "great pieces" of artillery; a band of morris-dancers; and "in a cart two white bears." Then the aldermen and dignitaries of the City of London; and after them the musicians of the queen's household—playing their loudest, and including a choir of "singing children." Lastly, the foreign ambassadors and their suites, and a great tail of common folk, cheering, shouting, and swarming after the royal show.

Chapter VIII

CHILDREN OF CAVALIERS AND PURITANS

WHEN "Good Queen Bess" closed her aged eyes one March day of the year 1603, an era ended which for children was a far happier time than the seventeenth century that was opening—a century of strife, culminating in religious fanaticism and civil war, from which youth suffered in every way. England was split between Cavaliers and Puritans, who tended to go to opposite extremes in their family lives. Puritan children were warped and terrified by a sour discipline and a "hell-fire" theology; while roistering, mocking Cavaliers set their offspring such bad examples that they grew up wild, hard-drinking young blades or vain fashionable beauties, with little in their heads but gossip and the latest styles.

A good example of family life at the beginning of the seventeenth century is the boyhood of Robert, later Earl of Leicester under King Charles I. Robert was born about the close of Elizabeth's reign, so he grew up in early Stuart times. One of a large family, he was brought up with his brothers and sisters on his father's country estate. We read of children's parties and dances in the old hall or

on the green lawns, of romps in the garden, and
of picnics in the park. A tutor gave them instruction, and we learn that the children did "much profit
of their books." When their parents were absent
from home, the children were well looked after by
the old steward, whose favorite was "little Master
Robert."

Robert was termed "a born courtier" at the age
of five. Shortly afterwards he was taken to Windsor Castle and presented on Saint George's day to
the knights assembled for that occasion. The
steward was his mentor, and the old man reports
proudly: "I brought in Master Robert while the
knights were at dinner. He played the wag so
prettily and boldly that all took pleasure in him,
but above the rest, my Lord Admiral, who gave
him sweetmeats, and he prated with His Honor
beyond measure."

Whatever may have been his shortcomings as a
king, Charles I was certainly a devoted parent, as
was also his wife, Queen Henrietta Maria. The
formal, opinionated monarch unbends in the nursery and romps both with his own children and with
their playmates, the Villiers children, of whom King
Charles was likewise very fond.

An amusing anecdote has come down to us about
Prince Charles, afterwards King Charles II. It
seems that the little prince strongly objected to taking medicine, and made such a fuss about it that
his mother (then away from him) wrote him a
letter telling him to take it like a good boy or she
would come herself and make him. But young

Charles was still touchy on the subject, for he gravely advised his tutor, the Earl of Newcastle, against the practice, citing his own sad experience, in the following childish note:

"My Lord:

"I would not have you take too much physicke, for it doth alwaies make me worse, and I think it will do the like with you. I ride every day, and am ready to follow any directions from you. Make haste back to him that loves you.

Charles P."

The civil war which broke out in 1642 ended this happy childhood. The queen fled abroad with some of the royal children, while two others fell into the hands of the parliamentary authorities. They were allowed to be with their father during his last imprisonment, and took an affecting leave of him on the eve of his execution. The king placed them on his knees and gave them some last fatherly advice. As an eye-witness of the scene describes it: "They gave him such pretty and pertinent answers as drew tears of love and joy from his eyes; and then, praying Almighty God to bless them, he turned about, expressing a tender and fatherly affection. Most sorrowful was this parting, the young Princess shedding tears and crying most lamentably, so as moved others to pity that formerly were hard-hearted; and at opening the bedchamber door, the King returned hastily from the window and kissed 'em and blessed 'em; so parted."

Many Puritan households were of the finest type —homes of love and devotion, which differed from the best Cavalier homes chiefly in a more quiet and earnest tone. Unfortunately, other Puritan households were of the sort already foreshadowed back in Elizabeth's reign by the mother of Lord Bacon. In such homes, parents crushed their children beneath the yoke of a fanatical discipline, and the unhappy children led lives so morbidly joyless that they seem to us a perpetual nightmare.

A picture of the better type of Puritan home comes to us from the pen of Lucy Apsley, who became the wife of Colonel Hutchinson, a noted parliamentary soldier. Describing her childhood, she writes: "As soon as I was weaned, a French woman was taken to be my dry-nurse, and I was taught to speak French and English together. By the time I was four years old I read English perfectly, and having a great memory, I was carried to sermons, and while I was very young could remember and repeat them exactly; and being caress'd, the love of praise tickled me, and made me attend more heedfully.

"When I was about seven years of age, I remember I had at one time eight tutors in several qualities, languages, music, dancing, writing and needlework; but my genius was quite averse from all but my book, and that I was so eager of that my mother, thinking it prejudiced my health, would moderate me in it. . . . My father would have me learn Latin, and I was so apt that I outstripped my brothers who were at school, although my father's chaplain, that was my tutor, was a pitiful dull fellow. My brothers, who had a great deal of wit, had some emulation at the progress I was making, which very well pleased my father, tho' my mother would have been contented if I had not so wholly addicted myself to that as to neglect my other qualities."

Little Lucy is far more puritanical than her own father and mother, for she goes on to say: "As for music and dancing, I profited very little in them, and would never practise my lute or harpsichords but when my masters were with me. Play among other children I despis'd, and when I was forc'd to entertain such as came to visit me, I tir'd them with more grave instructions than their mothers, and plucked all their babies [dolls] to pieces, and kept the children in such awe, that they were glad when I entertain'd myself with elder company; to which I was very acceptable, and living in the house with many persons that had a great deal of wit; and very profitable serious discourse being frequent at my father's table and in my mother's drawing-room. I was very attentive to all, and gather'd up things that I would utter again to great admiration of many that took my memory and imitation for wit.

"It pleas'd God that thro' the good instructions of my mother, and the sermons she carried me to, I was convinced that the knowledge of God was the most excellent study, and accordingly applied myself to it, and to practise as I was taught: I used to exhort my mother's maids much, and to turn their idle discourse to good subjects; but I thought, when I had done this on the Lord's Day, and every day performed my due tasks of reading and praying, that then I was free to anything that was not sin; for I was not at that time convinced of the vanity of conversation which was not scandalously wicked, I thought it no sin to learn or hear witty songs and sonnets or poems, and twenty things of that kind."

Another child more puritanical than his parents was John Milton. John had a comfortable home and might have led a pleasant, normal boyhood if he had chosen to do so.

But, like little Lucy Apsley, John Milton cared not for "childish things." Play seemed to him a vanity; his pleasures lay in books and in sedate walks with his father in the fields outside Londontown. So intense was this young Puritan's zeal for study that he would often pore over his books far into the night, while an unfortunate maid servant, charged with seeing Master John to bed, would nod and doze uneasily in her chair. Indeed, while still a mere child, Milton became aware of his talents and dedicated himself to an exalted mission. Undoubtedly he refers to his own boyhood when he writes in "Paradise Lost."

> "When I was yet a child, no childish play
> To me was pleasing: all my mind was set
> Serious to learn, to know, and thence to do:
> Myself I thought born to that end,
> Born to promote all truth, all righteous things."

So sternly serious a boy could hardly grow into an amiable man, and we are not surprised to find Milton's genius marred by a morose temper, which wrecked his early married life and made his household a place of harshness and cruelty. His first wife, a girl of Cavalier stock and sprightly temperament, soon left him and went back to her parents, alleging among other matters that she could not stand hearing her husband beat his poor little nephews, whom he was educating. Later on, Milton and his wife were reconciled, but they were never really happy together, and their daughters seem to have had a stern bringing-up. Despite their care of him during his years of blindness, these daughters were moved more by filial obligation than love, for there were many domestic jars, and when he died, Milton cut them off in his will, owing to their "undutiful" conduct, as he phrased it.

A contrast between the moderate Puritanism at the beginning of the seventeenth century and its more extreme phases some decades later is revealed by the boyhoods of Oliver Cromwell and John Bunyan.

The future Lord Protector was born in Elizabeth's reign, being four years old when she died. Though reared in a Puritan household and living in one of the stanchest Puritan regions of England, young Oliver was anything but a sour fanatic or learned prig. The fact that he was a good student didn't prevent him from being a hearty lad; for we read that "he was more famous for his exercises in the fields than in the schools, being one of the chief match-makers and players at football, cudgels, or any other boisterous game or sport." And throughout life, his fiery zeal was tempered by an underlying common sense.

Contrast the essentially sane, well-balanced character of Oliver Cromwell with Bunyan's morbid youth. John Bunyan was born in 1628, a whole generation later than Cromwell, and he grew up amid the strife and turmoil which culminated in the English civil war. He was of humble birth, his father being a tinker, and he was reared in a community of extreme Puritans.

A sensitive boy with a vivid imagination, John was early haunted by religious terrors. Before he was ten years old, his childish games were spoiled by doubts as to their righteousness, while his slumbers were disturbed by nightmares in which fiends tried to fly away with his soul. The older he grew, the more oppressed was he with the sense of sin. He accused himself of being a hopelessly wicked lad; but, as a matter of fact, he led a singularly blameless life. His "sins" boil down to the following: dancing on the village green, ringing the bells of the parish church, playing at tip-cat, and reading the history of Sir Bevis of Southampton!

Nevertheless, these strange transgressions preyed ceaselessly upon John's morbid mind. Unless he rid himself of them, he felt he was a lost soul. And the painful struggles of his purging he tells in his book, "Grace Abounding." The first to go was tip-cat. In the midst of a game he paused and stared wildly upward, his stick still in his hand; for he had heard a solemn voice asking him whether he would leave his sins and go to heaven, or keep his sins and go to hell; and as he gazed upward, he caught sight of an awesome face frowning on him from the sky.

Next, he renounced bell-ringing, but comforted himself by watching others pull the ropes until even that compromise was rendered impossible by the thought that if he coddled this sin much longer the steeple would fall on his wicked head. Thereupon he fled in terror from the spot and visited bell-ringings no more. We are not told when Sir Bevis went into the discard, but we do know that dancing on the green was renounced only after months of spiritual anguish, as it was his darling sin. Even then, the tortured youth was destined to years of brooding that nearly drove him insane.

We must not think of John Bunyan as an isolated, half-mad crank. He was merely typical of a large class of Puritan children, overwrought by the terrible discipline to which they were constantly exposed. What ultra-Puritan fanaticism was like becomes clear when we examine the books then written for the young.

A library of this "juvenile" literature was produced by eminent Puritan divines during the seventeenth century.

One of the most noteworthy is entitled "Spiritual Milk for Babes and Young Children." A more inappropriate title was never devised, for the whole of this formidable volume smells of sulphur and brimstone. Its spiritual quality is revealed in a preliminary exhortation to parents that: "Your child is never too little to go to hell." The author then addresses himself to his youthful readers by remarking: "Every mother's child of you are by nature Children of Wrath." He asks each child: "How dost thou spend thy time? Is it in play and idleness with wicked children? Do you dare to run up and down on the Lord's Day? Or do you keep in to read your book? Which of these two sorts are you?" Next the author enjoins the child to

THE STORY OF YOUTH 203

consort with godly people, attend sermons by "the most powerful ministers," and read the most "searching" books, his special advice being: "get your father to buy you Mr. Jole's 'Father's Blessing' and 'Guide to Heaven.'" And this to an audi-

ence whose ages were supposed to range from three to nine!

That John Bunyan was wrestling with his soul's salvation before he was ten years old does not seem strange when we read the histories of godly infants held up in this volume for children's emulation. One story is entitled: "Of a child that was admirably affected with the things of God when he was between two and three years old, with a brief account of his death." Another case-history is entitled: "Of a little Girl that was wrought upon by the Spirit when she was between four and five years old." Another child, a boy of three, objects to being put to bed before "Family Duty," as the Puritans termed family prayers; and, not content therewith, would often be found on his knees by himself in a corner. He learned to read the Scriptures "with groans, tears, and sobs," not because he was a slow reader but because of his conviction of sin.

Still another paragon of virtue walked into school of his own free will, at the tender age of two and a half, and urged to be taught. Perceiving his brother and sister delighted with new clothes, he proceeded "with a great Gravity to reprove their folly." After all these infant prodigies, we read with comparative indifference the case of a presumably backward child "eminently converted between eight and nine years old."

Lest this fearsome book seem exceptional, we will quote briefly from others written in a similar vein. A volume by one Thomas White contains the following: "Sleep not in church, for the Devil rocks the cradle. Be not proud of thy clothes nor curious in putting them on, for the Devil holds the glass. Fight not with thy playfellows, for the Devil will be thy second. Play not on the Lord's Day, for the Devil will be thy playfellow. Play not at cards, for they are the Devil's books. They that go to bed without praying have the Devil for their bedfellow."

This book tells a truly pathetic story of a little boy of eight who wept because he "thought he should go to hell though he did try to serve God as well as he could" And another boy, being found by his mother in tears, unburdens his tender conscience of the sin of having once whetted his knife upon the Lord's Day.

Another Puritan "juvenile," entitled "A New Book for Children," concludes a discussion of "original sin" with an exhortation to "all ye wicked children, who are of the seed of evil-doers," to amend their ways lest they meet the fate of the children who mocked the Prophet Elisha and be eaten up by bears.

The Puritans didn't succeed in taking the joy out of life all at once. As the month of April drew toward its close, the village would be astir with anticipation. To be sure, a few households held sternly aloof. But the majority could quote King James' proclamation bidding his subjects be merry as convincing proof that they were in the right in their celebration of May Day.

As the last April evening fell, parents had hard work putting their youngsters to bed, and only the threat of being kept at home next morning got the excited youngsters under the coverlets. For were they not to arise with the coming-in of May?

The last stroke of midnight had scarcely sounded from the belfry of the parish church when some light-slumbering boys and girls leaped from their beds, crying that the merry month was in. And long before the first streak of dawn, the lads and lassies of the village were romping and dancing in procession toward the greenwood, their way lighted by flaring torches, their steps quickened by music and blaring horns.

Their task was to gather flowers and greenery to bedeck the village on the following day. As the sun rose, the troop returned, and soon every cottage was hung with garlands, while in the village green, leafy booths and arbors arose.

Now a distant chorus of men's voices echoed on the fresh morning air. The May-pole was coming! The previous day, a party of lads had repaired to the forest, and had felled and trimmed a fine, straight tree. Drawn by several yoke of lumbering oxen, the long pole came in sight—painted in bands of bright colors and bound around with garlands tied with gay ribbons. Young and old, the villagers trooped forth to greet its coming; and soon the May-pole was reared in the center of the green, a flag flaunting from its tip in the spring breeze.

The maying was now in full swing. There was feasting and drinking in beneath the shaded arbors, and much dancing on the green. The climax of the festivities were the pageant of Robin Goodfellow and the morris-dance.

Out from behind a leafy screen strode Robin— none other than our old friend Robin Hood, followed by his Merry Men, with twanging bows and clad in Lincoln green. They shot right well at the butts, to prove that archery was not yet a lost art, even if gunpowder had grimed the world.

Robin and his faithful Maid Marian were hailed Lord and Lady of the May. Then—the morris-dance! Robin, Maid Marian, Friar Tuck, and Little John were the central figures, but about them capered a rout of jesters and mummers, bedecked with ribbons and tinkling bells, and riding hobby-horses whose multicolored trappings *swished* the grass and hid the dancers' feet.

But, as the Puritans rose to power, they imposed their discipline upon the rest of the population. From the very beginning of the seventeenth century a reaction set in against the gaiety and pleasure-seeking of the Elizabethan Age.

Almost the first things attacked by the Puritans were sports and games. Queen Bess had been dead only a few years when her successor King James I aroused the wrath of the Puritan party by encouraging his subjects to enjoy "plays and lawful games in May and good-cheer at Yule." Cavalier boys must have been strengthened in their loyalty to the king by the knowledge that their pastimes were threatened by the parliamentary cause. Perhaps that was one reason why they fought so well in the civil war; for Prince Rupert, the dashing young royalist cavalry leader, stated that lads of fifteen or sixteen were the most recklessly brave of his troopers. But the Puritans triumphed—and the "Merrie England" of Elizabeth passed into eclipse. May-poles were cut down, morris-dances were forbidden, and many sports and games were sternly prohibited. Some cruel pastimes like bear-baiting were wisely done away with. Yet in this the Puritans were not actuated solely by humanitarian motives; for, as Macaulay wittily put it, the chief reason was, not the pain suffered by the bear, but the pleasure given the spectators!

Indeed, during the Puritan Commonwealth, almost everything savoring of gaiety and good-cheer was put under the ban. In 1652, parliament decreed that "no observation shall be had of the five-and-twentieth Day of December, commonly called Christmas Day," and the same order forbade the making or consumption of mince-pies, plum-puddings, and similar delicacies. As an exasperated Cavalier expressed it:

> "All Plums the Prophet's sons defy,
> And spice-broths are too hot;
> Treason's in a December-pye,
> And death within the pot.
>
> "Gone are those golden days of yore,
> When Christmas was a high-day,
> Whose sports we now shall see no more;
> 'Tis turned into Good Friday."

With the fall of the Puritan Commonwealth and the restoration of the Stuarts, the pendulum swung as far in the direction of extravagant pleasure as it had gone toward excessive austerity under Puritan rule.

To the fashionable beauties of King Charles's court, children were either pets or nuisances. If pets, they were indulged almost as much as the ladies' lap-dogs, were tricked out in gorgeous finery, stuffed with unwholesome sweets, and allowed to sit up at late dinner-parties, in order to make the guests laugh at their pert sayings and precociously naughty remarks. Then, when the poor youngsters got upset stomachs and grew peevish, stubborn, or obstreperous, their mother would fly into a passion and whip them unmercifully.

If, on the other hand, my lady deemed children a nuisance, they were "planted out" with a foster-mother, usually an ignorant country-woman, and passed their early years in a peasant's cottage, growing up neglected and boorish, until, at the age of six or seven, they would be suddenly whisked off to some "genteel academy," where they would be taught little except the social graces and would often pick up bad habits.

Of course, many households kept to the traditions of former times. A good example of this type of home is revealed in Evelyn's Diary, where Mr. Evelyn thus describes his young daughter:

"She is a good child, religious, discreet, ingenious, and qualified with all the ornaments of her sex. She has a peculiar talent in design, as painting in oil and miniature, and an extraordinary genius for whatever hands can do with a needle. She has the French tongue, has read most of the Greek and Roman authors and poets, using her talents with great modesty, exquisitely shaped, and of an agreeable countenance."

Yet by the close of the seventeenth century, the old standards were sadly lowered.

Boys were somewhat less affected by the educational trend of the times. The grammar schools went on much as usual, with few outward changes in either studies or student life. One amusing incident occurred at Eton during the great plague of

1662. Certain learned doctors having declared tobacco to be a preventive against infection, all the Eton boys were ordered to smoke and were commanded to puff their pipes even in classroom, under dire penalties for disobedience!

The zest for learning which had quickened Elizabethan times was gone. Primary schools were especially neglected. The Puritans believed in popular instruction, but the Commonwealth lasted too short a time to accomplish much, and in the general collapse of standards under the Restoration, poor boys as a rule grew up uneducated.

The universities suffered greatly. At Oxford an important educational reform had been started in 1636, when the old medieval system of "disputations" had been replaced by a regular course of studies and lectures for the degrees of Bachelor of Arts and Master of Arts after oral examinations. But the promising beginning was nipped in the bud by the killing frosts of civil war, and Oxford sunk into an intellectual torpor that was destined to last until the opening of the nineteenth century.

During the early Stuart period the "finishing tour" abroad which had become so popular for young gentlemen in Elizabeth's reign continued to be very much the fashion. A play of the period makes the actor taking the part of an English ambassador declaim these exasperated lines:

"Gentlemen send me their younger sons to learn fashions, forsooth; as if the riding of five hundred miles and the spending of a thousand crowns would make 'em wiser than God meant to make 'em!

THE STORY OF YOUTH

Three hundred of these goldfinches have I entertained. . . . I can go in no corner but I meet some of my young Wifflers in their accoutrements. Six or seven of them make a perfect morris-dance; they need no bells, their spurs serve their turn. I am

ashamed to trail them abroad; they'll say I carry a whole forest of feathers with me, and I should plod before 'em in plain stuff, like a writing-school master before his boys when they go a-feasting!"

Seventeenth century dress offers a refreshing interlude between the absurdities of the preceding century and the exaggerations of the century to come. The graceful lines of the typical Cavalier costume of early Stuart times were marred only by too many ribbons, laces, and feathers stuck in the broad-brimmed soft felt hats.

The Puritans of course condemned the very word fashion. Puritan dress was austerely simple, with no ornamentation of any kind.

Under the Restoration, French styles became the mode. By the end of the century, young gentlemen were wearing long coats and enormous curled wigs, which replaced alike the love-locks of the Cavaliers and the Puritan Roundheads' close-cropped polls.

Seventeenth century boys and girls of well-to-do parents lived in substantial brick houses, sat on well-made chairs, ate at massive, handsomely carved tables, and looked out of long windows hung with heavy curtains. But there is as yet no bathroom!

As to food, a glimpse into the nursery of a well-regulated household gives us an idea of the diet of small children. Those of the North family, though indulged in extra treats on special occasions, were ordinarily kept to a diet "plain and rather short than plentyful." They were not pampered with "bits and curiosities," and were never allowed wine, though they were given as much small beer as they liked, a jug of it being kept in the nursery at all times for them to help themselves.

Older boys and girls ate with their parents at the family dinner table. Seventeenth century folk were inclined to be heavier eaters than Elizabethans had been. We hear less of salads and more of solid meat courses. In Cavalier circles hard drinking was common, and many young lads were indulged in the habit by roistering fathers. Three modern beverages, coffee, chocolate, and tea make their appearance.

Chapter IX

CHILDREN OF THE EIGHTEENTH CENTURY

THE eighteenth century was for most children a joyless period. Perhaps in no other age were they more repressed by their elders, who trimmed and pruned young minds as methodically as they did the trees and hedges of their stiffly formal gardens.

Children lived under such unhealthful conditions that fully one-half of them, even of the upper class, died before they were five years old. As late as 1820, the child death-rate was almost as high as it had been in the Middle Ages. Bad air, bad drainage, unsuitable food, ignorant nurses, and quack doctors killed off children wholesale, no matter in what social class they were born. The ancient prejudice against soap and water was still so strong that few children were given a thorough washing once in six months; for one of the pet ideas of the time was that frequent baths meant "catching cold" and other ills. Queen Anne gave birth to seventeen children, of whom all save one died in infancy, and that one lived to be only eleven years old.

Of course conditions in the eighteenth century were no worse than they had been. But children did not have as much of a "run for their money" as those of earlier times. The medieval child, reared in a damp, verminous hut or castle, rolled joyously in the dirt and played freely with pigs and dogs. But the child of the eighteenth and early nineteenth centuries had most of the dirt without the fun. He or she was brought up in a stuffy, unsanitary nursery; was crampingly clad, improperly fed, and tended by an ignorant nurse-maid. If sick, the child was usually dosed with home remedies or patent-medicines. If fractious and crying, he was stupefied by "soothing-syrups" and "elixirs" containing alcohol or even opium, which were prime factors in the heavy infant death-rate. If (as often happened) a child "went into a decline," it was "God's will." A competent physician (of whom there were then very few) was rarely called in. So the age-old slaughter of the innocents went steadily on, and was not really taken in hand much before the middle of the nineteenth century.

Relations between parents and children were never more chilly, harsh, and formal than during this period. Children were literally held at arms' length, and family life was marked by a formality which to us is almost inconceivable. When away at school, letters home usually began by addressing father or mother as "Sir," "Madam," "Honored Parents," and closed with such phrases as: "Your dutiful son."

Downright cruelty was only too common. Queen Anne is not usually thought of as a brutal person. Yet the treatment which she and her husband, the prince consort, meted out to their one surviving son seems to us monstrous. That unfortunate child, a sickly boy, was hardly able to get about, and objected to going upstairs without aid. He suffered from water on the brain, his head being so abnormally large that at five years of age he wore a hat big enough for an ordinary man. But his royal parents considered his attitude obstinate laziness, forbade the servants to "coddle" him, and finally shut themselves up with him in a room and gave him such a thrashing with a birch rod that the wretched little prince jumped about from pain and thenceforth dragged himself upstairs without daring to ask for help. When he died of scarlet fever in his twelfth year, Queen Anne grieved sorely for him, but did not apparently feel any remorse for her harsh conduct.

One of the few gentle rearings of the period which we know about is that of Edward Gibbon, the famous historian of the "Decline and Fall of the Roman Empire." Edward was a frail little boy, who was not expected to grow up. He probably would have died young if he had remained in his mother's care; for she, like so many fashionable ladies of the time, was too much engrossed in social pleasures to bother much about her offspring. Fortunately, little Edward had an aunt who took charge of him. This excellent woman watched over her nephew with an anxious tenderness very rare in those days.

No wonder that in later years Gibbon writes that at the bare mention of his aunt's name, "I feel a tear of gratitude trickle down my cheek." His devoted aunt certainly fed him well; for he became a regular "fat boy," and presently developed "cheeks of such prodigious chubbiness that they completely enveloped his nose and rendered it, in profile, absolutely invisible."

Those children who survived the ordeal of infancy were not without amusements. During this period, the modern wax doll appears. Some dolls were large and richly dressed. A newspaper advertisement of Queen Anne's day speaks of "large joynted dressed Babies" as prizes at a certain Widow Smith's raffle. Dolls were still called "babies," as they had been from olden times. Of course wax dolls were very expensive; so most little girls had to content themselves with "rag-babies."

Children's toys of the cheaper varieties were commonly hawked about the streets by venders, who blew upon a pipe or horn to call attention to their wares. Prime favorites were cardboard windmills and beribboned horses' heads, fastened to the ends of sticks. The hawkers' cry for the latter was: "Troope! Troope-horses! Warranted Chargers—every One!" There were likewise hawkers of sweets and fruit, who lured coins from children's pockets with seductive calls such as: "Hot baked Wardens!" "Buy Colly Molly Puffes!" "Ripe Strawberryes!" or "Six-pence a pound—fair Cherryes!"

Perhaps the most popular hawker, however, was the man who went through the streets calling: "Oh, Raree Show!" This man had a large flattish box strapped to his back. When he had collected a group of boys and girls about him, he would unsling his box, set it on a folding-stand like a high camp-stool, and for a ha'penny would let each child peek through a tiny hole in the box—in which they would see pictures and little figures wondrous to childish eyes in that simple age.

Notwithstanding the skepticism of "enlightened" circles, most people remained very superstitious. When gas-lighting was invented, several English cities like Bristol and even a university town like Oxford protested violently against having their streets illumined by means of what many persons considered an infernal agency, champions of gas-lighting being denounced as in league with the Devil. And this "anti-gas" campaign occurred between the years 1815 and 1820—only a trifle over one hundred years ago.

If such was the attitude of respectable townsfolk in the early nineteenth century, their superstitious bringing-up can be imagined. From the cradle onward, boys and girls had their heads filled with blood-curdling tales of spooks and bugaboos, and were always in fear of being "overlooked" by a witch. Wretched old hags were still executed for witchcraft—especially for the bewitching of children. One such case occurred in London in the year 1704; and part of the evidence that convicted the witch at her trial was that: "Some of the Neighbors' Children would be strangely effected with unknown Distempers, as vomiting of Pins, their Bodies turn'd into strange Postures and such like; many were frighted with strange Apperitions of Cats, which of a sudden would vanish away; these and such like made those in the Neighborhood both suspicious and fearful of her; till at last the Devil (who always betrays those that deal with him) brought the truth to light."

In the Spectator, Addison tells us of the Coverley Witch, Moll White; how he and Sir Roger visited her hovel, and found a broomstick behind the door, and the tabby cat, which had as evil a reputation as its mistress, and how "in our return home, Sir Roger told me that Old Moll had been often brought before him for making Children spit Pins, and giving maids the Night-Mare; and that the Country People would be tossing her into a Pond, if it was not for him and his Chaplain."

Most grown-ups believed in spooks and bugaboos, and children had implicit faith that fairies danced in the moonbeams and visited nurseries during the dark hours; that brownies and pixies gamboled in forest glades or played tricks on belated wayfarers; and that almost every old house or dark country lane was haunted by some "Boggle," "Boggart," "Clap-Can," "Gabble-ratchet," or other fearsome Thing. A Boggle was described by those who had "seen" it as a "human shape of gigantic size, with an enormous head and two eyes which flamed like beacons."

Since girls still married very young, and since every girl was in mortal dread of being an "old maid," the problem of matrimony intruded itself at what, to us, seems a ridiculously early age. Echoes of wedding-bells sounded literally in the nursery, for nurse-maids would tell little girls stories of "fine matches" and would gravely consult tea-leaves and coffee-grounds in the bottoms of their cups to predict the future "beaus" of their youthful charges.

Girlhood was filled with a host of silly rites and ceremonies supposed to ensure the catching of a husband. At early dawn on the first of May, young maidens would hie them to the woods and fields to listen for the call of the cuckoo—slipping off the left shoe at the precise moment when the bird uttered its peculiar cry. On Midsummer's Eve, the same girls would piously gather flowers and concoct love-charms. Most elaborate of all were the rites celebrated on St. Valentine's Day and St. Agnes' Eve.

The most singular of these rites was the making of the celebrated "Dumb-Cake," which an old writer thus describes: "Young girls desirous of dreaming of their future husbands would abstain through the whole of St. Agnes' Eve from eating, drinking, or speaking, and would avoid even touching their lips with their fingers. At night they made their 'Dumb-Cake,' so called from the rigid silence with which its manufacture was attended. The ingredients were supplied in equal proportions by their friends, who might also take equal shares in the baking and turning of the cake, and in drawing it out of the oven. The mystic viand was next divided into equal portions, and each girl, taking her share, carried it upstairs, walking backwards all the time, and finally ate it and retired to rest. A damsel who had duly fulfilled all these conditions, and had also kept her thoughts fixed on the weal of her future husband all day, confidently expected to see him in her dreams."

Meanwhile the growing evil of child-labor was unquestionably the darkest blot upon that age.

In every age and clime, many young children of poor peasant families have been forced to do hard field-labor or have had to pasture cattle, gather firewood, and do other tasks, in severe damp and cold, while underfed and thinly clad. Likewise, many children of poor townsfolk have been made domestic drudges or have been brought up in vicious, criminal ways.

But those ancient abuses were as nothing compared to the wholesale systematic exploitation of young life which is known as "child-labor," in the technical sense of the word. Child-labor was an evil by-product of the industrial system that began to develop in England during the latter part of the seventeenth century. People drifted steadily from the countryside into manufacturing towns and cities, and by the early part of the eighteenth century many districts were inhabited by a working-class population, which grew denser with every decade.

It was not long before underpaid, shiftless,

drunken parents learned that they could make a little extra money out of their very young children by putting them to work. At first, this child-labor was a domestic matter, because industry was at first carried on by families, working in their cottages with a few tools or a single hand-loom and selling their product to contractors. Even when children worked at home, however, they were harshly exploited. An English writer of those early days states that "the creatures [i e., the children] were set to work as soon as they could crawl, and their parents were their hardest taskmasters." As applied to conditions in the early industrial period, that statement is broadly correct. The only child-laborers then worse off were the unfortunate mine-boys, and the "climbing-boys" or chimney-sweeps.

As the development of machinery transferred industry from workers' cottages to mills and factories, young children likewise shifted the scene of their labors and were geared more directly to the industrial system. The more machines took the place of human hands, the more jobs could be filled by individuals possessing little strength or skill. From a brutally utilitarian standpoint, the ideal individuals for such jobs were young children, since they could be hired from poverty-stricken or grasping parents for a mere pittance, required less food than grown-ups, and would submit to harsher exploitation. So it came to pass that in all the spinning and weaving mills, which were so rapidly springing up, multitudes of little boys and girls of eight or nine, and even as young as six years old, were toiling under most dreadful working conditions, for pitiful wages, twelve, fifteen and sometimes even seventeen hours a day!

The much-used term, "wage-slavery," certainly fitted the child-workers of the eighteenth and early nineteenth centuries. Juvenile recruits for the industrial system were at first obtained directly from parents working in the mines and mills. But as time passed and expanding industry called for more, the increased demand was supplied by child-labor agents, who developed a sort of juvenile slave-trade.

One source of supply was the swarms of vagabond children abandoned by dissolute parents. These little "street Arabs," with no homes, and with no idea who their fathers and mothers were or where they might be, lived like savages, begging or stealing their food, and sleeping in doorways, ash-pits, and similar chance abodes.

Such waifs and strays were pounced upon by the labor-agents, much as we might today round up alley cats or mongrel dogs, and they were thereupon shipped in batches to mills needing child-labor. The town authorities were glad to be rid of the begging, thieving brats; the mill-owners paid the agents a good commission for their services; and the guttersnipes were duly "apprenticed," and might be legally held to their jobs until they reached the age of twenty-one. Since an abandoned child of six or eight would probably have no idea when he or she was born, and since under the unwholesome conditions of the factory such children would usually become stunted, wizened little creatures, those "apprenticeships" might last a lifetime—until, in fact, tuberculosis, smallpox, or some other of the diseases then prevalent in industrial centers should carry the victim off at a comparatively early age.

Further sources of supply were orphanages, poor-houses, and pauper families "on the parish"; that is, in receipt of public charity. The parish authorities were usually glad enough to be relieved of the burden of supporting pauper children, and so "bound over" many of them to mill-owners who might be at the other end of England. The go-betweens in these transactions were, of course, the labor-agents, who arranged all details and transported the children to their destination.

The horrors of this juvenile slave-trade, as it persisted down into the nineteenth century, are movingly described by Sir Samuel Romilly, one of the distinguished reformers whose efforts did away with these abuses. Writing in the year 1811, Sir Samuel states: "It is a very common practice with the great populous parishes in London to bind children in large numbers to the proprietors of cotton mills in Lancashire and Yorkshire, at a distance of two hundred miles. The children, who are sent off by wagonloads at a time, are as much lost forever to their parents as if they were shipped off to the West Indies. The parishes that bind them, by procuring a settlement for the children at the end of forty days, get rid of them forever, and the poor children have not a human being in the world to whom they can look for redress against the wrongs they may be exposed to from these wholesale dealers in them, whose object is to get everything that they can possibly wring from their excessive labor and fatigue."

The callous brutality of the system is revealed by two further statements in Sir Samuel's report. One of these refers to the "trade-practice" by which labor-agents had induced Lancashire manufacturers to take one idiot in every job-lot of twenty "apprentices," on condition that the other nineteen be warranted sane. A second appalling statement is that "instances not a few have occurred in our criminal tribunals of wretches who have murdered their parish apprentices, that they might get fresh premiums with new apprentices."

As far back as the sixteenth century there is occasional mention of "climbing-boys." But for a long time they were not numerous, for there were not many chimneys, and even where there were chimneys, people usually burned wood, and they seldom got foul.

By the eighteenth century, however, chimneys were universal, wood was expensive, and the new mines supplied most households with a soft coal which made a great deal of soot. This soot had frequently to be cleaned out, or the chimneys would catch fire and burn down the house. A grown man obviously could not squeeze his way into the chimney-flues. But a small boy, armed with a brush or scraper, could do the job very well. Hence, the multitude of little "climbing-boys" or chimney-sweeps, throughout the eighteenth and early nineteenth centuries.

They were probably the most pitiful, wobegone multitude of child-martyrs that the world has ever seen. Usually orphans or paupers, they were apprenticed when only five or six years old to master-sweeps. Even when not on duty, a sweep's existence must have been one of dull wretchedness. For he was grimed with soot, which was never cleaned from skin or ragged clothing; he dwelt in some filthy den with other sweeps, equally befouled; and he was half starved by his master, who beat him on the slightest provocation or for no reason at all when in an ugly mood.

But it was the chimney-sweeping which was the chief torment. The soot enveloped the sweep like a pall, stinging his eyes and choking his lungs; the rough bricks of the chimney scraped knuckles, knees, and elbows raw; while the inky darkness may well have set his shattered nerves aquiver.

The only merciful thing about a "climbing-boy's" martyrdom is that it was relatively short. A few years at most would almost always end his troubles (usually through tuberculosis), and the little chimney-sweep would be forever at rest.

So this abomination went on, generation after generation. Not until well into the nineteenth century were laws passed forbidding the employment of boys as chimney-sweeps, and compelling the use of long jointed brushes in their stead.

Practically speaking, there were no laws restraining such frightful cruelties to children before the Nineteenth Century. Furthermore, there was no indignant public opinion to protest against these abuses. For a long time, people of all classes seemed to think child-labor a good thing, and apparently cared nothing about the suffering involved.

A good example of the callous spirit of the age

THE STORY OF YOUTH 227

is the attitude of Daniel Defoe. The author of "Robinson Crusoe" was certainly not a hard-hearted wretch; on the contrary, he seems to have been a rather enlightened man for his time. And yet, when Defoe makes a tour of England early in the eighteenth century, he comments with especial satisfaction on the way very young children are being put to work in the manufacturing districts, and are thus helping to build up those new textile industries of which he is so proud. Of one district he writes admiringly: "There is scarce anything of five years old that does not earn its living in the woolen manufacture."

Toward the close of the eighteenth century, another celebrated Englishman, Arthur Young, made a similar tour. The cottage industry of Defoe's day had largely given way to mills, and working conditions had become worse. Young does note the misery of the working population, but does not express any particular sympathy with the children's lot. To him, it is evidently just part of the general picture.

With no care, no protection, and not a scrap of education, the low mental and moral level of chimney-sweeps, mine-boys, and mill-apprentices can be imagined. They were, as people then phrased it, "little heathens." At first, such children had absolutely no religious training; for the fires of sectarian zeal, so hot a century before, had cooled, and the church took no care of its stray lambs.

Later in the eighteenth century, however, a religious revival began, which foreshadowed better days. John Wesley, the founder of Methodism, started "Sunday Schools," where poor children were not only given religious instruction but were also taught their A-B-C's. Devoted evangelists like Hannah More became true apostles to the neglected children. So appalled were these evangelists by the conditions they encountered that they started a movement of protest and agitation which gradually bore fruit.

Yet it was a long, hard job converting public indifference into sympathy and effective legal action. Not until almost the middle of the nineteenth century were laws passed doing away with the worst aspects of child-labor and establishing a system of free elementary education for the children of the poor.

In the home life of children of the middle and upper classes, we find a marked difference between conditions in town and country. The homes of even squires and "county families" remained surprisingly backward and uncomfortable, judged by the rising standards of town life. A few pieces of massive furniture, a square of green baize beneath the dining table, narrow strips of carpet in bedrooms, and almost no pictures or ornaments gave country houses a bare, unhomelike aspect. Country bedrooms seldom had fireplaces. The chilly linen sheets were made endurable by warming-pans before retirers, having undressed in icy chambers, jumped shiveringly inside. About the only change from the preceding century in country houses was the increasing number of clocks. A tall eight-day "grandfather's clock" now solemnly sounded the hours, while one or more cuckoo-clocks ticked and called in lively fashion.

The homes of middle-class townsfolk were much more comfortable, while city mansions of the rich became really luxurious—with certain notable lapses, judged by modern standards. The rather gloomy wood-paneling and heavy draperies of the preceding epoch gave place to bright wallpapers and cheerful window-curtains. Wax candles were still the best method of lighting which had as yet been invented, and the wicks of these candles had to be frequently "snuffed" with a scissorslike utensil to prevent them from smoking and getting dim. However, by placing candles in wall-brackets with reflecting mirrors, and by chandeliers in the larger rooms, houses could be lighted in a manner that seemed positively dazzling to people of those days.

Town houses were now warmed by coal fires, not merely in open fireplaces but also in iron stoves set out into the rooms. Bedchambers in city mansions were usually thus heated; and since eighteenth century folk dreaded the night air and kept their windows tight shut, people slept in a stuffy atmosphere not conducive to health.

Besides the lack of fresh air, even the wealthy lived under sanitary conditions which no respectable family would now tolerate. The water supply was nearly always bad, and children, like their elders, rarely used water save for drinking purposes. People were, in fact, still very dirty, and needed all the powder and perfume of which they were so fond. Even the washstand probably did not appear till the latter part of the eighteenth century, while the bathroom was as yet quite unknown. Unsanitary homes were mainly responsible for the high death-rate which afflicted even the wealthiest families.

Two other primitive conditions persisted down to the days of our great-grandfathers—the clumsy methods of writing a letter and striking a light.

When you wanted to write a letter, you might sit down to a beautiful Chippendale desk; but you would have to scratch off the note with a spluttery cleft goose-quill pen, would sprinkle sand over the paper to dry the poor-quality ink, and would finally fold the sheet and fasten it with a lump of sealing-wax because there were no envelopes.

To strike a light was an even more cumbrous proceeding. Every time you wanted to light a candle, you had to get out your tinder-box. This was a box some eight inches long by four inches wide, divided into two compartments. In one section was kept flint, steel, and spills of paper. In the other section was the tinder—bits of scorched or half-burned linen rag. To get a light, you struck the flint and steel together, and the resulting sparks fell upon the tinder and ignited it here and there. You then touched a paper spill to the glowing tinder, breathed on it gently, and eventually got a flame with which you lighted your candle—if the wick caught before the spill burned down to the butt and scorched your fingers.

At the very end of the eighteenth century matches were invented. But—such matches! They were really wooden spills, several inches long, the tips of which were dipped in melted brimstone. You still used your tinder-box, and touched the tip of the "match" to the tinder as soon as it began to glow. Then you got a light—and also brimstone fumes which made your eyes water abominably if you got too close.

Except in circles which aped French fashions, people of the period were not dainty eaters. "The Roast Beef of Old England" was then in its heyday, and there were many other roasts—mutton, pork, game, and fowl. Meat was usually roasted on spits over an open fire; and the "turnspit dog" still did duty, as of yore. Dogs were trained to trot on a sort of treadmill, geared to the spit. This produced occasional domestic tragedies; for the dog sometimes slipped out just before dinner, and an old writer paints an amusing picture of cooks running frantically through the streets hunting for curs that had shirked their tasks.

The French traveler Misson, who spent much time in England, gives us a good description of British cookery in the early eighteenth century. "The English," he writes, "eat a great deal at dinner; they rest a while, and to it again, till they have quite stuff'd their Paunch. Their Supper is moderate: Gluttons at Noon, and abstinent at Night. I always heard they were great Flesh eaters, and I found it true. I have known several people in England that never eat any Bread, and universally they eat very little: they nibble a few crumbs, while they chew the Meat by whole Mouthfulls. Generally speaking, the English tables are not delicately serv'd. There are some Noblemen that have both

French and English Cooks, and these eat much after the French manner; but among the middling Sort of People they have ten or twelve sorts of common Meats, which infallibly take their Turns at their Tables, and two Dishes are their Dinners: a Pudding for instance, and a Piece of Roast Beef; another time they will have a Piece of Boil'd Beef, and then they salt it some Days before hand, and besiege it with five or six Heaps of Cabbage, Carrots, Turnips, or some other Herbs or Roots, well pepper'd and salted, and swimming in Butter: A Leg of roast or boil'd Mutton, dish'd up with the same dainties, Fowls, Pigs, Ox Tripes and Tongues, Rabbits, Pidgeons, all well moistened with Butter, without larding: Two of these Dishes, always serv'd up one after the other, make the usual Dinner of a Substantial Gentleman, or wealthy Citizen."

What Misson states about the hours of dinner and supper was not true a couple of generations later; for the eighteenth century saw the abandonment of the time-honored custom of having dinner around noon, followed by a light supper. When the nineteenth century opened, dinner had become an evening meal, fashionable folk taking it as late as eight o'clock, and the modern luncheon had arrived.

Tableware was not yet wholly modern in appearance. Forks had only three prongs, while knives were usually made with broad ends for eating peas and catching up gravy. Since chinaware was still expensive, the nursery table was often set with the wooden bowls and trenchers, which we encountered on grown-ups' tables back in medieval times. Certain grammar schools continued to use trenchers far into the nineteenth century. And the boys liked these medieval survivals so well that when trenchers were finally abolished at Winchester, the pupils protested, and the first time crockery plates were served, every boy with one accord threw his platter on the floor!

Schoolboy fare in those days was mainly beef and beer. Beer continued to be a favorite beverage, even in the nursery, though chocolate came to be much drunk for breakfast. Tea, despite its high cost, grew steadily in favor. Ladies' tea-parties were a prominent feature of social life, and young girls accompanied their mothers to these functions in order to learn polite ways. Similarly, young boys would be taken by their fathers to the coffee-houses, then so much frequented by gentlemen; and here the youngsters would not only sip cups of coffee but would probably further imitate their sires by smoking long clay pipes.

For tobacco had now become a well-nigh universal habit, and children were often indulged in it. They were frequently sent to school with pipes in their satchels, and at recess the whole schoolroom would light up, from the master to the littlest boy.

One of the well-known diaries of the period has this startling entry: "20 Jan. 1702. Evening with brother &c. at Garraway's Coffee House; was surprised to see his sickly child of three years old fill its pipe of Tobacco and smoke it as *audfarandly* as a man of three score; after that, a second and a third pipe without the least concern, as it is said to have done above a year ago."

Whilst young boys were smoking their pipes, their sisters were probably engaged in taking snuff. For snuff-taking was an art, with an elaborate ritual, which had to be observed in every detail. At social functions the gentleman would snap open his beautiful snuff-box, and with a low bow would offer the ladies a pinch. Each lady would take it, with much manner and deft manipulations of her dainty handkerchief. All these airs and graces had to be carefully learned, on penalty of social ostracism for bad breeding. So girls were taught snuff-taking at an early age—just as they were taught dancing, the coquettish management of the fan, and all the rest of the complicated eighteenth-century code of polite good manners.

In a whirligig of fashion, the dress of both sexes underwent many phases, which became more and more rapid, until by the close of the period styles changed markedly every few months. Women's dress, especially, was at times as grotesque (though not as ugly) as in Elizabeth's reign. And, as in former periods, children were clad like miniature men and women.

Not until the latter part of the eighteenth century do we note the beginning of distinctive "children's styles"—little girls in "Kate Greenaway" frocks and little boys in pinafores. But once out of the nursery, boys and girls were garbed like juvenile editions of their parents.

When the century opened, male attire was still reacting against the extravagant fripperies of the Restoration period. "Plain Dutch William" sat upon the English throne, and his sober influence persisted in men's styles throughout Queen Anne's reign.

How boys then dressed can be judged from a couple of newspaper notices describing two youngsters who had run away from school. Of the first, we read: "He is about 12 years of age, with light Cloaths lin'd with red, a well favour'd brisk Boy, with a fair Old Wig." The second boy is described as: "A little slim, fair hair'd handsome English Boy, who speaks French very well, between 11 and 12 years of Age, with a sad colour, coarse Kersay Coat trim'd with flat new Gilded Brass Buttons, with a whitish Calla-manca Waistcoat with round Plate Silver Buttons, and a little Silver Edging to his Hat, with fine white Worsted rowl'd Stockings, and with Silver Plate Buttons to his sad colour Sagathy Stuff Britches."

These "sad" styles, however, did not long endure. As time passed, gentlemen went in for bright-colored clothes, laced cravats, shirts, and ruffles, satin knee-breeches, silk stockings, silver-buckled, red-heeled shoes; and they doused their long hair or curled wigs with white powder. A writer of the period amusingly describes watching the "young gentlemen" of a boys' select boarding-school in London file into church Sunday mornings. They must have made a brave show as they marched along in pairs, for they were attired literally in all the colors of the rainbow. Sky-blue, pea-green, and flaming scarlet seem to have been the prevailing shades, and most of the boys wore gold-laced cocked hats atop of their powdered curls.

Boys thus reared naturally acquired foppish tastes which increased as they grew older. Lads of good family usually took the "grand tour" on the Continent—the custom having been revived after the Puritan interlude until it was as popular as ever. These young fellows returned from Italy or France giving themselves great airs and decked out in the most extreme fashions. Sensible men laughed at them, and some wit dubbed them "macaronies." This satirical term at first applied to fops returned from Italy, but was later extended to young bucks who aped French styles.

However, youths who had made the grand tour excited envious admiration in the breasts of many young fellows who could not go abroad. These admirers became fake macaronies, striving desperately to copy the genuine article. They could usually be detected by their absurd exaggerations in dress, and were even more ridiculed. Fake macaronies were humorously termed "jessamies," after a popular perfume which they used with reckless prodigality, whereas real macaronies scented themselves more discreetly and in better taste.

Toward the end of the eighteenth century the ranks of youth were split by a bitter feud over styles. The French Revolution brought with it a revolt against existing fashions. Young Frenchmen no longer curled and powdered their hair, but cut it relatively short, discarded knee-breeches for long trousers, and emphasized their break with the past in many other ways.

This sartorial revolution across the Channel was

feverishly watched by the macaronies and jessamies, who promptly aped the new republican modes. But most Englishmen detested the French Revolution, and soon began a war against France which lasted until Napoleon's defeat at Waterloo in 1815. Naturally, Paris fashions became widely unpopular. But the macaronies and jessamies blithely defied public opinion by flaunting republican styles in the teeth of their scandalized fellow countrymen.

Their bitterest opponents were the college boys. These arch-conservatives prided themselves on sticking to the old styles. In Oxford and Cambridge, knee-breeches and powdered hair reigned supreme. Every college maintained its "powdering-room," as of yore. Here, college students would first be wrapped in sheets, to spare their clothing. Then a valet, armed with a great can of powder and an enormous puff, would dust the students' heads till they were white as snow. When the air had cleared a bit, the sheets were carefully unwrapped, and the young gentlemen would walk out, leaving the place looking like a flour-mill.

As the years passed, a few young college radicals did brave custom by appearing with unpowdered hair and (horror of horrors!) long trousers. But these daring revolutionists had their troubles; much censure and many severe reprimands were administered to them, both by fellow students and by faculty members. In 1810, a youthful radical (who afterwards became a bishop) was thus accosted by a scandalized Cambridge don: "Young man! Young man! You'll never come to any good. You wear nankeen trousers and keep a dog!"

The eighteenth-century "flapper" was usually nicknamed Phyllis, Daphne, Chloe, or some other one of the Arcadian shepherdesses then the rage. Censorious critics peevishly dubbed her "a pert young Baggage!" Yet she abounded; and with all the vim of her early teens, she kept pace with the most

amazing series of feminine fashions that the world has ever seen.

The century opened with that formidable headdress known as the commode. It looked something like an Elizabethan ruff perched on top of the head instead of encircling the neck. The commode was fashioned of row on row of plaited muslin, stiffened with wire, and rising one on top of another. The number of rows increased or diminished arbitrarily with every social season. Addison writes in the Spectator: "There is not so variable a thing in Nature as a Lady's Head Dress. Within my own Memory I have known it to rise and fall above thirty Degrees. About ten Years ago it shot up to a very great Height, insomuch that the Female Part of our Species were much taller than the Men." And on another occasion he says: "The women were then of such enormous stature that we appear'd as grasshoppers before them."

The commode went out with Queen Anne. But worse was to follow. As the ladies shrank in height, they swelled in girth. The hooped petticoat now appeared, and soon rivaled the Elizabethan farthingale in size. Presently, fashionable damsels were often unable to get in or out of coaches and sedan-chairs. The grouch of one testy old gentleman has come down to us, as he pours forth the vials of his wrath upon "young baggages" in their early teens, flouncing along so airily that their hooped petticoats take up the whole sidewalk or *swish* the pews as they mince down the church aisle.

Another curious fashion was that of patching. At first it was not so bad. One or two bits of black court-plaster, artfully stuck upon a fresh young face framed with powdered curls, might give a decidedly piquant effect.

However, patching soon became a craze and was carried to the point of absurdity. Young ladies carried "patch-boxes" filled with patches cut into suns, moons, stars, and even grotesque figures like a miniature coach-and-four. As the afternoon or evening wore on, society buds would strive to outdo their rivals by adding patch after patch, until at a distance, a much-patched face had a curious "pepper-and-salt" appearance.

The French traveler, Misson, previously quoted, writes: "In England, young, old, handsome, ugly; all are *be-patched* till they are Bed-rid. I have often counted fifteen Patches upon a single Phiz."

More downright still is the line given a character in a comedy of the period: "You pert Baggages, you think you are very handsome now, I warrant you! What a devil's this pound of hair upon your paltry frowses for? What are those patches for? What, are your faces sore? I'd not kiss a Lady of this Age. By the Mass, I'd rather kiss my Horse!"

The "pound of hair" was another craze. By the aid of false-hair and "transformations," ladies' coiffures attained towering proportions. False hair became so expensive that peasant maids could get fancy prices for their long tresses. Indeed, *hair-thieves* now appeared, and little girls with tempting locks were not allowed to go to school unattended, lest they be temporarily kidnaped and return home close-shorn.

Coiffures were stiffened with pomade to make them retain their shape, and upon this sticky base layer after layer of powder was daily added—the accumulation sometimes not being removed oftener than once a month! A comic ballad of 1776 satirizing this craze begins:

"Give Chloe a bushel of horse-hair and wool,
 Of paste and pomatum a pound,
 Ten yards of gay ribbon to deck her sweet skull,
 And gauze to encompass it round."

For upon those coiffures were perched head-dresses. Some mimmicked flower-beds; others attempted to represent gardens of ornamental shrubbery; while, last but not least, there were—*the feathers!*

The feather-craze was the climax of eighteenth-century absurdities. At its height, ladies of fashion could be seen wearing head-dresses made of ostrich plumes, so spliced and lengthened that they rose several feet above the wearers' "cushion-coiffures."

Ladies equipped with such mammoth feathers had to use sedan-chairs with hinged lids, which were thrown back as they stepped in. A satirical entry in the London Times of December, 1795, reads: "A young lady, only ten feet high, was overset in one of the late gales of wind, in Portland Place, and the upper mast of her feather blown upon Hampstead Hill. . . . The Ladies now wear feathers exactly of their own length, so that a woman of fashion is twice as long upon her feet as in her bed."

In the eighteenth century, the whole educational system, from primary schools to universities, was in decay. It had sunk far below the level attained in Elizabethan days. The superstition, ignorance, and callous cruelty, which persisted well into the nineteenth century, and from which children so grievously suffered, were largely due to the wretched education which even the highest classes received.

An ill-taught, ill-used generation was bound to visit its shortcomings upon its unfortunate offspring; and this vicious circle was not broken until relatively recent times.

Children of the very poor got no education at all, were drafted into brutalizing labor, and grew up no better than savages. Children of country peasants and town artizans got a smattering of education in "dame schools," where little boys and girls learned their A-B-C's from some elderly woman. "Dames" could seldom teach anything beyond elementary reading, writing, and ciphering. However, when they were women of character, they might give their pupils a sound start in life. When they were doddering old crones, the children learned next to nothing.

Almost the only manual in these dame schools was the horn-book. It was really not a book, but a sheet of stiff paper or cardboard, on which was printed the alphabet, in both capitals and small text; a few simple combinations of letters; the numerals, from 1 to 10; and the Lord's Prayer. This printed sheet was covered with a thin plate of translucent horn, and bound in a wooden frame with a handle. This inexpensive "primer" would thus last a long time.

Only in London and a few of the larger provincial towns were there "charity schools" where children of certain parishes could receive a slightly better free education. Young children of middle-class parents either attended these institutions or were sent to private schools.

At the beginning of the eighteenth century, most

private establishments were day-schools. But in time, boarding-schools increased until they became much the more numerous. No boarding-schools were coeducational.

The head master of a boys' school was usually a broken-down, middle-aged man who had failed in other lines and had taken to schoolteaching as a last resort. Ordinarily, he could teach only reading, penmanship, and arithmetic of a very simple kind. Latin was usually taught (after a fashion) by the "usher"—often a half-starved creature with some pretentions to classical learning, who, through drink or lack of enterprise, had "come down in the world." The teaching staff might also include dancing and music masters, and perhaps a French teacher —all of a pretty low grade.

Such were the boarding-schools to which the average boy of parents with limited means would be sent. The boy was lucky if his masters were inefficient yet well-meaning men. Only too often, the poor little chap would find himself condemned to the tyrany of a villainous blockhead like Mr. Wackford Squeers, of Dickens's Dotheboys Hall. At such institutions, masquerading under the title of "genteel academies," the wretched boys not only learned nothing, but were half starved, knocked about, and forced to do menial labor, into the bargain.

The real genteel academies were high-priced boarding-schools, patronized by rich, socially ambitious parents, who sent thither their curled, bepowdered sons to make "fashionable" friendships with other rich boys and to learn fine manners. Here, boys were well-housed, well-fed, and sometimes too indulgently treated. But here, again, they seldom got much learning, in the true sense of the word. Their time was mostly taken up with dancing masters, fencing masters, riding masters, and "professors" of the social airs and graces. Having often entered spoiled children, the boys always graduated insufferable young snobs.

Beside all those private "academies," the old grammar schools, like Eton, Harrow, and Winchester, had come down from medieval or Elizabethan times. Outwardly, the grammar schools had just stood still; but spiritually, they too had decayed. A blind worship of the classics alone remained. Masters hammered Latin into their pupils' heads—and let it go at that. As for history, geography, science —all the new currents of thought which by the end of the eighteenth century were pulsing vigorously through the learned world—they might never have existed, so far as these ancient institutions were concerned.

Except in the few genteel academies where sons of the very rich were socially groomed and pampered, the typical schoolmaster is represented by "Pedagogue Thwackum" in "Tom Jones." And that eighteenth-century portrait was just as true a generation or two later; for in the early Nineteenth Century we get harrowing decriptions of school-life.

One eminent Englishman writes of his schooldays at that time: "The usher was a severe, cruel tyrant, and punished us just for the sake of doing so, as it it gave him a delightful pleasure. He had always by him two large bits of broken slate, with which he struck us on the hand, and if we dodged him when he ordered us to hold out our hands (which, I think, we all did), he would hit us under or on the knuckles."

That some of the most notorious "flogging masters" were found in famous grammar schools is shown by the painful reminiscences of George Keppel, afterwards Earl of Albemarle. Entering celebrated Westminster School in 1807, poor George put in seven dreadful years there. Discipline was harsh in the extreme, while the "fagging" system was at its worst. George fagged for a bullying senior and was so disgusted at the menial drudgery the bully made him perform that at length he struck work in desperation and hid himself away. But he was soon discovered, and what followed is told in his own poignant words.

"I was," he writes, "at length dragged out of my hiding-place and delivered over to the fury of my master. He made me stand at attention, with my little fingers on the seam of my trousers like a soldier at drill. He then felled me to the ground by a swinging blow on my right cheek. I rose, stupefied, and was made to resume my former position, and received a second floorer. I know not how often I underwent this ordeal, but I remember going to bed with a racking headache, and being unable to put in an appearance next morning at school."

As for the universities, they were as intellectually dead as the grammar schools. The same pedantic blight lay upon them. The classics were alone considered worth while, and a scholar's highest goal was ability to write stilted Latin prose or "elegant" Latin verses. The upshot was that students so trained usually became "drones, idlers, dull pedants, or portentous bores."

University graduates whose careers in after life proved they had a spirit which not even such a system of education could kill, almost unanimously condemned the college life of their youth. Gibbon, the historian, calls his college years "the most idle and unprofitable of my whole life." And he concludes: "To the University of Oxford I acknowledge no obligation; and she will as cheerfully renounce me for a son as I am willing to disclaim her for a mother."

A generation later, Adam Smith, the noted economist, states that in his day most of the professors had "given up altogether even the pretense of teaching." Another noted Englishman wrote during his varsity term at the close of the eighteenth century: "Except praying and drinking, I see nothing else that it is possible to acquire in this place." Finally, another student, later to become a famous scientist, describes Oxford in the year 1802 as "a perfect hell upon earth," and states that he often saw his tutor carried off dead-drunk to his rooms.

Hard drinking was, indeed, a besetting sin in university circles. Yet, with neither intellectual interests nor organized athletics to absorb their energies, it is not strange that college students should have drunk far too much. Cock-fighting seems to have been their chief sport, while "town-and-gown" rows occasionally enlivened their existence—as had been the case for centuries.

It is significant of the decay of English Universities in the eighteenth century that many upper-class fathers no longer thought of sending their sons thither, but sent them abroad for travel and study, as soon as they were out of grammar school. Lord Chesterfield did this with his son, remarking pithily that he himself had been to college—and that was enough!

However, even the grand tour does not appear to have functioned so successfully as it had in earlier times. The main reason seems to have been the poor quality of the "tutors" who accompanied the boys in their travels. Early in the century, Addison writes: "Nothing is more frequent than to take a lad from grammar and taw, and under the tuition of some poor scholar, who is willing to be banished for thirty pounds a year and a little victuals, send him crying and sniveling into foreign countries. Thus he spends his time as children do at puppet shows, and with much the same advantage, in staring and gaping at an amazing variety of strange things; strange, indeed, to one who is not prepared to comprehend the reasons and meanings of them, whilst he should be laying the solid foundations of knowledge in his mind, and furnishing it with just rules to direct his future progress in life, under some skilful master in the art of instruction."

Half a century later, things were no better, for Adam Smith states that such lads "commonly returned home more conceited, more unprincipled, more dissipated, and more incapable of any serious application either to study or to business than he could well have become in so short a time had he lived at home."

The boyhood of Charles James Fox is an equally good illustration of what was best and what was worst in the training of youth in his day. Charles's early years were spent in his father's London mansion, Holland House; and its trim gardens, broad lawns, and lofty avenues of trees must have made delightful playgrounds.

From his cradle, Charles displayed the art of getting his own way. His mother Lady Caroline adored him; his father, the celebrated Lord Holland, worshiped him; and the upshot was that little Charles was very much spoiled. Never was there a more indulgent father. When Lady Caroline deplored Charles's fits of temper, Lord Holland said soothingly, in his son's hearing: "Never mind. He is a very sensible little fellow, and will learn to cure himself." On another occasion, his lordship remarked: "Let nothing be done to break his spirit; the world will do that business fast enough." And when Charles announced one day with a stamp of his foot that he was going to smash his father's watch, the doting parent sighed resignedly: "Well, if you must, I suppose you must!"

Charles was amazingly precocious. With insatiable curiosity, he ransacked his father's ample library, and became well informed at a very early age. Lady Caroline at first undertook to instruct him, but an unlucky answer which she made to one of her son's questions on Roman history caused her to lose caste hopelessly as a teacher in his eyes, when he checked up on her and found she had blundered.

So, when Charles was seven years old, Lord Holland gravely consulted with him about the school he wished to attend. After pondering the merits of several institutions, Charles graciously assented to his father's suggestion that he go to a fashionable boys' school kept by a French head master. A year later, Charles decided he had been there long enough, and informed his father that he now wanted to go to Eton, and was promptly transferred to the famous public school.

Yet this overindulged, hot-tempered rich man's son was highly popular among his schoolfellows. There was an indescribable something about him which made him a leader everywhere he went, without effort on his part, or jealousy on the part of others. Eton being unusually given to sports for that period, he "went in for them" with his peculiar gusto, and was soon a remarkably good tennis player, as well as a great walker.

Even the severe masters could not resist his winning way. Charles studied hard and did splendidly in studies which interested him. But he let his instructors understand that he did not propose to drudge over matters which bored him. And so fascinated were the Eton masters by this headstrong yet obviously brilliant boy that instead of birching him they gave him his head and let him browse in the fields of knowledge where he chose.

From his sports and studies at Eton, Charles was suddenly plucked by his father in one of the most extraordinary freaks of conduct that ever entered a parent's head. Tired of political battles, Lord Holland decided to retire to the Continent for a high old time. And he proposed to take his young son along for good company. So fourteen-year-old Charles made the round of fashionable French watering-places as the boon companion of his gay father, who encouraged the boy in every sort of extravagance and folly. He fanned Charles's passion for gambling and every night would send the boy to the gaming tables with a pocketful of gold! Gambling became Charles Fox's besetting sin and in later life landed him in virtual bankruptcy.

After four months of riotous living, Charles grew bored with dissipation and asked his father to send him back to Eton. He arrived there sadly changed, and with a thoroughly swelled head. But for once in his life, Charles did not "get away with it." His schoolmates made fun of him unmercifully, while the head master gave him a flogging for some pert disobedience. Charles was taken down a peg—which did him no harm. Nevertheless, his wild pranks became notorious, and he kept up this conduct through college, where he was known as an inveterate gambler and one of the gayest young rakes of his day.

Yet these extravagances did not postpone the early beginning of his brilliant career as an orator and statesman. Fresh from Oxford, he took his seat in parliament before he was twenty, and became a force to be reckoned with there before he was twenty-five.

If boys' education in the eighteenth century was bad, that of girls was even worse. For here we encounter, not the decay of an old system, but the appearance of a thoroughly false and foolish new idea. The ideal woman in Elizabethan times had been a cultured, capable, high-spirited lady. That was the goal aimed at in the education of upper-class Elizabethan girls, whatever the practical shortcomings of educational methods.

The new eighteenth-century ideal may be best described as one of "genteel helplessness." Self-reliance, ability, intelligence, were all considered "ungenteel." From babyhood, girls were systematically taught to lean upon some masculine protector —father, brother, and finally the "suitable husband." Since girls "came out" socially at fourteen or fifteen, and hoped to be married a year later, it is not strange that their thoughts ran on "a good match" almost while they were still babies.

This feminine education took a little romping girl, and in a few years turned her into a mincing young "Miss," who would shriek at the sight of a spider and faint if a cow turned its bovine gaze her way.

Of course, the same girl who fainted at a cow's glance, and powdered her face chalk-white to give an impression of "delicate health," might dance, posture, ogle, and "languish" almost every night at balls and "routs"—and keep it up till dawn. It was all part and parcel of that artificiality which characterized eighteenth-century society.

The century saw a rapid spread of "select boarding-schools for young ladies," where girls were entered at the age of six or seven, to be socially polished. This, in itself, was a new thing; because girls had seldom been sent away from home since the suppression of convent-schools at the time of the Reformation.

Girls learned nothing solid at these institutions. A really educated girl would have been dubbed a "blue-stocking," and would never have caught a husband. Instead of genuine education, therefore, girls acquired "genteel accomplishments." Everything was fake. The "French" was a mere jumble of phrases with which to interlard witty conversation. English was so badly taught that fine ladies could hardly write a note without spelling absurdly. "Music" meant strumming a few "show pieces" on spinet or harpsichord and singing a few sentimental ballads with easy accompaniments.

But most amazing of all was feminine "art." Says an old writer on this point: "Deeming it unladylike to do anything well, a *mock-art* was invented. To model well in clay would have been considered strong-minded, but to model badly in wax or bread was quite a feminine occupation. Filigree and mosaic were imitated in colored paper, medals were made of cardboard and gold-leaf, Dresden china of rice-paper, cottages of pasteboard, flowers of lamb's-wool."

Fashionable girls were no longer taught even to be really good housekeepers. To be sure, they were drilled to make all sorts of showy pastry, cakes, and sauces, but the plainer household duties were slurred over.

The only two branches of a girl's schooling which were never neglected were deportment and dancing. That a girl should have a straight figure and a correct carriage were considered indispensable to her social success. So schoolgirls were put through a most unpleasant course of sprouts, including tight lacing, "straightening-boards" strapped to their backs, iron collars, feet-stocks, and neck-swings. One schoolmistress devised an ingenious but tormenting method of forcing her pupils to keep their heads up by pinning bunches of prickly holly in their dresses just under their chins!

The importance of dancing in those days is shown by a passage from Steele in the Spectator. "When," he writes, "a girl is safely brought from her nurse, before she is capable of forming one simple notion of anything in life, she is delivered to the hands of her dancing master, and with a collar round her neck, the pretty wild thing is taught a fantastical gravity of behavior, and forced to a particular way of holding her head, heaving her breast, and moving with her whole body; and all this under pain of never having a husband, if she steps, looks, or moves awry."

And of course we must remember that "dancing" then included all the arts of polite coquetry. In Steele's description of an expert dancing master, a certain fashionable lady "recommends Mr. Trott for the prettiest Master in Town, that no Man teaches a Jigg like him, that she has seen him rise Six or Seven Capers together with the greatest Ease imaginable, and that his Scholars twist themselves more ways than the Scholars of any Master in Town. He is a very extraordinary Man in his Way; for, besides a very soft Air he has in Dancing, he gives his Pupils a particular Behavior at a Tea-Table, and in presenting their Snuff Box; to twirl, flip, or flirt a Fan, and how to place Patches to the best advantage, either for Fat or Lean, Long or Oval Faces."

When a girl had been crammed with all this polite nonsense, she made her bow to society, and, if successful, she became a "toast." Her health having been publicly drunk by some well-known beau, her social standing was assured—and her matrimonial future as well. For, as a "toast of the town," a girl would ordinarily have her pick of several good "matches." And by the time the year's social season was over, she would probably have been led to the altar: a blushing bride of sixteen or seventeen.

Chapter X

CHILDREN OF YOUNG AMERICA

COLONIAL DAYS

A RUDE cabin stands in a clearing of the primeval forest. Its logs, rough-hewn at the corners and with the bark left on, are chinked with moss or clay. At intervals, loopholes have been cut, whence bullets can be fired at prowling Indians—the terror which is the abiding shadow of pioneer existence. The same fear accounts for the tiny windows barred with heavy shutters, and for the massive door which forms an effective barricade.

This is the typical home of numberless children all along the far-flung frontier of the American colonies, stretching from the rocky hills of northern New England to the semitropical swamps and savannas of Carolina and Georgia. Generation after generation, boys and girls grow up in log cabins as the frontier pushes slowly inland from the seaboard. Behind the frontier, towns and cities arise, with more varied and comfortable modes of life; but the life of the frontier, though ever shifting its scene westward, remains essentially the same. It is the constant factor in early American history.

The thrills and privations of early pioneer life are quaintly told by a New Englander, who describes his boyhood experiences in the Connecticut Valley toward the end of the seventeenth century. "Concerning of ye earlie days," he writes, "I can remember but little save Hardship." And, passing from young childhood to boyhood, he goes on: "Ye firste Meeting House was solid mayde to withstande ye wicked onslaughts of ye Red Skins. Its foundations was laid in ye feare of ye Lord, but its Walls was truly laide in ye feare of ye Indians, for many & grate was ye Terrors of em. I do mind me y't alle ye able-bodied Men did work thereat, & ye olde & feeble did watch in turns to espie if any Salvages was in hidinge neare, & every Man keept his Musket nighe to his hande. . . . Several Families wch did live back a ways from ye River was either Murderdt or Captivated in my Boyhood & we all did live in constant feare of ye like. My Father ever declardt there would not be so much feare iff ye Red Skins was treated with suche mixture of Justice and

Authority as they cld understand, but iff he was living now he must see that wee can do naught but *fight* em, and that right heavily.

"After ye Red Skins ye grate Terror of our lives at Weathersfield and for many yeares after we had moved to Hadley to live, was ye Wolves. Catamounts was bad eno' & so was ye Beares, but it was ye Wolves yt was ye worst. The noyse of theyr howlings was eno' to curdle ye bloode of ye stoutest & I have never seen ye Man yt did not shiver at ye Sounde of a Pack of em. What with ye way we hated em & ye goode money yt was Offered for theyre Heads we did not heare em now so much, but when I do I feel again ye yonge hatred rising in my Bloode, & it is not a sin because God mayde em to be hated. My Mother and Sister did each of em kill more yan one of ye gray Howlers & once my eldest Sister shot a Beare yt came too neare ye House. He was a goode Fatte onne & keept us all in meate for a good while. I guess one of her Daughters has got ye skinne."

For very young children on an exposed frontier the clearing around the log-cabin must have measured the confines of their little world. To stray even a short distance into the dark recesses of the forest which ringed the clearing so closely about would have involved too great a risk.

However, the clearing made a good playground. It was dotted with big tree-stumps ideal for hide-and-seek, and every year it grew larger, as the father and older boys with their sharp axes won fresh ground from the wilderness.

The clearing was also a primitve garden. Around the stumps trailed pumpkin-vines, while the more open patches were sown to beans and Indian corn. All three were native to the country and formed the staple vegetable food of the pioneers. Pumpkin pie adorned even the breakfast-table; the Indians taught the colonists to cook beans in earthen pots; while cornmeal as mush and "johnny-cake" was the "staff of life." Johnny-cake, by the way, is a corruption from "journey-cake"; because a bag of cornmeal was usually carried on trips through the woods, as a compact, sustaining food, easily prepared.

The wilderness teemed with game. Deer crashed through the woodlands on every side; ducks and geese quacked and honked on lakes and ponds; turkeys gobbled in the trees, partridges drummed on fallen logs, while flocks of wood pigeons (now extinct) were so enormous that their passing darkened the sky. A half-grown boy need not be a good shot to bring home a fine dinner. Hunting was, in fact, the chief sport of all pioneer lads—a sport which never grew stale, because always seasoned with a spice of danger from bob-cat, bear, or redskin.

Besides game, colonial children ate much fish. Every brook, lake, or river was abundantly stocked with the fresh-water varieties, while the ocean was alive with seafood. First and foremost came the "Sacred Cod." All good New England families ate it dutifully once a week, though, in order to avoid a taint of "Popery," the Puritans' fish-day fell on Saturday. Regular as clockwork, the Saturday noon-dinner consisted of boiled cod served with pork scraps, while Sunday breakfast included fried codfish balls. Many other kinds of fish were eaten, but curiously enough, salmon and shad were then despised. And there were shell-fish: oysters a foot long, giant lobsters measuring a yard from tip to tip, and sand-clams, quahogs, and crabs of monstrous size! The deep shells of giant quahogs were often used as tableware, while small clamshells, set in cleft sticks, served as spoons. Only a favored few had pewter, and there was almost no glass and crockery. Young and old ate off wooden trenchers and drank out of wooden bowls or dried gourds.

Except for abundant food, frontier children had few comforts and no luxuries. Outside of New England they seldom got any "book larnin," and they often grew up almost as wild as young Indians. The log cabin was one room, scantily furnished with a homemade table and stools. Beds would probably be mere straw pallets, covered with bearskins. Meals were cooked over the open fire; and happy was the family which owned a "great pot of iron." Such pots were prized possessions, handed down as heirlooms. On the Virginia frontier, an early settler wills to his son James his "Bible and big iron pot," and to his son Samuel his "next biggest pot," stipulating that his wife Agnes shall "have the use of both pots."

Early in the eighteenth century, Colonel William Byrd made a frontier trip in Virginia and pithily describes the crude but hospitable homes in which he lodged. Of one family he remarks: "We found the housekeeping much better than the house." He goes on to say: "The worst of it was we were obliged to lodge very sociably in the same apartment with the family, where reckoning men, women and children we mustered no less than nine persons who all pigged very lovingly together." Of another household, he comments on "that evil custom of lying in a house where ten or a dozen people are forced to pig together in one room, troubled with the squalling of peevish, dirty children into the bargain."

A generation later, young George Washington started his career as a surveyor of wild lands on the Virginia frontier. He writes: "After supper we were lighted into a room and I not being as good a woodsman as the rest stripped myself very orderly and went into the bed, as they called it, when to my surprise I found it to be nothing but a little straw matted together without sheet or anything else but only one threadbare blanket with double its weight of vermin. I was glad to get up and put on my clothes and lie as my companions did." Hardened to frontier discomforts, he writes some time later: "After walking a good deal all the day I have lain down before the fire upon a little hay, straw, fodder or a bearskin, whichever was to be had, with man, wife, and children; and happy is he who gets the berth nearest the fire."

Thus pioneer boys and girls grew up—rough, unlettered, and usually unwashed. But precious little they cared. Hardships and dangers were taken as a matter of course, while the wild, free, adventurous life had a charm all its own. The genuine frontiersman rarely settled down. As soon as the country began to fill up about him, he would usually sell his half-cleared land and move on into the wilderness, where he would build another log cabin and start life over again. Regular farm work he despised. What he liked was the hunting, trapping, and fishing to which he had been used ever since he was a boy. Even half-grown lads would make long trips into the wilderness after furs. Lying about the camp-fire at night, serenaded by a circle of wolves which howled and snarled just beyond the circle of firelight, or by a chorus of bullfrogs when the swamps thawed in the spring, those bold frontier lads drank in romance and mystery.

Boys and girls who grew up on the farms behind the actual frontier led a life very much like that which still survives in remote parts of rural New England or among southern mountaineers. The Indian rarely threatened, and game was getting less abundant; so the perils and pastimes of the frontier gave place to a relatively prosaic existence, with more comfort, but also with much more hard work. Farm boys and girls began their "chores" as soon as they could toddle; for there was a deal to be done, and parents saw to it that the youngsters did their full share. Stock and poultry had to be tended; fields had to be cleared of stumps and stones; substantial frame houses and outbuildings replaced log cabins; and the families who dwelt in those farmsteads did everything, from brewing their own beer to spinning and weaving the cloth for their "homespun" clothing. In those days, farm boys and girls never found time hang heavy on their hands!

The farmhouses of colonial America, whether

among the frugal New England Yankees, the thrifty Dutch of the Hudson Valley, or the solid Quakers and Palatine Germans of Pennsylvania, were homes of solid comfort, as the world then understood the term. A family gathered about the great open fireplace after supper made a cozy picture, though all were doubtless tired out from a long day's labor. Soon the younger members would be packed off to icy chambers, whence they would emerge next morning to splash faces and hands at the "sink" in the shed next the kitchen—after breaking the ice in a bucket of water. As for the toothbrush, it was unknown on the farm in colonial times.

When they trooped back from the cold shed into the warm kitchen, they sat down to a breakfast which, if in New England, would probably start with ham and eggs, fish balls, or salt fish in cream, with bean porridge cooked with a ham-bone, and cold corned beef and hot potatoes on the side. Wooden trenchers would be heaped with steaming johnny-cake and hot biscuits or muffins, together with rye bread and quarters of pumpkin pie. An old New England bard sings feelingly:

"We have pumpkins at morning and pumpkins at noon,
If it were not for pumpkins we should be undone."

To wash down this substantial breakfast there would be, not tea or coffee, but mugs of cider for most of the family; though "father" might start his day with a stiff cannikin of grog—watered rum.

On the stroke of noon, the family would draw up their stools or splint-bottomed chairs to the homemade table for dinner. Except on Saturday, earmarked for the Sacred Cod, the main dish would probably consist either of salt pork or a "boiled dinner." To cook that New England specialty was quite an art. It was all cooked together in the big iron pot hung on a crane over the open fire. Into the pot went, first, the corned beef. Then, at nicely timed intervals, the traditional vegetables were added. Potatoes, beets, squash, turnips, cabbage—each had its special boiling-period, so that the whole dinner might come on the table cooked just right. Meanwhile, the family would have probably been eating Indian pudding—cornmeal and butter, sweetened with molasses. This was served first, not last, for dessert, as it is today.

Supper also was a substantial meal, much like breakfast in character. In winter, hot drinks would probably be served—hard cider, "flip," or rum-toddy. Our colonial forebears liked their liquor, and boys and girls were allowed to partake, in moderation, from a relatively early age.

Clam-shell spoons and clasp-knives alone aided the fingers in early Puritan days. Nevertheless, the Puritans believed in "seemly" conduct at table, as elsewhere. A manual of etiquette was composed by a Boston schoolmaster, in which children were admonished as follows: "Smell not of thy Meat, nor put it to thy Nose; turn it not the other side upward to view it upon thy Plate or Trencher. Throw not anything under the Table. . . . Foul not the napkin all over, but at one corner only. . . . Gnaw not Bones at the Table but clean them with thy Knife (unless they be very small ones) and hold them not

with the whole hand, but with two Fingers. . . .
When thou blowest thy Nose, let thy Handkerchief
be used. . . . Spit not in the Room, but in the
Corner,—and rub it with thy Foot."

"Nov. 6, 1692. Joseph threw a knop of Brass
and hit his Sister Betty on the forehead so as to make
it bleed and swell; upon which, and for his playing
at Prayer-time, and eating when Return Thanks, I
whip'd him pretty smartly. When I first went in
(call'd by his Grandmother) he sought to shadow
and hide himself from me behind the head of the
Cradle: which gave me the sorrowfull remembrance
of Adam's carriage."

This entry in the diary of Judge Samuel Sewall
is refreshing. It shows that even in the household
of one of Puritan New England's stanchest pillars,
children were still human. For in New England,
as in old England, Puritan children at that time were
often subjected to a discipline calculated to crush the
spirit and terrorize the mind.

Less than a year after Joseph's naughtiness, Judge
Sewall narrates the following incident concerning
Betty, then barely fourteen: "When I came in, past
seven, at night, my wife met me in the Entry and
told me Betty had surprised them. I was surprised
with the abruptness of the Relation. It seems Betty
had given some signs of dejection and sorrow; but
a little after dinner she burst out into an amazing
cry, which caused all the family to cry too. Her
mother ask'd the reason; she gave none; at last,
said she was afraid she should goe to Hell, her Sins
were not pardon'd."

Betty had been reflecting over some recent sermons. About a month later, "Betty comes into me almost as soon as I was up and tells me the disquiet she had when she waked; told me she was afraid she should go to Hell, was not Elected. . . . I answered her Fears as well as I could, and pray'd with many Tears on either part; hope God heard us."

Young Increase Mather got to brooding over the Unpardonable Sin and passed through a long torment of spiritual anguish almost as poignant as John Bunyan's search for "Grace Abounding." Another New England Puritan boy, Nathanael Mather, speaks for himself.

"When very young," he writes, "I went astray from God, and my mind was altogether taken with *Vanities* and *Follies;* such as the remembrance of them doth greatly abase my Soul within me. Of the manifold sins which then I was guilty of, none so sticks upon me, as that being very Young, I was *whitling on the Sabbath-day;* and for fear of being seen, I did it behind the door. A great Reproach of God! A Specimen of that *Atheism* that I brought into the World with me!"

The Puritan Sabbath began on Saturday at sundown. All that afternoon, mother and daughters had been busy finishing up domestic tasks. Supper was eaten early, that the dishes might be washed and put away in "secular" time.

As soon as the sun had set, a solemn hush fell upon the household. The Sabbath was ushered in with an hour of prayer. Then followed an elaborate ceremony—the Saturday Night Bath. Pots and kettles had long been steaming over the fires. The kitchen was now partitioned off by quilts or blankets, and great tubs were filled with hot water in which the whole family would scrub or be scrubbed, so as to rise immaculate on Sunday morning. Sunday brought lengthy services at the meeting-house, with sermons which boys and girls had to remember, since they would afterwards be "catechized" upon them by their elders.

At sunset the Sabbath was over, and the family relaxed from the strain. Mother and the older girls prepared Sunday night supper—the best meal of the whole week. Father unbent and perhaps even romped a bit with the children, who were allowed liberties permitted at no other time. The New England conscience was eased with the sense of duty well done, and the farmhouse rang with shouts and laughter as the youngsters joked and played games long past the usual hour for going to bed.

Except in the households of a few very austere divines, the New England Puritans took a more liberal attitude toward games and pastimes than the Puritans of old England. Seldom do we find in New England that morbid fanaticism against all recreation which characterized John Bunyan and his fellows. Though cards were sternly prohibited as the "Devil's Books," New England children were allowed to play checkers, chess, and backgammon, and many old English games like blindman's-buff, prisoner's base, and even tip-cat—the pastime against which young Bunyan imagined he had been solemnly warned from Heaven.

Dancing was never banned in New England. Even in the early days we find so prominent a religious leader as John Cotton stating that he does not condemn dancing, "even mixt," provided it be decorous and decent. There were dancing schools in old Boston, though the ministers kept a sharp eye on them, and saw to it that a dancing master lost his license if his teaching methods failed to win their approval.

During the eighteenth century, dancing became almost as widespread in New England as in the other colonies, and gay balls and parties took place both in the towns and at country taverns. These social events were confined mainly to the "upper circles." They sometimes roused the ire of extreme Puritans, and divines like Jonathan Edwards thundered from the pulpit against the wickedness of the rising generation, which Edwards pleasantly termed, "Young vipers and infinitely more hateful than vipers unto God."

In Puritan times there was a redeeming sense of justice and forbearance on the part of elders toward their sons and daughters. There seems to have been much less beating and downright cruelty in New England than in old England at the same period. Cotton Mather condemns excessive punishments, for he writes in his diary: "I would never come to give a child a *Blow;* except in case of *Obstinacy;* or some gross Enormity. To be chased for a while out of *my Presence,* I would make to be look'd upon as the sorest Punishment in the Family. . . . The *slavish* way of *Education,* carried on with raving and kicking and scourging (in *Schools* as well as in *Families*) 'tis abominable; and a dreadful Judgement of God upon the World." Notorious "flogging masters" were much rarer in Puritan New England than they were in either England or the other English colonies; for New England schools were carefully inspected by the authorities, and we know of several cases where masters deemed guilty of needless severity were forbidden to have further charge of youth.

New England parents seem to have tried conscientiously to be just and kind. Puritan children suffered, not so much from harsh acts, as from a general home atmosphere of austerity and gloom. Play was permitted, and was recognized by parents as necessary; but it was not encouraged, and it was strictly subordinated to study and religious devotions.

Of his children, Cotton Mather states in his diary: "I am not fond of proposing *Play* to them as a Reward of any diligent Application to learn what is good; lest they should think *Diversion* to be a better and nobler Thing than *Diligence.*" His little son Sammy, aged ten, was a problem much pondered, for Mather writes: "I must think of some exquisite and obliging Wayes to abate *Sammy's* inordinate Love of Play. His play wounds his Faculties. I must engage him in some nobler Entertainments." Some months later the problem had become still more pressing, for Mather asks himself: "What shall be done, for the raising of *Sammy's* Mind above the debasing Meannesses of Play!" Home studies outside of school hours offered a partial solution, and the anxious father goes about the matter in no uncertain way. He says: "Entertain *Sammy* betimes, with the first Rudiments of Geography and Astronomy, as well as History; and so raise his Mind above the sillier Diversions of Childhood. . . . Heap a great Library on my little *Samuel.*" A year later, Mather's paternal heart seems to beat contentedly, for he tells us: "*Sammy* is united with a Society of sober and pious lads, who meet for Exercises of Religion. I will allow them the Use of my Library, for the Place of their Meeting; and give them Directions and Entertainments."

Probably the reverend doctor discoursed upon death more than once to those boys. For death was then deemed a peculiarly fitting subject of contemplation for the young. Puritan writings are filled with the topic. Jonathan Edwards writes a long letter to his young daughter, Mary, who is away from home on a visit. The girl is in perfect health, yet her father covers pages assuring her how he and her mother would be comforted in their affliction, should they never see her again, to know that she had "died in the Lord." On Sundays, during the noon interval between sermons, fathers would take their children through the graveyard and point out pious epitaphs upon the tombstones. An old New England primer recalls this practice with these cheerful lines on "the Uncertainty of Life":

> "In the burying-place may see
> Graves shorter there than I;
> From Death's arrest no age is free.
> Young children, too, may die.

>   My God, may such an awful sight
>   Awakening be to me.
>   O! that by early grace I might
>   For Death preparèd to be."

Brought up to contemplate death, it is not surprising that in Puritan New England, funerals were "enjoyed" by both young and old. Judge Sewall states that his children went to funerals when only five or six years old, and young children often acted as honorary pall-bearers to playmates who had died. Funerals were real community festivals. The whole neighborhood attended; there was much food served, with cider, home-brewed beer, and rum.

There were other festivals on less somber occasions. And since the community spirit was very strong in old New England, the youngsters came with the rest of the family as a matter of course. A "raising" was a great event; for then the frame of a new house was raised by the united efforts of all the men and boys in the neighborhood—with a feast and dance afterwards.

In autumnal husking-bees young people of all ages gathered in some big barn to shuck corn-ears; boys kissed the girls whenever a red ear was shucked; and after a mighty supper of baked beans, pumpkin pies, and other delicacies, they danced to the scrape of a fiddle. Husking-bees seem to have been chiefly an excuse for a good time. An old writer complains that the celebrators "will not husk clean," and adds this canny bit of advice: "If you make a husking, keep an old man between every two boys; else your husking will turn out a losing."

The long, cold New England winter was enlivened for the women and girls by quilting-parties and knitting-bees; the men and boys had logging-bees and fishing-parties through the ice; while youth of both sexes enjoyed skating, coasting, and sleigh-rides. The approach of spring was celebrated by "sugaring-off," when the maple-sap was boiled down.

The New England Puritans, like their "Roundhead" brethren in England, objected to the long ringlets and love-locks of the Cavaliers. The "Blue Laws" of Connecticut ordained that every male should "have his hair cut round by a cap." Leather caps being scarce, the hard shell of a pumpkin was substituted. Every Saturday night boys had their hair trimmed around the edge of the pumpkin-shell as part of the general cleaning-up for a godly appearance at the meeting-house on the morrow. From this custom the derisive New England epithet "punkin-head" is derived.

At first "The Little Red Schoolhouse" was a mere log cabin. Later on, it became a one-room frame building, painted red and with a shedlike entry where the wood was piled and where coats, mufflers, hats, and dinner-pails were stored. In winter, the schoolmaster arrived at daybreak to build the fire, since children could not be expected to write or recite properly in a temperature below zero.

The pupils were boys only, in the early days, since girls were then given scant "book-larnin." The boys were of all ages, from those of five and six to hulking youths in their teens. Sometimes a new master had to "rassel" a youthful bully before he could assert his authority and maintain proper discipline.

In those district elementary schools of early New England, the pupils learned their "Three R's" and little else. Not much education, judged by modern standards; yet far more than poor boys of the period got, either in England or in the southern colonies. For the New England Puritans had grasped the modern ideal of primary education for all future citizens of the commonwealth. By the Massachu-

setts school-law of 1642, the selectmen of every town were required to keep a "vigilant eye over their brethren and neighbors, and see that none of them shall suffer so much barbarism in any of their families, as not to endeavor to teach their children and apprentices so much learning as may enable them to read the English tongue and obtain a knowledge of the laws." And it was further enacted that children of parents who neglected this duty might be taken from them and given into the charge of others not so "unnatural."

The religious disturbances kicked up by that strong-minded woman Mrs. Anne Hutchinson seems to have prejudiced the New England Puritans against "female education." Governor Winthrop of Massachusetts expresses the general feeling in his day when he relates in his diary the sad case of a young lady who had lost her wits "by occasion of her giving herself wholly to reading and writing. . . . If she had attended her househeld affairs, and such things as belong to women, and not gone out of her way and calling to meddle in such things as are proper for men, whose minds are stronger, she had kept her wits and might have improved them usefully and honorably in the place God had set her."

Girls were usually taught to read (often at home by their fathers) that they might study the Bible; but writing was deemed so superfluous that in early colonial days not one woman in ten could sign her name.

But conditions improved. Girls began to go with their brothers to the schoolhouse, or attended dame schools, where they learned to sew, knit, and embroider, as well as to read and write. During the eighteenth century, "Select Academies for Young Ladies" were opened for upper-class girls, much like those in England at the same period. Here girls were taught chiefly "genteel accomplishments," and were subjected to the same Spartan training in deportment and manners.

Oliver Wendell Holmes wrote the following comic poem about the torments suffered by an aunt in her girlhood:

"They braced my aunt against a board
To make her straight and tall,
They laced her up, they starved her down,
To make her light and small.
They pinched her feet, they singed her hair,
They screwed it up with pins—
Oh, never mortal suffered more
In penance for her sins."

Above the Little Red Schoolhouse, in the Puritans' educational system, stood the Latin School. This was designed to prepare lads of exceptional promise for college. And college, in turn, was meant to recruit that one really worth-while profession—the ministry.

The early Latin Schools of New England were grave seats of learning attended by infant prodigies like the Cottons, Mathers, and Edwards, who were studying not only Latin but Greek and Hebrew by the age of ten, and who entered Harvard or Yale at twelve or thirteen.

Besides the state-aided Latin Schools, various private institutions in time grew up, ranging from "Genteel Academies" for upper-class boys to small establishments where boys of humbler birth were given a practical business training. Also, in Boston and a few other towns, there were night schools where apprentices were taught after their day's labor.

Benjamin Franklin gives us an excellent picture of all this in his account of his own schooldays. "My elder brothers," he writes, "were all put apprentices to different trades. I was put to the grammar school [Boston Latin School] at eight years of age, my father intending to devote me, as the tithe of his sons, to the service of the Church. My early readiness in learning to read (which must have been very early, as I do not remember when I could not read) and the opinion of all his friends that I should certainly make a good scholar, encouraged him in this purpose of his. My uncle Benjamin, too, approved of it, and proposed to give me all his short-hand volumes of sermons, I suppose as a stock to set up with, if I would learn his character.

"I continued at the grammar school, however, not quite one year, though in that time I had risen gradually from the middle of the class of that year to be the head of it. . . . But my father, in the meantime, from a view of the expense of a college education, which having so large a family he could not well afford, and the mean living many so educated were afterwards able to obtain, altered his first intention, took me from the grammar school, and sent me to a school for writing and arithmetic. . . . There I acquired fair writing pretty soon, but I failed in the arithmetic, and made no progress at it. At ten years old I was taken home to assist my father in his business."

Franklin goes on to tell the story of his apprenticeship to various trades, and relates the process of self-education during which he devoured every worth-while book he could lay hands on, thus fitting himself for his great career.

Harvard and Yale were the only New England colleges during most of the colonial period, Brown and Dartmouth being founded shortly before the

Revolution. Founded in 1636, Harvard was at first practically a theological seminary where young men were trained for the ministry. In those early days it was a small college, with very strict rules. Students guilty of "profane swearing" were publicly whipped by the president, and undergraduates were forbidden to use tobacco. At Yale (founded in 1701) life was at first almost as austere.

In both colleges the course of study was modeled closely on that of English universities. Far more interesting are the student life and customs. In 1750, a traveler records his impressions of Harvard: "Went to see Cambridge, which is a neat Pleasant Village and Consists of ab't an Hundred houses and three Collages, which are a Plain Old Fabrick of no manner of Architect and the Present much Out of Repair is situated on one Side of the Towne and forms a Large Square, its Apartments are Pretty Large. The Library is very large and well Stored with Books, but much Abused by Frequent use."

Boys often entered Harvard or Yale at fourteen, and sometimes as young as eleven or twelve. Freshmen were compelled to "fag" for seniors, as in the English public schools. At Harvard, a freshman must take off his hat in a senior's presence, must furnish "batts, balls, and footballs" for seniors' use, and had to run errands for seniors, except in "study-time." At Yale, freshmen were forbidden to wear their hats within ten rods of the president, eight rods of a professor, and five rods of a tutor, unless the weather was stormy; and they were likewise forbidden to run in the college yard or up and down stairs, or to call to anyone through a college window. Harvard boys were ranked according to the social status of their parents, and one form of punishment was "degrading" a boy several places on the class list. This was a very practical matter, because high-rank students were assigned the best rooms and also had the right to help themselves first at table. Since the food at "commons" was none too abundant, those entitled to first helpings fared best. Each student, by the way, carried his own knife and fork to table, wiping them on the table-cloth at the end of the meal.

By the middle of the eighteenth century, college life was not so austere as might be supposed. Pungent extracts from the diary of a Harvard boy throw light upon the times. One Nathaniel Ames writes, on various occasions:

1758:
Came to college, began Logick.
Fit with the Sophomores about Customs.
Had another Fight with the Sophomores.
Declaimed this morning. Left off my wigg.
President's Grass mow'd.
Finished the President's hay.
Did not go to Prayers.
Sot in the Sophomores Seat.

1759:
Disputed forensy on Soul is not extended.
Acted Tancred & Sigism'da, for which we are like to be prosecuted.

1760:
Disputed. Freshmen rake President's Hay.

President sick, wherefore much Deviltry carried on in College.

1 Schol'r Degraded this Morning, 2 adm'shd, 1 punished.

Kneeland's & Thayers Windows broke last night.

Gardiner & Barnard admonish'd Stealing Wood.

1761:

Lost 2 Pistare'ns at Cards last Evening.

First game of Bat & Ball.

Dependents on the Favors of the President and Tutors sign an agreement to inform of any scholar that is guilty of profanity.

Joseph Cabot rusticated. As soon as the President said he was rusticated, he took his Hat & went out of the Chapel without staying to hear the President's Speech out. After Prayers he bulrags the Tutors at a high rate & leaves College his Mother faints at the News.

Chapel rob'd of the Cushing & Bible Cloths.

The last Friday that we are ever to be pun'sh.

Commencem't. Many Dedhamites present.

A Dance in Town House Camb'ge.

A genteel Set-down at Prentices. Prentices account for Trouble & a few things taken by Negroes.

Devouring the remains of Commence't.

A Yale boy, Ezra Clap, gives us a detailed description of a rough party pulled at Yale in 1738: "Last night some of the Freshmen got six quarts of Rhum and about two paylsfool of Sydar and about eight pounds sugar and mad it in to *Samson,* and evited every scholer in Colege in to Curtis is Room, and we mad such prodigius Rought that we Raised the tutor, and he ordred us all to our one rooms and some went and some taried and they geathered a gain and went up to old father Monsher dore and drumed against the dore and yeled and screamed so that a bodey would have thought that they were killing dodgs there, and all this day they have bien a counsling to geather, and they sent for Woodward and Dyar and Worthenton, Briant and Styles. . . ."

Apparently, Ezra's spelling and punctuation were affected by the party of the previous evening!

West of New England lay the Dutch colony of New Netherlands—presently conquered by British arms and renamed "New York." Dutch family life was genial and easy-going, with a high standard of comfort and enlightened views on education. Boys and girls had good schooling in Dutch days, though education suffered somewhat under English rule, chiefly because British governors did not favor the Dutch language and many parents were indifferent to having their children taught in the English tongue.

However, the neat, thrifty, contented Dutch home-life went placidly on, as before. The trim brick towns of New York and Albany, the solid farmsteads along the Hudson River, and the spacious country mansions of the patroons were alike filled with sturdy children, encouraged by their parents to games and sports of many kinds.

At Albany (formerly Fort Orange), the steep road leading from the river to the fort was alive in winter with young people coasting. The sport was watched by their elders sitting wrapped in furs on the stoops of their brick houses and laughing loudly whenever a sled upset in the snow. In summer, the Albany children formed themselves into picnic-bands for excursions on the river or among the surrounding hills.

Every boy or girl was allowed to entertain his or her playmates at least once a season. On these occasions the parents would leave home for the day, turning the house entirely over to the young people for dancing and a feast of cakes, cider, and chocolate—that beverage of which the Dutch are so fond.

The sons and daughters of patroons were reared partly on their parents' great landed estates and partly in town mansions in New York City. Such children were well educated by private tutors or at select schools in and around New York. These schools were often kept by Huguenots, who taught the children French and fine manners.

A good example of the placid yet effective domestic discipline in patroon households is the childhood of Philip Schuyler. His father having died when Philip was only eight years old, the boy was brought up by his mother, a kindly but calmly firm lady, who spared the rod yet stood no nonsense. Philip had a stubborn streak in him, as befitted his Dutch blood. On one occasion he obstinately refused to eat a certain dish. His mother uttered no reproof, and a servant took the dish away. But next morning the same dish was set before him, and the process was repeated for four consecutive meals—Madam Schuyler all the time not indicating by word or look that she was aware anything was taking place. At last, at the fifth meal, Philip's stubborn spirit broke.

He devoured the food, craved his mother's pardon, and was forgiven with a smile.

As for child-life in the other middle colonies, colonial New Jersey was largely Dutch, while the households of Quakers and hard-working Palatine Germans in Pennsylvania were puritanical, though milder than in New England.

In the South, however, the lot of children was governed by class distinctions far sharper than in the other American colonies. Negro slavery split the population into planters and poor whites (so far as the settled coastal regions were concerned), with virtually no middle class between; although the backwoodsmen of the Southern frontier led a free pioneer life.

The social gulf between children of planters and poor whites is nowhere better shown than by the difference in their educational opportunities. Poor white children had almost no chance of getting even primary schooling, and grew up as a rule unable to read or write. The planter aristocracy did not intend they should learn anything. Governor Berkeley expressed the prevailing view when he "thanked God" there were neither free schools nor printing-presses in Virginia. As time passed, this ceased to be literally true; for some liberal-minded planters did establish schools, here and there, where poor boys might get at least primary schooling. Yet, broadly speaking, poor white children remained illiterate and backward throughout the colonial period.

On the other hand, children of the planter aristocracy were often finely educated. The same Governor Berkeley who denounced free schools for the poor warmly favored higher learning for the sons of the rich and well-to-do. In 1693, William and Mary College was founded—the second college to be established in America, and more richly endowed than Harvard at that time. To it went the sons of wealthy Virginia and Maryland planters, with Negro body-servants to attend them, and with plenty of money to spend. Yet even William and Mary College was often not considered good enough by parents who wanted to give their sons the best the world afforded; so a surprisingly large number of Southern lads completed their education at Oxford or Cambridge—sometimes after having graduated from an English public school.

Planters' sons frequently made fine scholastic records in England, since from their earliest years they had very likely been carefully educated at home by private tutors, or had attended boarding-schools and academies conducted by competent masters. Planters' daughters were likewise educated by private tutors, along with their brothers, and often grew up accomplished young gentlewomen.

Boys and girls born in the manor-houses of Virginia and Maryland, or on the even more luxurious plantations of South Carolina, with wonderful dolls and toys imported from England, with devoted black nurses to attend them, and with a healthful life in the open, were really little lords and ladies of the manor, as in old feudal days. Their parents were usually persons of culture, with family traditions of good breeding which they instilled into their sons and daughters. One such father gives his little daughter Frances, afterwards Mrs. Custis, the following advice:

"Do not learn to romp, but behave yourself like a gentlewoman. . . . Be calm and obliging to all the Servants, and when you speak doe it mildly, even to the poorest slave; if any of the Servants commit small faults yt are of no consequence, doe you hide them. If you understand of any great faults they commit, acquaint yr mother, but do not exaggerate." A New Jersey teacher who set up a select boys' school in Virginia declared that his pupils were more polite to the servants who waited on them than many ladies and gentlemen in his own colony were to each other.

That training in self-control was needed is evident from this entry in the diary of little Sally Fairfax: "On Friday the 3d of Jan. that vile man Adam at night killed a poor cat of rage, because she eat a bit of meat out of his hand & scratched it. A vile wretch of New Negrows, if he was mine I would cut him in pieces, a son of a gun, a nice negrow, he should be killed himself by rites."

Besides the fine old estates of Tidewater Virginia, there were many properties in the newer regions where conditions still smacked of the frontier. On such a plantation in the half-settled Shenandoah Valley grew up young John Sevier. Like most lads along the frontier, John had a passion for hunting, and scant regard for books. And small blame to him, considering the guise in which learning was first presented, the only school in the neighborhood being a log cabin presided over by a crotchety old fellow who birched his pupils in and out of season. Later on, John was sent to an academy newly opened at Stanton; but he was restless, and presently forsook the paths of learning for the adventurous life of a scout in the French and Indian War, where he killed redskins in hand-to-hand conflict long before he was out of his teens.

Another boy destined to become a famous son of the Old Dominion was Patrick Henry. Patrick's father and uncle were educated Scotchmen, but the boy was captivated by the lure of the wilderness. He hated books as much as he loved guns, dogs, and fishing-tackle. Roaming the woods with rough hunters and trappers or loafing on some river-bank, waiting for a "bite," Patrick seemed bent on becoming a shiftless, happy-go-lucky "character," and showed no signs of his later brilliant career. Indeed, his uncouth youthful associations always cropped out in his speech. For though a born orator, he retained a strong backwoods accent, and strangers who heard the distinguished orator were astonished to hear him talk of "the *yearth*" and affirm that "men's naiteral parts are improved by larnin'."

Stripped of the cherry tree and other absurd fables concocted by Parson Weems, the boyhood of George Washington gives us a good idea of child-life in Virginia during the later colonial period. Though the Washingtons were of good stock and belonged definitely to the planter aristocracy, George's father was only moderately prosperous, and the future Father of His Country was born in an unpretentious four-room farmhouse with a long sloping roof and a great outside chimney at either end. George's father had gone to school in England, but his mother was not well educated. Furthermore, George did not fare well educationally, because he was a younger son. His elder half-brother Lawrence (destined to inherit the bulk of the property) had been sent to an English school and given every advantage his father could afford, but George had to be content with decidedly makeshift schooling.

George's first teacher was a certain Mr. Hobby, the sexton of the parish church. A queer sort of schoolmaster, yet the best there was in a district which had no regular school. From Mr. Hobby, George learned his A-B-C's out of a horn-book, a smattering of arithmetic and rudimentary handwriting—also, a weird system of spelling which so bothered George to the end of his days that he could not write a letter without making mistakes like "blew" for blue, "lye" for lie, and "oyl" for oil.

Presently, George was sent to his half-brother Augustine, much older than himself, who lived near a fairly good day school for boys. Here George revealed his talent for mathematics, which was ultimately to decide his choice of a career. The boy loved to count and measure, and he presently began to measure land, and showed that he had in him the makings of a good surveyor.

Land-surveying was then an important profession. That was lucky for George; because when his father died, the bulk of the property went to the older half-brothers, and the second wife and her five young children (including George) were left with little.

Fortunately, his half-brother Lawrence (now the head of the family) liked George and took the boy to live with him. Lawrence Washington was quite a hero in George's boyish eyes. Educated in England, with a creditable war record of foreign service, and married to a charming lady of excellent family, Lawrence was a cultured man of the world, who lived in style on a fine country estate and moved in the best society. For fourteen-year-old George, this was a new experience. The sturdy, serious boy soon blossomed out into a gravely fashionable lad who rode well to hounds, danced and flirted rather awkwardly with the girls—and indulged his surveying talent on every possible occasion.

At fourteen and fifteen he was busy plotting out parcels of his brother's estate. A plan of the turnip-field done by him at that time still exists. One of Washington's recent biographers has described how George showed off his talents, while some guests looked on. "It makes an interesting picture. Late in the afternoon, after dinner, which was at three o'clock. The ladies and gentlemen stand in groups on the edge of the field while young George, with a negro to help him, peers through his surveying instrument, motions authoritatively right and left, and jots down memoranda. The guests are somewhat bored, they had rather be playing at cards, but there is a patronising spirit among them; they think George is wonderful, and say so. Afterwards, he appears among them at the card tables with the turnip field finely plotted and drawn to scale on a piece of paper." (W. E. Woodward, *George Washington: The Image and the Man*, p. 29.)

Indeed, it may have been this very occasion which resulted in giving George his professional start. For one of Lawrence Washington's neighbors was Lord Fairfax, a wealthy old nobleman who owned great tracts of wild land on the Virginia frontier, and it is quite possible that he may have been among the guests that day of the turnip field.

At any rate, Lord Fairfax took a liking to young Washington—as most people did, for George was a good-looking lad, tall beyond his years, with reddish brown hair and honest gray-blue eyes. Also, George could hunt, ride, and shoot with the best— all of which were passports to the fox-hunting old nobleman's favor.

In the spring of 1748, Lord Fairfax offered sixteen-year-old George Washington the job of assistant surveyor in an expedition bound for his lordship's land beyond the Blue Ridge Mountains. And so it happened that George set out for the backwoods, well pleased with his prospects in the world.

AFTER THE REVOLUTION

Towheaded boys and girls—crowds of them past counting—keep step with their elders in a nation's westward march. Peering from covered wagons; perched atop piles of household goods, on flatboats floating down the rivers; trudging along rough roads and forest trails, the sturdy pioneer youngsters brave the hardships of the wilderness and perils from wild beast or savage redskin. The frontier, which advanced so slowly during colonial days, now moves forward by leaps and bounds. From the Revolution to the Civil War, most of America is a land of pioneers.

As in colonial times, the log cabin was still the typical pioneer home. There the children grew up, self-reliant and fearless, in the hard but stimulating school of privation and danger. At what seems to us an impossibly early age, boys and girls handled a rifle, and became forest-wise. Flitting silently through the woods, they knew how to bring game to their call. Hidden behind a log, they would gobble like turkeys, drawing a whole flock within range of their guns. Bleating like fawns, they might soon bring down a doe. Their chattering would fill the tree tops with excited squirrels, while far away a wolf would howl in answer to their cry.

Like young Indians, pioneer boys could throw the tomahawk and shoot with the bow and arrow. And when besieged by Indians, boys and even girls only ten or eleven years old took their turn at the loopholes, rifle in hand, and did good service. They were a scrappy breed, those youngsters of pioneer days.

One of the early settlers in the Ohio Territory tells of his boyhood in that region, then known as the "Old Northwest."

"The Indian meal which we brought with us," he writes, "was used up too soon, so that for a long time we had to live without bread. The lean venison and the breast of wild turkey we were taught to call bread. I remember how narrowly we children watched the growth of the potato tops, pumpkin, and squash vines. How delicious was the taste of the young potatoes when we got them! What a jubilee when we were allowed to pull the young corn for roasting ears! Still more so, when it got hard enough to be made into johnny-cake by the aid of a tin grater. The furniture of the table consisted of a few pewter dishes, plates, and spoons, but mostly of wooden bowls, trenchers and noggins. If these were scarce, gourds and hard-shell squashes made up the deficiency.

"I well remember the first time I ever saw a teacup and saucer. My mother died when I was seven or eight years old. My father then sent me to Maryland to attend school. The first tavern we reached on the way back to civilization was a frame house, and to make the change still more complete, it was plastered on the inside, both walls and ceiling. I was struck with astonishment. I had no idea that there was any house in the world that was not built of logs. But here I looked around and could see no logs, and above could see no joists. Whether such a thing had been made by the hands of man, or had grown so of itself, I could only conjecture. I had not the courage to inquire anything about it. When supper came on, my confusion was worse confounded. A little cup stood in a bigger one, with some brownish stuff in it, which was neither milk, hominy, nor broth. What to do with these little cups I could not tell, but I was afraid to ask anything concerning the use of them."

The painted savage was a very real bogy-man to pioneer children. Any night, a red glow in the sky might give warning that playmates in some neighboring cabin had been barbarously murdered. Or a panting messenger might pound on the door, bidding the family fly for their lives to the shelter of the district stockade.

Yet even the youngsters were prepared to fight with quick-witted courage. One anecdote tells how about sundown three Indians suddenly emerged from the forest and approached a cabin inhabited only by a widow and her two little children. The mother was sick in bed, and the family were quite defenseless, their rifle being broken. The older boy, a boy of ten, discovering the Indians, hurriedly barred the door just in the nick of time. The Indians first tried to wheedle him into opening it, claiming to be friends, then began angrily to batter on it. The brave youngster picked up the broken rifle-barrel, poked it through a loophole, and threatened to shoot unless the Indians instantly got out. The startled Indians took cover, and before they could renew the attack, two woodsmen approached and scared them away.

Even more striking was the bravery of a boy thirteen years old. One night when the father was away from home, the family was roused by the furious barking of their dog, and on peering cautiously out they were horrified to see five Indians creeping toward the cabin. This time, however, the family rifle was in working order, and the boy knew how to use it. Silently he drew a bead upon the leading Indian and shot him dead. The Indians ran

THE STORY OF YOUTH 291

around to the other side of the cabin, but the boy caught sight of them through a loophole on that side and fired a second shot with fatal effect. Mad with rage, the remaining three Indians got a log and tried to batter down the door, but the boy shot one of them, and the surviving pair of savages hid behind the wood-pile. Presently, the siege was raised by a party of settlers, alarmed by the shots.

Another time a widower, who lived in a lonely cabin with his three children, had to go to a distant mill to get his corn ground. He expected to get back by afternoon, but was so delayed at the mill that he did not return at nightfall. Warily the children—the eldest was a girl of fourteen—barricaded the cabin door, bringing in their big dog as a protector. It was well they did so, for presently they heard soft footsteps, and, peeking out, saw three Indians skulking about the cabin. Apparently the savages had been watching the house and knew the father was away, for they first tried to get the children to open the door. This failing, two of the Indians climbed onto the roof and started to descend the wide-throated chimney, having noted that the fire burned low. Quick-wittedly, the elder girl emptied upon the glowing coals the contents of a feather-bed she had been repairing. A moment later, an Indian came tumbling down the chimney, half-suffocated, landing in the fire where he was so roasted that he presently died. The other Indian, after trying desperately to climb out of the chimney, likewise slid down, half-choked, and rolled out onto the floor of the cabin, where the dog pounced upon him and tore out his throat. The third Indian must have fled, for the father presently rode up, unmolested, and was astonished to find the cabin a grim battleground.

One autumn afternoon, two brothers, aged fourteen and eleven, were sent into the woods by their father to look for a strayed cow. After hunting for a couple of hours they sat down to rest under a hickory tree and began to crack nuts. The autumn twilight was falling, and they did not notice the approach of two figures until a pair of rifles were leveled at them. They had been taken prisoners by Indians.

The elder boy John concealed his fright. Indeed, he put a good face on the matter, and when he found that the Indians could talk English, he told a plausible tale. His father, said he, was a hard master, who treated them harshly and never let them have a good time. He therefore hoped the Indians would let them become mighty hunters, which was their great desire. At this, the Indians became quite friendly, for it sometimes happened that white boys did actually join the Indians and become renegades.

After going some miles into the deep woods, the Indians stopped, built a small fire, and cooked their supper. The boys were then bound, and the Indians went to sleep, one on either side of them. Toward morning one of the Indians, becoming cold, caught hold of John in his arms and turned him over to the outside. In this position, the boy, who had kept awake, was able to get his hands loose. Stealthily sitting erect, he suddenly grasped the Indian's tomahawk and brained first him and then his comrade. The boys then made the best of their way home, laden with the rifles and other weapons of their captors.

The slain Indians were noted warriors, and the boy's heroic act made a great sensation, not only among the settlers but among the Indians themselves. Far from seeking vengeance, the redskins apparently honored their youthful bravery. Years later, when the Indians had been cleared out of the region and peace had been established, an old Indian passed that way and inquired what had become of the young heroes. He was told that they still lived with their parents. The old warrior shook his head, remarking gravely: "You have not done right; you should make chieftains of those boys!"

Davy Crockett, the hero of the Alamo, was born in Tennessee, shortly after the Revolution. His family had terrible times with the Indians. His grandparents were scalped in their own cabin; one uncle was crippled for life in a desperate hand-to-hand fight with the redskins; while another uncle, taken prisoner by Indians when a boy, was a captive among the savages for seventeen years. Davy's childhood was enlivened by warlike alarms and rumors of Indian raids.

One of a large family, Davy grew up wild and untaught. When a man finally did open a backwoods school in a log cabin not far from his home, Davy went with the other neighborhood children, but his schooling lasted only four days. Picked on by an older boy, Davy flew at him like a young wildcat, right in the schoolroom; so the master, after birching him soundly, sent him home with a message to his father advising a further licking. Since Davy knew by experience that the schoolmaster's advice would be acted upon, he determined to run away from home. Accordingly, he hired out to a passing cattle-drover and began his adventurous life among cattlemen and wagoners.

The rough life of the frontier produced a plentiful crop of "bad boys," who often grew up to be notorious "bad men" like the immortal Jesse James. Yet some of the wildest youngsters got a grip on themselves and turned out well. A good example of the reformed bad boy is David Glasgow Farragut, the distinguished admiral of the Civil War.

David's father was an army officer who was stationed at various military posts along the Southern border. His mother was a woman of the true frontier type; for Admiral Farragut often related the following incident of his early childhood: "I remember that on one occasion, during my father's absence, a party of Indians came to our house, which was somewhat isolated. My mother, who was a brave and energetic woman, barred the door and sent all of us trembling little ones up into the loft, while she guarded the entrance with an ax. The savages attempted to parley with her, but she kept them at bay, until finally they departed. My father arrived shortly afterward with his command (he was a major of cavalry), and immediately pursued the Indians, whom he overtook and punished."

This incident occurred at an army post back of

New Orleans. Unfortunately, Davy's mother died soon afterwards of yellow fever, and the seven-year-old boy, deprived of home guidance, became an unusually "tough kid" for his tender years. To get David away from the bad surroundings of frontier Louisiana, his father got a close friend, Commodore Porter, to take the boy with him into the navy, and he was made a midshipman when only nine and a half years old.

Little David was certainly a rough customer for his age. The Admiral thus frankly describes his juvenile self at that time: "I could swear like an old salt, could drink as stiff a glass of grog as if I had doubled Cape Horn, and could smoke like a locomotive. I was great at cards, and was fond of gambling in every shape."

Happily, Commodore Porter had his eye on David and knew just how to treat him. Seeing that the boy had good stuff in him, he appealed to his family pride and professional ambition. Commodore Porter told David that if he went on as he was going, he would never get to be an "officer and a gentleman," but would become "a poor, miserable, drunken sailor before the mast, kicked and cuffed about the world, to die at last in some fever hospital in a foreign clime." David, who loved Commodore Porter like a father, was "stunned by the rebuke and overwhelmed with mortification." Then and there he abandoned his wild habits, devoted himself to his profession, and rose rapidly to an admiralship.

The story of young Abraham Lincoln and his forebears is a beautiful illustration of the life of the old frontier. The Lincolns were typical pioneers. The family landed first in Massachusetts as early as 1638, but the pioneer strain was always "moving on" into the wilderness. Wandering from New England to Pennsylvania, Lincoln's forebears moved to the backwoods of Virginia, where they tarried awhile. Thence, Abraham's grandfather (after whom the future President was named) trekked over the mountains into Kentucky, building his log cabin when Kentucky was well named the "Dark and Bloody Ground."

Although the Lincoln homestead stood almost in the shadow of a stockaded fort built to protect the new settlement, the family was soon stricken by the ever-lurking Indian peril. One day when the elder Abraham was working in his clearing, assisted by his son Thomas, a boy of six, an Indian brave crept to the edge of the forest and fired a shot which killed the father at his task. With a yell, the Indian ran into the clearing, seized little Tom, and made off with him toward the woods. Tom's half-grown brothers had been chopping wood close by. Mordecai, the elder, leveled his long-rifle, and an instant later the Indian went sprawling in his death-throes. Freed from the savage's grasp, Tom jumped to his feet, ran to the cabin, and sought shelter in his mother's arms.

Tom's boyhood was a hard one. The father's death plunged the widow and her five children into bitter poverty. The tragedy was deeply taken to heart. Standing over the father's body, young Mordecai swore a great oath to avenge that blood many-fold. And Mordecai Lincoln kept his word, for he

THE STORY OF YOUTH 297

became a noted Indian-fighter and many a redskin died through his unerring aim.

Meanwhile, the Lincoln family grew up poor and uneducated. Abraham's father Thomas was a typical pioneer—an expert woodsman and a dead shot with the rifle, but lacking in industry and always inclined to "pull up stakes and move on." He did move on, taking his young wife, Nancy Hanks, to a rude log cabin in a region of half-cleared wilderness, and here Abraham Lincoln was born on a February morning of the year 1809. Shortly afterwards, Thomas Lincoln moved again to another log cabin where Abraham spent his childhood.

His mother was a woman of unusual character and some education. She it was who first taught her husband to read, and her son Abraham tells us that his earliest recollection of his mother was of sitting at her feet drinking in tales which Nancy was reading to him out of a story-book that she had been fortunate enough to lay hands on. For books were rare and precious things in the backwoods those days.

Little Abraham's childhood was as poor and primitive as his father's had been. His easy-going sire was not a "good provider," so Nancy not only did the housework but often took the rifle and went out after a deer, bear, or raccoons, bringing back food for the table and pelts which her deft fingers wrought into buckskin shirts and leggings, moccasins, and coonskin caps for the family. Determined that her children should not grow up illiterate, Nancy taught them their A-B-C's, and when a master opened a backwoods school near at hand, she eagerly sent seven-year-old Abraham to him to learn the scant knowledge he had to impart.

Abraham's Kentucky schooldays, however, were destined to be brief. For meanwhile, Thomas Lincoln was getting the *wanderlust* once more. Glowing tales were filtering through the backwoods about the new territory of Indiana, described as a paradise of rich soil and teeming game. The lure of golden opportunities just beyond the horizon beckoned him, as it had his pioneering forebears.

Poor Nancy was full of foreboding, but she followed her man bravely, as a pioneer wife should. The Kentucky home was sold for twenty dollars cash and ten barrels of whisky—whisky being backwoods currency at the time. After a long, hard journey, the Lincoln family with their scanty belongings landed in the wilderness of southern Indiana, the site for the new home being a grassy knoll in the heart of the primeval forest.

A time of grim privation followed. Winter was coming on, and the Lincolns were forced to huddle in a rude shanty, hastily knocked together from branches, split-wood slabs, and hides. The family lived chiefly on game, and were so poor that they had to use thorns for pins and bits of bone for buttons on their buckskin or homespun clothing.

Such hardships proved too much for the devoted mother. She fell ill, and, in default of any medical attendance, died when Abraham was only ten years old. The sole bright spot in this gloomy time was the arrival of some relatives of Nancy's, who settled near the Lincolns and thus gave the motherless children neighbors who were also blood kin.

One of these, Dennis Hanks, a lad almost ten years older than Abraham, proved a welcome companion and a stanch friend, and Dennis's recollections, phrased in his backwoods dialect, give us a vivid picture of Abraham Lincoln's boyhood days.

Indeed, Dennis Hank's memories go back to Abraham's birth. He says: "I rikkilect I run all the way, over two miles, to see Nancy Hanks's boy baby. Her name was Nancy Hanks before she married Thomas Lincoln. 'Twas common for connections to gather in them days to see new babies. I held the wee one a minute. I was ten years old, and it tickled me to hold the pulpy, red little Lincoln. The family moved to Indiana when Abe was about nine. Mr. Lincoln moved first, and built a camp of brush in Spencer County. We came a year later, and he had then a cabin. So he gave us the shanty. Abe killed a turkey the day we got there, and couldn't get through tellin' about it. The name was pronounced 'Linkhorn' by the folks then. We was all uneducated. After a spell we learnt better. I was the only boy in the place all them years, and Abe and me was always together."

Dennis Hanks claims to have continued his young cousin's education. "He knew his letters pretty wellish, but no more. His mother had taught him. If ever there was a good woman on earth, she was one—a true Christian of the Baptist church. But she died soon after we arrived, and Abe was left without a teacher. The boy had only about one quarter of schooling, hardly that. I then set in to help him. I didn't know much, but I did the best I could. Sometimes he would write with a piece of charcoal or the p'int of a burnt stick on the fence or floor. We got a little paper at the country town, and I made some ink out of blackberry brier-root and a little copperas in it. It was black, but the copperas ate the paper after a while. I made Abe's first pen out of a turkey-buzzard feather. We had no geese them days.

"After he learned to write his name he was scrawlin' it everywhere. Sometimes he would write it in the white sand down by the crick bank and leave it there till the waves would blot it out. He didn't take to books in the beginnin'. We had to hire him at first, but after he got a taste on't, it was the old story—we had to pull the sow's ears to git her to the trough, and then pull her tail to get her away. He read a great deal, and had a wonderful memory—wonderful. Never forgot anything.

"His first reading book was Webster's Speller. When I got him through that, I had only a copy of the Indiana Statutes. Then Abe got hold of a book. I can't rikkilect the name. It told a yarn about a feller, a nigger or suthin', that sailed a flatboat up to a rock, and the rock was magnetized and drawed all the nails out, and he got a duckin' or drowned or suthin',—I forget now. [It was the *Arabian Nights*]. Abe would lay on the floor with a chair under his head and laugh over them stories by the hour. I told him they was likely lies from beginnin' to end, but he learned to read right well in them. I borrowed for him the life of Washington and the speeches of Henry Clay. They had a powerful influence on him. . . .

"And my, how he could chop! His ax would flash

and bite into a sugar-tree or sycamore, and down it would come. If you heard him fellin' trees in a clearin' you would say there were three men at work, the way the trees fell. Abe was never sassy or quarrelsome. I've seen him walk into a crowd of sawin' rowdies, and tell some droll yarn and bust them all up. It was the same after he got to be a lawyer. All eyes was on him whenever he riz. There was *suthin' peculiarsome* about him."

So young Abraham Lincoln struggled upward, through boyhood and youth, moving once more with his visionary, impractical father to Illinois; educating himself under the greatest handicaps; but firmly laying the foundations of his future greatness.

While boys and girls on the westward-moving frontier were living in log cabins and fighting Indians, children in the older parts of America were leading a life less thrilling but more comfortable—and with their share of good times.

Between the Revolution and the Civil War, New England was becoming much less strict than it had been in colonial days. To be sure, boys like Henry Ward Beecher might still be brought up as sternly as young Mathers and Edwardses; yet, on the whole, Puritanism was mellowing and living conditions were getting easier.

The change from frontier conditions is well shown by the boyhood of Daniel Webster. Daniel's father had cleared his farm among the New Hampshire forests. But when little Daniel came into the world at the close of the Revolution, the first pioneer hardships were over. In one of his speeches, he tells us: "It did not happen to me to be born in a log cabin; but my elder brothers and sisters were born in a log cabin, and raised amidst the snow-drifts of New Hampshire at a period so early that when the smoke first rose from its rude chimney and curled over the frozen hills there was no similar evidence of a white man's habitation between it and the settlements on the rivers of Canada."

Daniel was an unusually bright boy, and his father was determined he should get an education. But the path of learning in the New Hampshire "North Country" was no easy one. Sometimes Daniel had to follow his teacher about from hamlet to hamlet, boarding away from home at various farmhouses, to keep up his schooling. Books were scarce as schools; such volumes as Daniel could lay hands on he read over and over until he had practically committed them to memory. In later life he said: "In my boyish days there were two things I dearly loved; namely, reading and playing. We had so few books that to read them once was nothing; we thought they were all to be got by heart." Once his teacher offered a jackknife as a prize to the pupil who would learn and recite within a given period of time the greatest number of passages from the Bible. When Daniel's turn came, he arose and recited chapter after chapter, until the teacher cried: "That's enough! We haven't time to hear the whole Bible." Similarly, when a large handkerchief was given him on which the Constitution of the United States was printed in colors, he studied it until every word and phrase was his own.

An exceedingly likable boy, Daniel had a knack

of making firm friends. His elder brother Ezekiel was devoted to him, and some amusing anecdotes show how Ezekiel backed up Daniel on every occasion. One day, when the two boys were out in the barn, their father, suspecting they might be up to some prank, called out: "Daniel, what are you doing?" "Nothing," called back the future orator. "And what are you doing, Ezekiel?" "Helping Daniel," came the quick answer.

Another time, the two brothers were allowed to attend a fair in a neighboring village, and each was given a little money to have a good time with. They had a great day, but when they came home that night their mother, being a thrifty New Englander, asked them how they had spent their money. Daniel replied vaguely that he had "just spent it." "And you, Ezekiel?" went on their mother disapprovingly. "Lent it to Daniel," confessed the elder brother, with a sheepish grin.

Spendthrift Daniel Webster was far from being a typical Yankee in money-matters. But this was emphatically not true of another New England boy who later blossomed into fame as that prince of showmen P. T. Barnum, creator of the Greatest Show on Earth. Phineas was born in Connecticut, the region famed for its wooden nutmegs, where the farmers were said to file down their sheep's noses to crop the grass between the rocks of their boulder-strewn pastures.

Little Phineas soon qualified as a good Connecticut Yankee, for he showed an understanding of the value of money before he was out of his babyhood.

In this he was abetted by his grandfather, a canny, humorous soul, who would occasionally "loosen up" to the extent of giving Phineas a cent to buy candy —coupled with an injunction to ask the storekeeper to sell at the "lowest cash price."

Coached by such guides to thrift as his grandfather and an even more penurious father, Phineas early began to branch out in speculative ventures which proved good business. While schoolmates were playing ball or birds-nesting, young P. T. Barnum would purchase a gallon of molasses, boil it down, work it up into candy, sell it to the neighbors and pocket a neat dollar by the transaction. Having proved his mettle in molasses candy, Phineas soon branched out into gingerbread cookies, sugar candies, and cherry rum—the last item going big with the militiamen encamped near his home at "muster-time." By the time he was ten years old, he was so affluent that, as he himself drolly expressed it, his thrifty father "considerately allowed me to purchase my own clothes." And at twelve years of age he appears to have been quite a boy-capitalist—certainly much richer than any of his juvenile neighbors.

Leland Stanford, destined to become famous as one of the pioneer builders of California, was another boy with a phenomenally keen eye for business. He showed this at the age of six, when his father was talking about getting rid of the horseradish weed with which the garden was overrun. Leland and his brothers were given the job. The garden was presently cleared, and a pile of horseradish lay to one side. Then Leland had a bright idea—wash it and sell it in the town of Schenectady near by. The horseradish fetched the sum of $1.50, Leland's share being fifty cents.

The autumn Leland was eight he proposed to his brothers that they gather chestnuts, store them, and await a favorable moment to sell in the Schenectady market. The boys gathered several bushels and hoarded them, waiting for the right moment to sell. At length the hired man returned from a trip to town, bringing the tidings that chestnuts were very high. The boys lost no time getting their produce to town, and realized no less than twenty-five dollars!

Though Leland's father was a farmer in comfortable circumstances, the family was large and he could not see his way to send Leland to Albany to study law, as the son desired. Accordingly, the sturdy lad in his mid teens, proceeded to solve the problem in his own fashion. His father had recently purchased a tract of woodland adjoining his farm, but had not yet cleared it for lack of ready money to pay for labor. Leland proposed to take the contract, if he could have the profits to pay for his legal education. Not only was he a good woodsman himself, but he had saved up a small sum which he spent on hiring woodchoppers—wages at that time being only twenty-five cents a day. Leland's profits were $2,600—a handsome sum in those days. He had earned enough to go forth into the world—paying his own bills.

The rapid change from pioneer conditions to settled life comes out strongly in the memoirs of a well-known Confederate soldier. General Basil Duke was born in Kentucky only a trifle over twenty years later than Abraham Lincoln. Yet the contrast between their boyhoods is an amazing one. When Lincoln first saw the light, Kentucky had barely ceased to merit its original name of the "Dark and Bloody Ground." The echoes of Indian raids were still ringing through the half-cleared forests, and rough frontier hardships still prevailed. A generation later, Basil Duke grew up in a settled land of prosperous farms and comfortable homes. The painted savage was a dim memory, and the frontier had passed on far to the west.

It is a singularly happy, care-free childhood which General Duke describes. In those days, almost every boy had his horse, dogs, and rifle as soon as he was "knee-high to a grasshopper." Horsemanship became second nature, while the hunting of small game was a never-failing pastime.

The genial social life of Old Kentucky made for a wide circle of youthful friendships. There was much "visiting" among families, and many neighborhood festivals—especially the "barbecues" for which the South is famed. An entire neighborhood, from old men to toddling children, would gather amid a shady grove by a running stream, and while the roasting meats slowly "barbecued," the expectant feasters would work up an appetite by sports such as horse-races and shooting-matches. The boys would display their skill with their squirrel-rifles. After a mammoth picnic-dinner there would be more horse-racing, dancing, flirting, and a fair consumption of corn liquor—though if the minister were present, "cuss-words" were taboo, and any young blood who wanted a drink was supposed to consume it behind a tree!

Two Southern belles have written recollections of their girlhood which give us vivid pictures of Southern life in the early nineteenth century. The first of these ladies was born on a Carolina plantation, and her earliest memory was of her black nurse, who told her creepily fascinating stories of "sperrits an' ghostes, and of Old-Blue-Eyes-an'-Bloody-Bones who would come out of the plum orchard and carry me off to the graveyard if I did not go to sleep quickly."

When she was six years old, her parents migrated to Tuscaloosa, the new capital of Alabama. "Migration" is the proper word to describe that journey, for the family traveled in a cortège of queer old carriages, followed by a long wagon-train containing their household goods. Much of the journey lay through almost uninhabited wilderness, and the heavy carriages jolting along over the rough roads to the nightly bivouacs in tents grouped about a roaring camp-fire made a deep impression on the little girl.

Another Southern lady (afterwards Mrs. Roger A. Pryor), who spent most of her girlhood, in the early thirties, on a big estate in Virginia, writes: "The general impression I retain of the world of my childhood is of gardens—gardens everywhere; abloom with roses, lilies, violets, jonquils, flowering almond trees. . . . And conservatories!" These charming surroundings were a setting for a delightful social life. Guests were always coming and going in the great mansion, and gay parties, sports, and picnics were the order of the day.

Of the varied, colorful activities of plantation existence this little girl says: "The life we led was busy beyond all parallel. Everything the family and the plantation needed was manufactured at home, except the fine fabrics, the perfumes, wines, etc., which were brought from Richmond, Baltimore, or Philadelphia. Everything, from the goose-quill pen to carpets, bedspreads, coarse cotton cloth, and linsey-woolsey for the servants' clothing was made at home. . . . Miss Betsey, the housekeeper, was the busiest of women. Besides her everlasting pickling, preserving, and cake-baking, she was engaged with my aunt in mysterious incantations over cordials, tonics, and home remedies. . . . I was intensely interested in all this busy life—and always eager to be a part of it."

In the cities of the North, as on the plantations of the South, children of wealthy parents grew up amid luxurious surroundings inconceivable to children on the farm and the frontier. If ever there was a boy "born with a silver spoon in his mouth," it was John Watts de Peyster. The scion of a noted Dutch patroon family, he was born in the year 1821, in his grandfather's fine old residence at Number Three Broadway! And he has told us the story of his fascinating boyhood with a wealth of lively detail.

Of his early childhood he writes: "I wore ample frills, almost ruffs, around my neck, and long aprons almost to the ankles; but underneath were very respectable imitations of trousers and jackets. I slept on feathers in a room heated with sea-coal, which I consider injured my health; and I was generally pampered. I had heavy plum cake, *ad libitum,* and mince pies, in season, at all hours. . . . Mamie, the nurse, and her cronies used to delight in ghost stories, and I used to get down in the bed, to the very foot, under the covering, with every fiber quivering, —and then had such dreams!"

John's special playmate was his cousin, Phil Kearney, who later became a famous general of the Civil War. Both boys had military tastes and commanded armies of lead soldiers—literally armies, several thousand strong. And with those toy armies they fought entire campaigns (according to elaborate codes of rules) which sometimes lasted for weeks. These wars nearly drove the housekeeper distracted, for they ranged over several rooms, and books, rugs, and tables were conscripted wholesale for fortresses and mountain-ranges.

Like most boys of wealthy families at that period, John de Peyster was educated in private schools. Later on, he went to a select military academy located in uptown New York, where the pupils wore amazing uniforms and had a variety of foreign instructors. Yet the absence of organized athletics is strange to our eyes.

Long summer vacations were spent on grandfather's big estates up the Hudson River. Little John, as the old patroon's heir, was treated almost like a young prince. Riding about on his pony, he would be greeted by the tenants with affectionate respect, while their sons would be eager to show him the best trout-pools, the favorite swimming-holes, and the likeliest spots for birds' nests and small game.

Such were the varied lives led by boys and girls of farm and frontier, of city and plantation, in that springtime of the young Republic which lay between the Revolution and the storms of the Civil War.

Chapter XI

CHILDREN OF THE DAWN OF TODAY

S the eighteenth century drew toward its close, signs could be observed of the dawn of better days for childhood and youth. The temper of the age was stubborn, yet gradually the influence of new ideas transformed the harsh, callous, unimaginative attitude of elders into one of broadening sympathy for, and intelligent understanding of, the young. By the middle of the nineteenth century, cruel parents and flogging masters, though still numerous, were beginning to be considered old-fashioned, and by another generation our own age had, practically speaking, begun.

All this meant changes more deep-going even than

those between the close of the Middle Ages and Elizabeth's reign. During the nineteenth century, youth entered into a new life, far happier (and on the whole better) than anything it had previously known. This transformation took nearly a hundred years and went through several distinct phases.

Toward the close of the eighteenth century, when most parents were chastizing or neglecting their children, a few enlightened young couples began rearing their offspring along startlingly novel lines. These "Superior Parents," impressed by the liberal ideas then spreading, adopted a correspondingly new attitude toward family life. They took their parental responsibilities very seriously, often withdrawing from the frivolous round of society and devoted themselves mainly to the care of their children. "Superior" parents scorned current practices like "planting out" babies with foster-mothers and packing children off to boarding-schools when only five or six years old.

It was upon the infant and the very young child that the Superior Parent's attention was at first concentrated. The schools long remained wholly untouched by the influence of these new ideas.

Even the most superior parents did not realize what we now know—that the child's mind and attitude toward life is vastly different from that of the adult's. Like everyone else in those days, they looked on children as little men and women who, by some strange perversity, refused to act like grown-ups.

However, Superior Parents held that this unfortunate perversity should be remedied by a different

THE STORY OF YOUTH 313

method from that commonly employed. Instead of beating children into grown-up behavior, Superior Parents proposed an "appeal to reason." And, to get the child started right, this appeal should begin almost in the cradle. That was why Superior Parents insisted on home training. And the product of this new theory was—the "Rational Child."

Whipping was abolished in enlightened households. Beatings, it was argued, excite only the emotions, and are thus clearly irrational. To develop the reason, appeal to it alone and carefully avoid every irrational tendency. Do not tell a child it *must* do thus-and-so, on penalty of a thrashing. Instead: carefully explain *why* it *ought* to act thus, *for his own best interests*. If the child will not listen, and persists in his naughty conduct, let him go ahead and learn by bitter experience the folly of his actions.

Superior Parents did not hesitate to carry their beliefs to extremes. Does your child break a window in the nursery? Do not spank it; let him sit in a draft and catch cold. Does your little girl dawdle in dressing for her afternoon walk? Just leave her behind and let her miss the fun. Is your little boy deaf to warnings about too much jam? Let him stuff himself and get a stomachache. That very "enlightened" matron Mrs. Ruskin deliberately allowed her small son to lay his finger on a hot grate, in order to let him learn once and for all that fire will surely burn.

All those sad experiences would be followed as well as preceded by long discourses from parents, in which children would be encouraged to "talk back," argue, chop logic, and generally "develop their reasoning faculties."

Children were seldom left alone to play by themselves. They were forever trotting around with father and mother, having all sorts of things explained to them, from the boiling of a teakettle to the puffing of a mechanical marvel like the newly invented steam-engine. Such children lived in an ultra-rational world. Their imaginations were starved, by parents so disdainful of the emotions that they carefully pointed out the foolishness of fairy-tales and all kinds of make-believe, because they were not literally "true."

Superior Parents often quizzed their children to make them give logical reasons for their likes and dislikes. A rhyme has come down to us about a father who keeps at his little son to state precisely *why* the boy wants to return to a certain seaside resort named Kilve, where the family has been the summer before. The child has no "logical reason" for his childish emotional preference. Yet his father keeps on quizzing him, until at last, in desperation, the child happens to glance at the vane on a near-by church-steeple, and cries:

> "At Kilve there was no weather-cock
> And that's the reason why!"

These "enlightened" ideas are reflected in the flood of children's books which now appeared. Like the previous "juveniles" of Puritan days, these books were designed to instruct, rather than amuse and stimulate, the youthful mind. But the Puritan tracts of the seventeenth century had been full of hell-fire and brimstone, these of the early nineteenth century said little about dogmatic religion, but were usually chock-full of practical information on such worldly topics as minerals, birds, geography, and machines. Since the authors always condescendingly "wrote down to" their audience and seem to have been devoid of a sense of humor, these "instructive" volumes must have been repellant reading to any child who had not been warped into a little intellectual prig.

The top-lofty attitude of such authors is amusingly revealed by a remark of a certain clergyman to his sister, who had written several such books. He graciously informs her that, although she has been "censured for employing talents of so superior a kind in the composition of books for children," such a task is "by no means an ignoble employment." Perhaps further to reassure his sister, the reverend gentleman himself tries his hand at the game by composing a manual of useful information. His thrilling style (addressed especially to children between the ages of six and ten) may be gaged by his statement that "Hailstones are drops of rain suddenly congealed into a hard mass, so as to preserve their figure." Later on, he states that the woodlark and skylark "are the only two birds which are known to sing flying." And, lest the mention of larks might spur childish imaginations to picture their carolings high in the heavens, and so interrupt the reading of his useful information, the author hastens to nip romance in the bud by adding: "They are considered very excellent eating."

There were also many books telling about "good"

little boys and girls who talk like walking encyclopedias and who are always starched models of decorum. One of these volumes, composed by the head master of a boys' school about 1840, advises the youthful reader that "his looks should be complacent and composed, modest yet confident, affable and condescending." He is reminded that "the circumstance of your being sent to school places you above numbers of indigent and vulgar children who are suffered to wander about the streets." The boy is exhorted "to invite, implore, and cherish the advice of parents and teachers." Finally, he is to be "affable and condescending" in replying to everyone "according to the rank and sex of the person addressed."

There were even books of stilted verse along the same lines. To quote two examples:

> "Miss Lydia Banks, though very young,
> Will ne'er do what is rude and wrong;
> When spoken to, she always tries
> To give the most polite replies.
>
> "Observing what at school she's taught,
> Turns out her toes as children ought,
> And when returned at night from school
> She never lolls on chair or stool."

As for the model good little boy, he is made to say:

> "The things my parents bid me do
> Let me attentively pursue.
> I must not ugly faces scrawl
> With charcoal on the whitewashed wall.
> I must not blow the candle out,
> Or throw the smutty snuff about."

Yet the boys and girls of those days did have one great advantage over children of former times—they stood a better chance of living to grow up. As the decades passed, the nineteenth century witnessed a revolution in health and sanitation. Dirt and disease vanished from well-appointed nurseries, along with the fairies and bogies of old wives' tales. Children now had their cold morning tub, and were scrubbed with soap and hot water in that formidable proceeding the Saturday-night bath. Water became fit to drink, drains were looked after, while plumbing and the modern bathroom at length appeared.

Beer and improper foods became tabu. Nursery tables were set with simple fare such as porridge, eggs, milk, cocoa, and bread or toast sparingly spread with marmalade or jam. Nurses had to have some professional training, while competent doctors were called in as a matter of course whenever illness appeared.

All this notably reduced the child death-rate. After the middle of the century, progress in sanitation and medical science was so rapid that by 1880 most epidemic diseases of childhood had been brought under some sort of control, and a large majority of children born to upper- and middle-class families survived.

After 1840, especially, children of the wealthy and well-to-do grew up in a domestic atmosphere of solid comfort and rather pompous well-being. It was an age of massive furniture, overstuffed chairs and sofas, heavy draperies, thick carpets, and amazingly ugly ornaments and gas-light chandeliers. The typical Victorian mansion breathed an oppressive air of wealth and overcrowding. Wallpapers, sober in color but powerful in pattern, were interspersed with tall pier-glasses reflecting the somber magnificence of the rooms, from ornate plasterwork ceilings to red-and-green figured carpets. Everywhere was a profusion of bric-à-brac—on tables, in curio-cabinets, and even ranged along wide moldings around the walls. Finally, domestic felicity would be emphasized by conspicuous mottoes such as:

EAST, WEST,
HAME'S BEST.

The young people were clad as befitted their surroundings. However, distinctive children's styles had appeared.

Those juvenile fashions had their vagaries. Beginning with boys in big tasseled caps and long trousers, and girls in poke-bonnets, leg-o'-mutton sleeves, and befrilled ankle-pantalets, children's styles get more and more ugly, until by the seventies and eighties they are indescribable.

An elderly lady still living states of her girlhood: "My coming-out dress had a bustle. Not, I think, the 'cushion' bustle, but one with wires tied together with tapes to make a half-hoop which waggled as one walked. Sometimes a steel poked through, which was most embarrassing. One of my brothers as a boy staying with a large family of cousins hid all their bustles on a Sunday morning (these were the horse-hair cushion bustles), and none of them would go to church because they 'felt so flat and indecent.'

The daughter who played the organ *had* to go and hastily made a bustle out of a white petticoat."

(Quoted from Mrs. C. S. Peel's *A Hundred Wonderful Years*.)

Nineteenth-century girls, with their bustles, hoop-skirts, pantalets, and voluminous bathing-dresses requiring twelve yards of serge, had ideas as finicky as their clothes. The ideal of genteel helplessness persisted until almost the close of the century. Generation after generation, girls were warned against "strong-mindedness" and were trained to accomplishments of a silly, pretentious character.

The "genteel" ideal is well set forth in a book written by an estimable lady, which had a considerable vogue in the forties. In its prim pages, girls were told that: "There is something unfeminine in independence. It is contrary to Nature, and therefore it offends. A really sensible woman feels her dependence; she does what she can, but she is conscious of inferiority, and therefore grateful for support. In everything that women attempt they should show their consciousness of dependence. . . . Women in this respect are something like children— the more they show their need of support, the more engaging they are."

To children of the first half of the nineteenth century, the most awe-inspiring figure on their mental horizon was probably "Papa." True to the traditions of the Superior Parent fathers then usually took their parental position very seriously. They conscientiously looked after their children's health and training; indeed Papa was liable to pop into the nursery mornings, clad in dressing-gown and slippers, to enforce discipline and see to it that reluctant youngsters took their cold tub and ate their simple breakfast in approved fashion. And when he returned home, he would be apt to demand a report of the day's behavior. If satisfactory, this majestic personage might have the children into the dining-room, dressed in their best, to remain stiffly seated on chairs ranged against the wall, without moving or speaking, until the dessert course was served. Then they would be summoned to the table, and given some fruit, a biscuit, and a tiny glass of wine.

After dinner, if all still went well, Papa would unbend and there would be a "children's hour." Games (of a genteel sort) would be played, and the children might dance and sing—Mama furnishing the accompaniment on the harp, or upon "the instrument"—an upright piano with candle-sconces and a front of fluted silk. The children were expected to be decorously merry. In a story-book of the period, a father states that he never permits a child to remain in his presence "whose company is rather calculated to inspire gloom than cheerfulness."

Albert, the prince consort of Queen Victoria, is a good instance of the portentous Papas of the age. The little Prince of Wales, afterwards King Edward VII, stood much in awe of his formidable parent. Albert did realize, however, that little Edward needed some "recreation." So, once in a while, duly selected Eton boys were invited to spend an afternoon at Windsor Castle, to "play" with the Prince of Wales. But, since the "play" went on under Papa Albert's chilly eye, we can imagine the joyous vim which the boys put into their games. Indeed, one of those Eton boys has informed us about the "feeling of dread" with which the prince consort filled him and his companions.

Writings of the time give glimpses of fathers more genial and companionable, and the number of these increases with every decade of the nineteenth century.

Save for a few old fairy-tales and literary classics like "Pilgrim's Progress," "Robinson Crusoe," and "Gulliver's Travels," none of which had been especially written for children, children's reading had been a dreary waste up to this time.

The little girl destined to become Queen Victoria is a good instance of how young children of the early nineteenth century were crammed with dry-as-dust reading. Her tutor was a kindly man, genuinely anxious to give his charge the best and most stimulating books of the day. Yet poor little Victoria's reading consisted mainly of the inevitable manuals of useful information. The juiciest literary titbit to which she was introduced seems to have been a collection of poems called "The Infant's Minstrel" —a title which, of itself, would damn the book in the eyes of a modern child.

Before the middle of the century, however, things had begun to change for the better. Several gifted authors had written books which children hailed with delight and eagerly devoured.

Sir Walter Scott, who lamented that "the minds of children are, as it were, put into the stocks, like their feet at the dancing school," wrote purposely for children, in his "Tales of a Grandfather," and also produced the Waverley Novels, which delighted readers both young and old. Charles Lamb was introducing boys and girls to Shakespeare and the great Greek epic poems by his celebrated "Tales" and "Adventures."

And, in the footsteps of these successful pioneers, a throng of other authors soon trod. The second half of the century saw a host of books which boys and girls might read with equal pleasure and profit. Lewis Carroll's "Alice in Wonderland" and Stevenson's "Treasure Island" are but highlights in the extensive literature of youth which then appeared. The boresome "juveniles" of former days were buried and forgotten.

Although the lives of boys and girls in the upper and middle classes became progressively more healthful, comfortable, and interesting, below them were vast multitudes of children whose existence was a veritable hell of hunger, cold, cruelty, dirt, and disease. The grinding poverty and terrible child-labor abuses increased rather than diminished during the early nineteenth century. The life-and-death struggle against Napoleon, which ended only at Waterloo in 1815, left England crippled with taxes and loaded down with debt. Food, clothing, and other necessaries of life were abnormally high, while wages were very low. The children of the poor suffered the worst consequences of all this.

Dickens describes the state of the London slums in "Oliver Twist," and some of these slums persisted until after the middle of the century. There children grew up in filth, disease, and crime. Young boys and girls convicted of petty thefts were flung into jail among hardened criminals, and were often hanged or transported to penal colonies.

The general misery of the working-classes probably reached its climax in the "hungry forties." During that gloomy period, a charity-worker tells us that whole families endured slow starvation, and says: "Parents sat in their clothes during the whole night for weeks together in order that their only bed and bedding might be reserved for the use of their large family. Others slept upon the cold hearthstone for weeks in succession, without adequate means of providing themselves with food or fuel. In many cases money insufficient for food was used to buy opium to still the cravings of hunger and bring forth forgetfulness."

Even more poignant is this story, told by one who himself had suffered. "Poor mother," he states, "died when I was between two and three. My eldest sister went to work in the factory very early. I soon had to follow, I think about nine years of age. What with hunger and hard usage I bitterly got it burned into me—I believe it will stay while life shall last. We had to be up at 5 in the morning to get to factory, ready to begin work at 6, then work while 8, when we stopped ½ an hour for breakfast, then work to 12 noon; for dinner we had 1 hour, then work while 4. We then had ½ an hour for tea, then work again on to 8.30. If any time during the day had been lost, we had to work while 9 o'clock, and so on every night till it was all made up.

"Then we went to what was called home. Many times I have been asleep when I had taken my last spoonful of porige—not even washed, we were so overworked and underfed. I used to curse the road we walked on. I was so weakley and feeble, I used to think it was the road would not let me go along with the others.

"We had not always the kindest of masters. I remember the master's strap, 5 or 6 feet long, about ¾ in. broad, and ¼ in. thick. He kept it hung on the ginney at his right hand, so we could not see when he took hould of it. But we could not mistake its lessons; for he got hould of it nearly in the middle, and it would be a rare thing if we did not get 2 cuts at one stroke. I have reason to believe on one occasion he was somewhat moved to compassion, for the end of his strap striped the skin of my neck about 3 in. long. When he saw the blood and cut, he actually stoped the machine, came and tied a handkerchief round my neck to cover it up. I have been fell'd to the floor many times by the ruler on the top of the carding, about 8 or 9 feet long, iron hoop at each end. This was done as a change from the strap."

This description of a boy's life in a Yorkshire textile-mill in the forties shows that child-labor abuses were still almost as bad as they had been a century before. Attempts at reform were, to be sure, being made. The first legal restriction on child-labor was an act passed by parliament in the year 1802, when *young* children were not allowed to *work more than twelve hours a day*—exclusive of an hour and a half for meals, so that the working-day really covered more than thirteen hours; say from six in the morning until between seven and eight o'clock at night. A decade later, a second law was passed forbidding the employment of children under nine years of age in mills, though little boys and girls were still allowed to be employed in mines. Not until the late thirties was much more done in the way of reform, and the problem of child-labor was not really tackled till after the middle of the century.

How bad conditions were, not merely in the mills but in most trades, can be seen by the description of the shop of a master file-maker named Hatton, in a book written by Benjamin Disraeli in 1845.

"One of Hatton's apprentices, a lank and haggard youth, ricketty and smoke-dried, and black with his craft, was working on a file. Behind him stood a stunted, meager girl, with a back like a grasshopper; a deformity occasioned by the displacement of the blade-bone, and prevalent among the girls of Woodgate from the cramping posture of their usual toil. . . . The lad says, 'He's wery lib'ral too in the wittals. Never had horse-flesh the whole time I was with him. . . . Never had no sick cow, except when meat was very dear. He always put his face against stillborn calves; . . . there never was any sheep that had bust in the head sold in our court. And then sometimes he would give us a treat of fish, when it had been four or five days in town and not sold. No, give the devil his due, say I!'"

Since mining is an industry naturally remote and hidden from public attention, the wrongs of boys and girls employed in mines went unredressed long after the woes of chimney-sweeps and mill-apprentices had stirred public opinion.

Yet the sufferings of mine children called for drastic legal action. Tiny boys and girls, four and five years old, were carried to the mines on their fathers' backs, acted as "fanners" working in inky darkness for sixteen and eighteen hours, and were then carried home and put to bed, stupefied from exhaustion. Children of six sat at doors in the mine galleries, their duty during a twelve-hour shift being to pull a door open to let coal-trucks pass and close it again. To allay their fear of the dark, these children were at first given candle-ends which burned a couple of hours at most. If the children cried or went to sleep on duty, they were severely beaten. Since work began at four in the morning and lasted till late afternoon or evening, mine children, except in summer, never saw the light of day.

As they grew older, mine children were "promoted" to more laborious tasks. Boys and girls of ten or twelve, clad alike in short trousers, and nothing else, acted as "drawers" and "thrutchers." The drawer-boy or girl had a belt tied round the waist to which was fastened a chain attached to a coal-truck, which was thus dragged through the long galleries from the workings to the loading-stage. Since galleries were cut low, drawers usually had to go on all fours. They were aided by the "thrutchers," who pushed the truck along with their heads as the drawers pulled. Thrutchers wore a thick cap, but the work soon made them bald on the top of the head. When boys grew up, they might become full-fledged miners. But the unfortunate girls and young women, many of whom worked on in the mines, remained drawers and thrutchers all their days.

Though much poverty and suffering persisted, the lot of poor children grew steadily better after 1850. The worst child-labor abuses were done away with by law, while the general situation of working-class families improved. The series of inventions which was transforming every-day life contributed greatly to the comfort and well-being of even the humblest homes. Steamships, railways, cold-storage, and canning combined to make food cheap and give a diet more varied than ever known before. Working folk got better wages, and with rising standards of living they no longer sought to make extra money out of their young children, but wanted them to go to school and get a fair start in life.

Heartless, shiftless, or drunken parents were not only legally forbidden to apprentice their young children to mines and mills, but could also be fined or imprisoned for cruelty to children in their own homes. Thus the age-old "right" of parents to beat and abuse their little ones was abolished. Yet it is astonishing to realize how recently this took place. The British Society for the Prevention of Cruelty to Children was founded only in the eighties, and excited considerable opposition. One prominent newspaper sneeringly remarked that "the Reverend Benjamin Waugh and a few benevolent old women of both sexes are desirous of forming a Society for the Purpose of Washing the Faces of Dirty Children." The traditional idea had been that children were "chattels," which belonged to parents, much like domestic animals and other forms of property; and that "a man had a right to do as he willed with his own." State protection of children against parental cruelty and exploitation is a very modern idea.

Until after the middle of the nineteenth century, English boys and girls of the poorer classes grew up ignorant, many being unable even to sign their names or spell out a few lines in a newspaper.

However, in 1861 a parliamentary commission investigated the situation. The commission reported that primary schools were "often taught by discharged servants or barmaids, outdoor paupers, small traders, washerwomen, cripples, drunkards, consumptive and very aged persons—those, in short, who had no more profitable resource than such a school afforded. Many of the schools were held in lofts, bedrooms, cellars, kitchens, shops, or other available but unsuitable places; where the children, generally little more than infants, tumbled over one another like puppies in a kennel. Attendance, always irregular, ceased altogether at an early age, and the pupils, who had learnt next to nothing, forgot even this within the next twelve months."

At last, English public opinion was shocked broad awake. In 1870, a state system of public schools was begun, and before the close of the century, poor children could get a good education and a fair start in life.

Meanwhile a new spirit was stirring the old grammar schools from the lethargy into which they had fallen. The nineteenth century witnesses a fresh flowering of Eton, Harrow, Rugby, Winchester, and the founding of new "public schools," as the English term these educational institutions. Head masters like Arnold of Rugby set high standards of scholarship and character; boys respond with enthusiasm; and the "public schools," expanding rapidly in size and spirit, set the tone of British educational life.

In "Tom Brown's School Days" is a wonderfully vivid picture of Rugby under Arnold, with all its rough yet exhilarating flavor; trials endured by "new" boys; woes of "fags" and their revolts against bullying seniors; pranks and punishments; sports and games.

Perhaps the most noteworthy feature of school life during this period is the development of organized athletics. During the eighteenth century, athletic sports had been out of fashion. Of course, schoolboys did play games, and Eton was not alone in its celebrated cricket-field. But athletic sports were not encouraged, and were for the most part unorganized. With the nineteenth century, however, conditions rapidly altered, and cricket, football, rowing, running, and other sports came into their own. The English public-school boy became a lover of outdoor sports, and the athletic spirit transformed university life as well.

What Rugby was like in the early nineteenth century is told us in the reminiscences of an "old boy" who entered the school in the year 1813. He arrived as a little shaver dressed in what was then known as a "skeleton suit," consisting of a close-buttoned jacket, a frilled collar around his neck, and long trousers. Rugby still had an antique flavor, for the head master wore a cocked hat and did his hair in a powdered queue, though the boys were attired in white duck trousers, green or blue swallowtail coats with metal buttons, and tall felt hats. They must have had a considerable wardrobe, for sport clothes were unknown, the only preparation for a game of football or a cross-country run being to discard the swallowtail and the tall hat. After a hike, the winners would stand treat at an inn, and some boys were quite overcome by the potations, while those who did not like beer climbed into a farmyard and milked somebody's cow—to be soundly birched by the master if complained of by the farmer.

New boys had to go through a stiff hazing, known as "chairing." Another ordeal was called the "buffets"—a form of running the gantlet, in which the victims would be buffeted by large handkerchiefs tied into hard "Winchester knots." The more wary would prepare themselves for the ordeal by tying boards or book-covers under their clothes. However, that would help little in another ordeal, termed "clodding." Here, boys were pelted with clods of mud from a marshy pool near by, and fags were kept busy getting ammunition.

Fags had many duties, not the least of which was smuggling in supplies of food and drink for clandestine feasts, which they had to cook in dormitories or senior studies. Battered collections of pots, pans, forks, and spoons were secreted for these occasions, until confiscated by a master's untimely raid.

An ordeal much dreaded by new boys was "singing in hall." Before the assembled house, the newcomers mounted a table, one by one, candle in hand, and were sternly commanded to sing a song. If the victim's voice trembled, or he sang off-key, jeers and hisses broke forth, while throughout the performance he was pelted with bread-crusts or stung by missiles from pea-shooters, which frequently knocked the candle out of his hand and covered him with tallow. Finally the boy was allowed to get down from the table and pledged the assembled company in a bumper of salt and water stirred with the tallow candle. Though doubtless squeamish in the stomach, he now had the "freedom of the house."

The Spartan simplicity of those early days was later celebrated in a ballad praising the "good old times," which runs as follows:

"In the days when twenty fellows drank out of one large mug,
And pewter were the dishes, and a tin can was the jug;
In the days when shoes and boot were thrice a week japanned,
And we sat on stools, not sofas—there were giants in the land!

"When new boys on the pump were set to pelt at and to sing,
Or sent from Close to Pendred's for a pennyworth of string;
In the days when fags a long hour in the passage had to stand,
In the days of happy night fags—there were giants in the land!

"When Sixth and Fifth-form fellows had all been duly 'chaired,'
And he who told a falsehood was 'cobbed' and never spared;
And we walked around the School-field with our breakfast in our hand,
Ere the days of tea and coffee—there were giants in the land!"

Such was Rugby when Dr. Thomas Arnold became head master in the year 1829. According to Rouse, the school historian: "The system as Arnold found it at Rugby was not unlike the administration of a conquered state. The Headmaster was an autocrat, dispensing punishments with no sparing hand. He and his colleagues alike were looked on as the natural enemies of boyhood, set over them by a mysterious dispensation of Providence to interfere with personal liberty and enjoyment. To these rulers the boys rendered a grudging obedience, which ceased when it ceased to be enforced. They had their own organization, by which the weaker were slaves of the stronger; and their own code of honour, mercilessly strict among themselves, but lax towards their masters. A lie told to a schoolfellow was a very different thing from a lie told to a master. Differences between themselves were settled by an appeal to brute force, not only amongst the younger, where it was natural, but amongst older boys already on the verge of manhood. Ideals of conduct were otherwise low, and intemperate indulgence of various kinds was not condemned by public opinion."

With equal tact and insight, Dr. Arnold set about his reforming task. He did not abolish the boys' cherished customs; instead, he modified them and infused them with a new spirit. The ideals he set before his boys were: Character, gentlemanly conduct, and sound scholarship—with the emphasis always on character. Boys were put on their honor; their word was unquestioningly taken until proved false; and boys were soon ashamed to tell him a lie. Flogging was restricted to grave moral offenses, such as lying, persistent idleness, and wilful disobedience. Incorrigible boys were promptly expelled. The fagging system was retained, but seniors were taught a sense of responsibility for their fags, and mere bullying came to be looked on by the boys themselves as "bad form."

One of Dr. Arnold's most effective ways of influencing his boys was through his addresses in chapel. Instead of preaching long, dull sermons away over the heads of the audience, Arnold gave short, stimulating talks, which hit the nail on the head every time. His favorite motto was: "Always expect to succeed, and never think you have succeeded." This earnest, honest, genial soul inspired his boys with a devotion which lasted all their lives.

Let us take a first-hand glimpse of school life at Rugby under Dr. Arnold, as described in "Tom Brown's School Days":

On the last Tuesday but one of the half-year Tom was passing through the Hall after dinner, when he was hailed by shouts from Tadpole and several other fags seated at one of the long tables, the chorus of which was, "Come and help us tear up scent."

Tom approached the table in obedience to the mysterious summons, always ready to help, and found the party engaged in tearing up old newspapers, copybooks, and magazines, into small pieces, with which they were filling four large canvas bags.

"It's the turn of our house to find scent for big-side Hare-and-Hounds," exclaimed Tadpole; "tear away, there's no time to lose before calling-over."

"I think it's a great shame," said another small boy, "to have such a hard run for the last day."

"Which run is it?" said Tadpole.

"Oh, the Barby run, I hear," answered the other; "nine miles at least, and hard ground; no chance of getting in at the finish, unless you're a first-rate scud."

"Well, I'm going to have a try," said Tadpole; "it's the last run of the half, and if a fellow gets in at the end, big-side stands ale and bread and cheese, and a bowl of punch; and the Cock's such a famous place for ale."

"I should like to try too," said Tom.

"Well, then, leave your waistcoat behind, and listen at the door, after calling-over, and you'll hear where the meet is."

After calling-over, sure enough, there were two boys at the door, calling out, "Big-side Hare-and-Hounds meet at White Hall"; and Tom, having girded himself with a leather strap, and left all superfluous clothing behind, set off for White Hall. . . .

At the meet they found some forty or fifty boys, and Tom felt sure, from having seen many of them run at football, that he and East were more likely to get in than they.

After a few minutes waiting, two well-known runners, chosen for the hares, buckled on the four bags filled with scent, compared their watches with those of young Brooke and Thorne, and started off at a long slinging trot across the fields in the direction of Barby.

Then the hounds clustered round Thorne, who explained shortly, "They're to have six minutes' law." . . . Then the watches are pocketed, and the pack is led through the gateway into the field which the hares had first crossed. Here they break into a trot, scattering over the field to find the first traces of the scent which the hares throw out as they go along. The old hounds make straight for the likely points, and in a minute a cry of "forward" comes from one of them, and the whole pack quickening their pace make for the spot, while the boy who hit the scent first and the two or three nearest to him are over the first fence, and making play along the hedgerow in the long grassfield beyond. The rest of the pack rush at the gap already made, and scramble through, jostling one another. "Forward" again, before they are half through; the pace quickens into a sharp run, the tail hounds all straining to get up with the lucky leaders. They are gallant hares, and the scent lies thick right across another meadow and into a ploughed field, where the pace begins to tell; and then over a good wattle with a ditch on the other side, and down a large pasture studded with old thorns, which slopes down to the first brook. The great Leicestershire sheep charge away across the field as the pack comes racing down the slope. The brook is a small one, and the scent lies right ahead up the opposite slope, and as thick as ever; not a turn or a check to favor the tail hounds, who strain on, now trailing in a long line, many a youngster beginning to drag his legs heavily, and feel his heart beat like a hammer, and the bad plucked ones thinking that after all it isn't worth while to keep it up.

Tom, East, and the Tadpole had a good start, and are well up for such young hands, and after rising the slope and crossing the next field, find themselves up with the leading hounds, who have over-run the scent and are trying back. . . . Then comes the cry of "Forward" again, from young Brooke, and the pack settles down to work again steadily and doggedly. . . .

Now comes a brook, with stiff clay banks,

from which they can hardly drag their legs, and they hear faint cries for help from the wretched Tadpole, who has fairly stuck fast. But they have too little run in themselves to pull up for their own brothers. Three fields more, and another check, and then "forward" called away to the extreme right.

The two boys' souls die within them; they can never do it. They struggle on across the next field, the "forwards" getting fainter and fainter, and then ceasing. The whole hunt is out of ear-shot, and all hope of coming in is over.

"Hang it all!" broke out East, as soon as he had got wind enough, pulling off his hat and mopping at his face, all splattered with dirt and lined with sweat, from which went up a thick steam into the still cold air. "I told you how it would be. What a thick I was to come! Here we are dead beat, and yet I know we're close to the run-in, if we knew the country."

"Well," said Tom, mopping away and gulping down his disappointment, "it can't be helped. We did our best anyhow. Hadn't we better find a lane?"

"I suppose so—nothing else for it," grunted East. "If ever I go out last day again,"— growl—growl—growl.

While Rugby was thus breaking new ground, Eton, perhaps the most celebrated of English public schools, continued under Dr. Keate's long reign. "Old Keate" was a "character." He had a terrible temper and "red, shaggy eyebrows, so prominent that he habitually used them as arms and hands, for the purpose of pointing out any object toward which he wished to call attention." A holdover from the eighteenth century, Keate was a "flogging master" of the old school, and, until he resigned in 1834, Eton was notorious for harsh discipline and cruel fagging, punctuated by rebellions of the boys against both.

A retired assistant master at Eton in a recent book (James's "Seventy Years") cites some interesting reminiscences of his father, who was at Eton toward the close of Old Keate's reign. "Eton boys," he writes, "were allowed more variety in dress those days than they are now, but the line was drawn somewhere. My father went to Eton in a tight jacket with rows of shiny buttons, but the buttons were incontinently cut off by an outraged senior. Life in College was incredibly rough, and food was inadequate, both in quantity and quality. Some ancient cronies were allowed into Hall to gather for their own consumption whatever scraps were left. They sometimes tried to snatch morsels from the tables during the meal, and my father once saw a boy drive his fork into a too-intrusive hand. In those days cricket, football, and rowing were in a very elementary stage of organization, and I believe that the first code of rules for the Wall game was drawn up in my father's day."

Even more detailed are these memories of an "old boy" who went to Eton at about the same period, when he was barely ten years old. He was assigned to the main dormitory, the terrible "Long Chamber." "I was told," he writes, "that I should find my sheets and bedding in Long Chamber, and that as 'lag of the School' [i.e., new boy] my bedstead was at the bottom. On entering that renowned dormitory, a scene of indescribable confusion greeted me. It was nearly dark, and there were no lights except a few tallow candles carried about here and there by the boys. The floor was covered with bedding, each bundle being wrapped in a coarse horse-rug, far inferior to what would now be used in a gentleman's stable. This was intended to serve as a counterpane. The noise and hooting of nearly fifty boys, each trying to identify his scanty stock of bedding, combined with the shouts of the elder boys calling their fags, gave me a foretaste of my future lot. There were no servants, nor was there anyone to give us assistance. At 8 P. M. after prayers in the Lower School, the doors were closed and we were left prisoners for the night, to settle down as best we could. At 7 A. M. Dr. Keate's servant set us free, and after pacing the Long Chamber twice, armed with a lantern in winter, left us to our morning duties. A person styled a 'bed-maker' came to put the clothes straight, but he did little more, and, at nightfall we had to make the beds of our fag-masters as well as our own. . . .

"The conditions of a junior Colleger's life at that period was very hard indeed. The practice of fagging had become an organized system of brutality and cruelty. I was frequently kept up until one or two o'clock in the morning waiting on my masters at supper, and undergoing every sort of bullying at their hands. I have been beaten on my palms with the back of a brush, or struck on both sides of my face, because I had not closed the shutter near my master's bed tight enough, or because in making his bed I had left the seam of the lower sheet uppermost. When I was kept up fagging late at night, I had to look forward to the probability of a flogging next day for not knowing my lessons. I say nothing of the minor discomforts of having the tassel of one's nightcap set on fire in the night, or having one's bed turned up on end and finding one's heels in the air. Notwithstanding the frequent obstacles to study, my tutor, who had himself been a Colleger, would listen to no excuses, and Dr. Keate was always ready with the birch on complaint of idleness. The rioting, masquerading, and drinking that took place in College after the doors were closed at night can scarce be credited. . . .

"In Hall there was mutton for dinner daily. The boys helped themselves in rotation, and my share, when I was at the bottom of the school, was the last cut of the invariable shoulder. By the time the joint reached me, there was little left but bone, and my dinner generally consisted of the excellent hot new bread, of which there was an abundant supply. I used to put some of it in the pocket of my gown and eat it in the Playing Fields. Most of the bread supplied was wasted, as the elder boys used to pelt each other with it directly after dinner, leaving very little for the almswomen, who were allowed by the College all the bread and meat that remained over." (Quoted from Lyte's *History of Eton College*.)

Of public school customs the celebrated Eton Montem was the most spectacular. The Latin term *Ad Montem* refers to a certain hill where the culminating ceremonies took place. Thither the entire school would parade, dressed in fantastic uniforms, with a band of music and a great fluttering standard. The Montem Captain was always the ranking senior of the school. His confirmation in the exalted post was made the excuse for a hilarious preliminary celebration, termed "Montem-Sure." On a certain evening, Long Chamber was packed with boys. Just before midnight, they all took up their appointed stations. Some raised beds in the air; others stood by the windows. As the clock struck twelve, the heavy wooden shutters were slammed to, the beds dropped to the floor with a crash, and all hands joined in a deafening: "Montem sure!"

The great day at last dawned—usually a fine summer morning, since the season was early June. Long before the parade assembled, several pairs of boys would come forth from the dormitories, attired in strange costumes and carrying satin bags and painted staves with mushroom-shaped tops inscribed with Greek or Latin texts. These were the "Salt-Bearers" or Gatherers of Tribute. The Salt-Bearers were posted at bridges and prominent crossroads in the neighborhood, and every traveler on the highways that morning was compelled to pay toll in exchange for a "pinch of salt"—in later times, a ticket, to show to other Salt-Bearers as proof that the traveler had already paid his score. Since generous "old boys" and curious sightseers flocked from far and near to witness the proceedings, the Salt-Bearers took in tidy sums. After payment of the day's expenses, the net proceeds were turned over to the captain. In the Montem of 1841, the "salt" brought in nearly £1300.

Meanwhile the mock-military parade was on the

march to the sacred mount. Arriving about noon, the standard was waved on the summit of the hill, a humorous ode was recited to the boys and crowd of spectators, and after some other ceremonies the parade returned to the town. Here dinners were given at the principal inns, attended by considerable drinking and much skylarking.

Here is a description of the "military maneuvers" executed by the mock-soldiers in the vegetable-garden of a certain inn, during the Montem of 1841: "The first onset took place against a hollow square of cabbages, which they charged as furiously as did the Cuirassiers against our own human parallelograms at Waterloo, and in two minutes nothing but stumps remained. Potatoes, lettuces, and asparagus followed, without appeasing their fury; on the contrary, the taste of sap seemed to have given fresh edge to their swords; and when not even a currant or gooseberry bush was left, half a dozen of the most stalwart warriors directed their attack upon a large apple-tree, which after being much hacked about, tumbled to the ground amidst the cheers of the bystanders. In another quarter of an hour, the blooming Eden was converted into a blank desert."

This Etonian custom, centuries old, was then in its last days. The school authorities had already restricted it to once every three years. The hard drinking, the riotous demonstrations, and the unsettling effect upon studies and discipline over a considerable period were regarded by masters as most undesirable. The final blow was the opening of the new railway, which brought crowds of "trippers" down from London. The last Montem was held in

1844. Thereupon, after much debate and heart-burning, it was formally abolished.

Thus went another relic of the past. And soon flogging, fagging, blanket-tossing, cock-fighting, formal combats with bare knuckles, and many other customs, good, bad and indifferent, joined Montem in the limbo of forgotten things.

THE END

INDEX

Abuses, terrible child- labor, 334
Academies, 272, 282–84
Age of Youth, 175
Age, marriageable, 21
Alabama, 318
Albany, 290, 305
Alcibiades, 30, 37
Alexander, 40
Alice in Wonderland, 333
American boys, 70
American colonies, 256, 281
American girls, 47
Ames, Nathaniel, 277
Anglo- Saxons, 103
Anglo-Norman noble, 141
Anglo-Saxon child-life, 108
Anglo-Saxon craftsmen, 101
Anglo-Saxon monasteries, 140
Anglo-Saxon pupils, 100
Anglo-Saxon type, 130
Apprentices, 25, 145, 199, 191–92, 225, 272–74, 336–39
Apprenticeship, 91, 106, 193, 223, 286
Apsley, Lucy, 208–199
Aquitaine, 118–08
Arabian Nights, 300
Archelaus, 33
Aristophanes, 33
Arnold, Thomas, 332
Ascham, 169, 184
Ascham, Roger, 169–71
Athenian bride, 36
Athenian citizens, 44
Athenian diet, 45
Athenian life, 32
Athenian men, 35
Athenian women, 35
Athenian youth, 40
free-born, 43
Athletics, 40, 43, 105
organized, 65, 144, 246, 309, 340
Augustus, Emperor, 66
The Babees' Boke, 128, 142
Babies, boy, 299
Babylonia, southern, 7
Babylonian boy, 3
Babylonian children, 3
Babylonian cities, 2
Babylonian history, 6
Babylonian schoolroom, 12
Backwoodsmen, 281
Bagdad, 168

Baltimore, 319
Banks, Lydia, 316
Baptist church, 299
Barby, 334–35
Barnum, showmen P. T., 303
Bath
frequent, 226
hot, 85
Bathing, 85, 121
Bathroom, 212, 317
Becket, 141
Bees, 86, 89–90
Benedict, Abbot, 98
Berkeley, Governor, 281
Bertrand, 127
Bess, Queen, 168, 207
Blacksmiths, 17, 101, 121
Blue Ridge Mountains, 287
Boston, 266, 274
Bower-maidens, 128, 133, 135, 149
Boyhood, 83, 90, 106, 127, 176–68, 205, 199–200, 256, 284, 296, 301, 317, 319
Boys, upper-class, 274
Bugaboos, 218–19
Bulla, 61–62, 67
Burgundians, 158–60, 163
Cabot, Richard, 358
Caesar, 85, 77, 87, 121
Caius' day, 58, 67
California, 304
Calvinism, 176
Cambridge, 143, 237, 276, 282
Canada, 302
Canterbury, 176
Canterbury Tales Chaucer, 114
Carew, Peter, 170
Carolina, 256
Carolina plantation, 318
Cavalier boys, 207
Cavalier circles, 213
Cavalier costume, 212
Cavalier stock, 199
Cavaliers, 24, 205, 212, 270
Chariot races, 76
Charles James Fox, 247
Charles, Prince, 195
Child
medieval, 226
primitive Nordic, 87
Child- laborers, 222
Child-labor agents, 223

Children, lower-class, 128
Chimney-sweeps, 222, 225–27, 337
Christians, 102, 109, 148, 299
Christmas, 208
Christmas tree, 147
Circus Maximus, 72
Citizens, 49–40, 44, 67, 156, 271
  free, 49, 46
  wealthy, 184, 232
Civilization, 12, 7, 108, 124, 300
Clap, Ezra, 278
Classics, 183, 255–56
Clay, Henry, 300
Clement, 148
Code, eighteenth-century, 234
College lads, 185
Colleger, 339–40
Cologne, 149–62
Colonel William Byrd, 259
Colonial days, 266, 272, 287, 301
Colonial New Jersey, 281
Colonial period, 286, 281, 284
Colonial times, 262, 288
Colonies, southern, 271
Columbus, 175
Commodore Porter, 295
Confederate soldier, 317
Connecticut, 270, 303
Constantinople, 96
Cotton, John, 266
Crockett, Davy, 293
Cromwell, 200
Cromwell, Oliver, 200
Darc, Jacques, 159–60
Darc, Jeanne, 168
Dartmouth, 286
Daughters, 21, 35, 66, 139–40, 159–60, 166, 168, 183, 200, 257, 265–67, 294
David Glasgow Farragut, 294
Dearden, 358
Defoe, 227
Defoe, Daniel, 227
Demosthenes, 33
Devil, 109–21, 112, 162, 161, 173, 204, 218–19, 240, 337
Devil's Books, 266
Dickens's Dotheboys Hall, 254
Domremy, 168–58, 160, 163
Dresden china, 263
Duke, Basil, 317
Dutch, 291–81
Dutch family life, 290

Education
  boys', 250
  medieval, 140
  sons', 139
Educational system, medieval, 184
Edward I, 121, 134
Edward III, 137
Edwards, 122, 216–28, 267, 274, 301, 320
Edwards, Jonathan, 268
Egyptian families, 22
Egyptian girl, 16
Egyptian houses, 19
Egyptian master, 168
Egyptian woman, 26
Eighteenth-century flapper, 249
Elizabeth, 199, 193, 207
Elizabethan attitude, 181
Elizabethan boys, 178
Elizabethan children, 173
Elizabethan fashions, 178
Elizabethan ladies, 182
Elizabethan literature, 171
Elizabethan nursery, 171
Elizabethan period, 176
Elizabethans, 176, 212
England boy, 303
England children, 266
England families, 258
English civil war, 200
English colonies, 267
English games, 266
English girls, 47
English lady, 126
English soldiers, 162
Ethelwolf, King, 104
Etiquette, 126–16, 145–35, 263
Eton College, 340
Eton Montem, 340
Etonian, 342
Euphrates, 12
Euripides, 40
Europe, 116, 146–49, 168
  continental, 44, 176
Evelyn's Diary, 220
Ezekiel, 302–3
Fagging, 339, 343
Fagging system, 256, 333
Fagging, cruel, 338
Fairies, 172–73, 189, 219, 317
Fairy-tales, 314, 321
Farms, 84, 272–62, 301, 305, 319–10

Fellah mothers, 25
Fellaheen, 12
Ferrule, 58, 142, 169
Finland, 96
First Crusade, 148
Fish, 24, 31, 101, 105, 116, 134–24, 177, 258, 337
Flogging, 101, 169, 250, 333, 343
Flogging masters, terrible, 170
Football, 43, 145, 187, 200, 341, 335, 338
old-fashioned, 187
old-time, 145
Fox, Charles, 250
French, 162, 183, 263, 284
French child crusaders, 152
French lady, 179
French manner, 232
French styles, 212
French woman, 208
Frontier children, 259
Frontier discomforts, 260
Frontier hardships, 317
Games, 49–50, 69–70, 101–3, 133–45, 186–99, 201–191, 207, 258, 272, 298, 320–21, 340–41
Ganger, 94–96, 109–21
Gaslighting, 218
Gentleman, 141, 142, 232–34, 339
Gentlemen, 21, 33, 71, 95, 191, 199, 193, 210, 244–46, 294, 286
Georgia, 256
Gerhard, 83
German tribes, 87, 93
German women, 85
Germanic peoples, 82
Germany, 102, 149, 168, 186
Giants, 173, 332
Gibbon, Edward, 216
Girlhood, 220, 273, 318
Girls
educated, 263
pious, 161
upper-class Elizabethan, 262
Gladiators, 70, 77–78
Golden Age, 199
Good Queen Bess, 176, 205
Goodfellow, Robin, 173, 206
Greece, 32, 40, 45–46, 54, 59
Greek heroes, 42
Greek life, 40
Greek Olympic Games, 66

Greek poets, 42
Greek slave, 68
Greek towns, 46
Greenland, 96
Gulliver's Travels, 321
Hanks, Dennis, 298–99
Hanks, Nancy, 308, 299
Harvard, 286–76, 282
Hatton, 336
Hell, 169, 201–4, 264
Helots, 45–46, 54
Helping Daniel, 303
Henry VI, 126
Henry Ward Beecher, 301
Henry, Patrick, 284
Holland, 140
Holland House, 247
Holy City, 155
Holy Land, 109, 150, 155
Holy Sepulcher, 148–50
Home
best Cavalier, 208
medieval, 166
northland, 82
upper-class, 31
Homer, 35, 42
Hood, Robin, 206
Horses, 27, 37, 71, 85–86, 78, 87, 94, 103, 161, 240, 317
Household slaves, 62
Households, medieval, 135
Hudson River, 290, 309
Hunters, 24, 90, 149, 284, 303
Husband, 47, 83, 89, 200, 216, 220–21, 263–53, 308
Iceland, 96
Ideals, 35, 319, 333, 358
educational, 183
new eighteenth-century, 262
Imperial Rome, 71
Incorrigible boys, 333
Indian brave crept, 296
Indian raids, 293, 317
Indian War, 284
Indiana, 298–99
Indiana Statutes, 300
Industrial system, 221–23
Infancy, 67, 226, 228
Ireland, 94
Italy, 94, 104, 152, 185–86, 236
northern, 93, 152
southern, 62

James, King, 207
Jarrow, 98
Jerusalem, 154
John Watts de Peyster, 319
Johnny-cake, 258, 300
Jones, Tom, 255
Judge Sewall, 264, 269
Juvenile slave-trade, 223–24
Keate, 337–40
Kentucky, 296, 317
Kentucky mountaineers, 87
Keppel, George, 256
King Charles I., 205
King Charles II, 195
King Edward VII, 320
King Henry V, 121, 137
Knighthood, 122, 131, 149
La Tour- Landry, 140
Ladies, 71, 145–35, 149, 168, 191, 199–201, 206–20, 234, 240–41, 263–53, 291–94
educated, 183
elderly, 318
Lads, 24–27, 67, 91–93, 137, 168, 186–99, 201–192, 200–201, 205–7, 247, 286
medieval, 137
Lady Caroline, 248
Lady Chatelaine, 128
Lady Jane, 169
Lady Jane Grey, 169, 183
Lamb, Charles, 333
Latin, 99, 118, 131, 140–41, 166, 183, 208, 254, 274
Latin mothertongue, 69
Latin School, state-aided, 274
Laws, 5–6, 52, 59, 99, 143, 181, 226–28, 272, 305, 336, 327
Leland, 304–5
Lewis, 118–08
Lincoln homestead, 296
Lincoln, Mordecai, 296
Little Abraham's childhood, 308
Little Caius, 69, 59
Little John, 206, 309
Little William, 121
Lollius, 69–86, 79
London, 189–93, 199, 219, 224, 242, 342
London slums, 334
Lord Admiral, 195
Lord Bacon, 183, 208

Lord Chesterfield, 247
Lord Francis Bacon, 176
Lord High Chamber- lain, 193
Lord Protector, 200
Lord Steward, 193
Loyalty, 21, 44, 88–89, 109, 207
Madcap Harry, 137
Maid Marian, 206
Maids, 149, 160–63, 173–86, 182, 198, 219
Marriage, 35, 140, 181–82
Marseilles, 152, 155–56
Maryland, 282, 300
Massachusetts, 272, 295
Mather, 265, 268, 274
Nathanael, 265
Mather, Cotton, 267–68
May Day, 205
May-pole, 147, 206–7
Mead, 84–85, 95, 105
Medieval children, 120
Medieval period, 124
Medieval primary schools, 141
Medieval system, 210
Mediterranean Sea, 150–52
Michael, Saint, 158–59, 162
Middle Ages, early, 118
Middle classes, 281, 334
medieval, 139
Midsummer's Eve, 220
Milton, 199–200
Milton, John, 199
Money, 6, 47, 162, 282, 303–5
Monks, 96–108, 100, 104, 118, 140, 162, 156–68, 166
Montem, 341–43
Mulcaster, 183–84, 187
Mulcaster, Richard, 169, 183
Music, 22, 21, 39–40, 42–43, 62, 55, 144, 199–89, 208–198, 205, 263, 340
Nancy, 308–298
New Hampshire, 301
New Netherlands, 290
New Orleans, 294
New World, 177
New York City, 291
Newcastle, 195
Niebelungenlied, 89
Nineteenth-century girls, 319
Nobles, 21, 85, 93, 140, 139
Nordic boy, 90
Nordic child-life, 84

Nordic woman, 91
Nordic youth, 93
Normandy, 93, 109–22
Normans, 109
Norse noblewoman, 83
Norse sea-kings, 125
Norsemen, 88
Northmen, 93, 96–98, 104, 108
Nurses, 4, 26, 42, 36, 60, 102, 120–21, 171, 253, 309, 317
black, 282, 318
Odin, 83, 94, 109
Old Germany, 82, 103
Old King Cole, 102
Old-Blue-Eyes-an Bloody-Bones, 318
Oliver Wendell Holmes, 273
Olympic Games, 40
Orleans, 159–60
siege of, 159–62
Oxford, 143–45, 186–87, 210, 218, 237, 246, 250, 282
Oxford University, 176, 246
Paida, 36
Paida- gogoi, 52
Paidadogoi lounged, 37
Paidagogoi, 69
Paidagogos, 36, 62, 69
Palestine, distant, 12
Parents
medieval, 127
middle-class, 242
royal, 216
upper-class, 141
Paris, 159, 186
Paston Letters, 127–28
Paterfamilias, 69, 60
Pauper children, 224
Pauper families, 224
Paupers, 225
outdoor, 339
Paynim Saracens, 148–50
Peasant boys, 16
Peasant class, 26
Peasant families, 221
Peasant girl, 161
Peasantry, 22
Peasants, 17, 121, 139, 145, 153, 158, 220
Penates, 61
Pharaoh Tutankhamen, 19
Philadelphia, 319
Phineas, 303–4

Pilgrims, 162, 154–55
Pilgrim's Progress, 321
Pioneers, 49, 257, 288, 295–308, 333
Plantation, 294, 318–10
Plantation existence, 318
Plantation, luxurious, 282
Planter aristocracy, 281, 284
Planters, 281
Plato, 37, 40
Plutarch, 37, 55
Poorhouses, 224
Prince consort, 216, 320–21
Puritan days, 263, 314
Puritan dress, 212
Puritan home, 208
Puritan party, 207
Puritan Roundheads, 212
Puritan rule, 208
Puritan times, 267
Puritan writings, 268
Puritanism, 176, 301
moderate, 200
Puritans' educational system, 274
Puritans, extreme, 201, 267
Queen, 149, 166, 169, 181, 201, 193, 196
Race, 2, 45, 49, 85–86
Ragnar Lodbrok, 88
Red Skins, 256
Redskins, 258, 293, 308
Reformation, 182, 184, 189, 262
Reims, 159, 163
Religious observances, 131, 140, 166, 182
Revolution, 276, 287–88, 293, 301, 310, 316
Rifle, 288–90, 303–293, 308, 317
Roman authors, 220
Roman child, 59
Roman children, 69
Roman citizens, 71
Roman civilization, 108
Roman culture, 175
Roman education, 69
Roman Empire, 93, 108, 216
Roman gentlemen, 69
Roman girl, 66
Roman manhood, 67
Roman system, 59
Roman youth, 67
Romance, 24, 135, 272
Rugby, 184, 340–41, 332–34, 337

Rupert, Prince, 207
Saint George, 195
Saint Nicholas' Eve, 147
Salt, 147, 177, 232, 295, 331, 341
Salt-Bearers, 341
Samuel, 224–25, 259, 268
Saxon mothers, 102
Scandinavia, 82, 87
Scandinavians, 6, 82, 87, 90
School
church, 146
medieval, 142
monastic, 140, 176
Schoolboys
medieval, 141
ordinary, 23
Schoolgirls, 253
Schooling, 7, 21, 24, 101, 104, 139, 143, 263, 290, 293, 299, 302
early Rome, 59
Sea, 40, 43–44, 101, 152, 154–55, 176
Sea-kings, 93–95
Semitic blood, 2
Servants, 21, 27, 59, 69, 105, 130, 127, 199, 216, 291, 294, 339
Seventeenth century boys, 212
Seventeenth century dress, 211
Sevier, John, 294
Shakespeare, 181, 191, 333
Siegfried, 89
Sir Bevis, 201
Sister Caia, 69, 65–66
Slaves, 5, 26, 21, 35, 49, 45, 62, 60, 70–71, 78, 333
Smith, Adam, 246, 247
Soldiers, 25, 44, 50, 54–55, 65–66, 108, 162, 170, 256, 309
Songs, 42, 95, 149, 152–54, 199, 331
South Carolina, 282
Southern lads, 282
Southern lady, 318
Southern life, 318
Spartan army, 55
Spartan authorities, 46
Spartan breed, 62
Spartan citizenship, 55
Spartan dwelling, 47
Spartan family, 59
Spartan house, 47
Spartan simplicity, 332
Spartan soldier, 55
Spartan state, 45, 53

Spartan training, 273
Spartan training system, 53
Spartans, adult male, 49
Sports, 21, 24, 47, 50, 53, 65, 145, 207–8, 260, 258, 290, 317–18, 340–41
St. Agnes' Eve, 220
Stephen, French, 162
Stuart period, 210
Stuart times, 205, 212
Switzerland, 152
Syria, 26–27
Tadpole, 334, 336
Tales of a Grandfather, 333
Teens, early, 106, 249–39
Teutonic, 130
Teutonic tribe, 85
Thames, 189–201
Thorne, 335
Thracians, 77
Titus, 85, 76
Titus, Emperor, 67, 69, 72–85
Townsfolk, middle-class, 229
Treasure Island, 333
Trumpeters, 64, 137
Tumbler, Tom, 173
Tutors, 21, 104, 121, 131, 169, 176, 195–208, 246–47, 276–90, 333, 340
Valhalla, 83
Valkyries, 83
Venerable Bede, 98, 141
Venice, 185–86
Victoria, Queen, 320–33
Viking Age, 93
Virginia, 259, 281–84, 296, 318
Wagons, covered, 86, 287
Wales, 320
Wantage, 103
War, 42, 46, 62, 54–55, 65, 84–86, 93, 106, 145, 158, 237, 309
Warriors, 30, 32, 45–46, 84–85
Warwick, 126
Washington, 284–86, 300
Washington, Lawrence, 286–87
Waterloo, 237, 334, 342
Webster, Daniel, 301
Wesley, John, 228
White, Thomas, 204
Windsor Castle, 195, 320
Witches, 42, 50, 62, 162, 172–73, 218–19
Xerxes, King, 52
Young Frenchmen, 236

Young maidens, 91, 220
Young Spartan, 62
Young wife, 89, 308
Youngsters, 12, 103, 112, 141, 208, 244–46, 272, 266, 269, 288–90, 294, 319

www.ingramcontent.com/pod-product-compliance
Lightning Source LLC
Chambersburg PA
CBHW071300110426
42743CB00042B/1113